Time and Traditions

TIME AND TRADITIONS

Essays in Archaeological Interpretation

BRUCE G. TRIGGER

Columbia University Press
New York 1978

Published in 1978 in Great Britain by Edinburgh University
Press and in the United States of America by Columbia
University Press

Printed in Great Britain

Library of Congress Cataloging in Publication Data
Trigger, Bruce G
  Time and traditions.

  Bibliography: p.
  Includes index.
  1. Archaeology—Methodology—Addresses, essays,
lectures. 2. Archaeology—History—Addresses, essays,
lectures. I. Title.
CC75.T68 1978   930.1   77-28524
ISBN 0-231-04548-4

Contents

Introduction

THE PUBLICATION OF A collection of papers written over a period of thirteen years is a challenge to author and readers alike both to judge the quality of these essays and to decide whether or not they chart some recognizable course. Because my work has not been aligned explicitly with any of the more easily identifiable positions in contemporary archaeology, some readers have found it difficult to relate the arguments in particular essays to specific current debates (Longacre 1973 : 333) and this has given rise to some suspicion of internal contradiction (Stjernquist 1972 : 24). Publishing these old and new essays as a set may help to clear up some of the problems that have arisen from having to deal with individual papers in isolation.

Most of the essays in this collection are characterized by multiple perspectives. Many criticize both the Old and the New Archaeology. Some of them attempt to understand current debates in archaeology from an historical perspective. Some try to distinguish what is essential in archaeological theory from what is accidental, by comparing and contrasting the British and American traditions.

The general orientation that characterizes these essays can perhaps best be explained biographically. As an undergraduate at the University of Toronto in the late 1950s I was influenced strongly by the tenets of British social anthropology, which then seemed to offer a progressive alternative to Boasian anthropology. By that time, many social anthropologists had accepted Ernest Nagel's (1953) argument that a functional relationship was a statement of cause and effect, and micro-historical studies were seen by some as a source of sociological insight. Yet, most social anthropologists retained Radcliffe-Brown's (1952) faith that all necessary generalizations about human behaviour could be made on the basis of the brief time frames that are accessible to the observation of the ethnological fieldworker. Archaeology was viewed at best as a manifestation of Radcliffe-Brown's pseudo-history and as such as no serious part of any social science. Nevertheless, from my exposure to social anthropology I acquired an awareness of the social system as an analytical tool, and also a certain contempt for the concept of culture, which I regarded as a German mystification of the nineteenth century that was of dubious value for understanding human behaviour. Along with this I developed an awareness of far-reaching cross-cultural regularities in social systems and in human behaviour generally.

At the same time that I was learning about social anthropology, I had the privilege of following a course in ancient economic history given by F.M.Heichelheim in the Classics Department. He encouraged me to pursue an old interest in the work of V.Gordon Childe. From Childe's writings I learned that the aim of prehistoric archaeology was to examine the dynamics of social change and of long-range trends in the life of societies. Childe also argued that archaeological phenomena should be shown as specific instances of general principles. Applying such an approach to the differences as well as to the cross-cultural regularities that were exhibited in the archaeological record produced a 'truly historical explanation' and made archaeology a valid historical discipline. Through Childe I also became aware of the important economic studies of Grahame Clark, as well as of the British concept of prehistory as a discipline drawing upon both archaeological and non-archaeological data in order to understand the past better.

All of this was far removed from the concern with cultural classification and chronology that then constituted the mainstream of North American archaeology. As a graduate student at Yale University I became very dissatisfied with traditional American archaeology, although I did not yet realize how many other graduate students across the United States shared this dissatisfaction. To remedy these defects I drew upon the work of Childe, Clark, and the social anthropologists and viewed archaeological evidence as fossilized elements of social systems. These systems were made up of clearly recognizable elements and, even if no two were precisely alike, they were shaped to a considerable degree by regularities that applied cross-culturally. In my early work I was interested in utilizing the concept of

viii

settlement pattern to gain a better understanding of social systems. This work is discussed in Chapter XI of the present volume and also in my doctoral dissertation *History and Settlement in Lower Nubia* (Trigger 1965). In the latter, I attempted to demonstrate that for over four millennia the population density of Lower Nubia had been determined by four main variables: flood height, agricultural technology, foreign trade, and war. Although it is currently fashionable to treat population as an independent rather than as a dependent variable, I would still defend the basic accuracy of my analysis of the Nubian data. In any case I was clearly concerned with explaining processes of socio-cultural change. It is a pleasure to record that in my work I received the support and encouragement of Professors Chang, Coe, and Rouse. Later essays stressed the concept of society as an analytical tool (Chapters VI and VII), examined cross-cultural regularities in economic and political subsystems (Chapters IX, X, and XIII), and discussed the role of communication in the development of social hierarchies (Chapter XII). These essays embodied a functional and systemic view of human activities, not a particularist or 'shreds and patches' one, such as is associated with traditional American archaeology. At the end of Chapter IV I have even considered a possible predictive role for archaeology.

In spite of this, I did not espouse the New Archaeology as it developed. The reason may be partly temperamental. Like Shakespeare's Cicero, I may be inclined never to 'follow anything that other men begin'. Accident too played a part. During the 1960s my work on Iroquoian prehistory had compelled me to consider the role of population movements as one aspect of societal development. As a result, in 1968 I published a not very successful effort to compare and in part to reconcile the traditional approach in American archaeology and my own societal approach (Trigger 1968a). This study, which was more evenhanded than some more recent attempts to compare old and new approaches have been (e.g. Martin and Plog 1973 : 337-368), was widely interpreted as indicating greater support for traditional concepts than in fact I had intended (Plog 1968 ; Wendorf 1969). This too perhaps inhibited contact with the New Archaeology. I was also aware of the intellectual debt that I owed to Childe, Grahame Clark, and many other British and European archaeologists whose interpretation of the evidence of prehistory had long since transcended cultural chronology. I was therefore necessarily repelled by the ahistoricity and provincialism that characterized much of the early New Archaeology. Chapters IV, V, VI and IX, which view current problems from an historical and often from an international perspective, are efforts to correct this deficiency.

Apart from these problems, a number of significant theoretical orientations continue to differentiate my position from that of the New Archaeology. To a large degree the work of the New Archaeology in the United States, like that of David Clarke in Great Britain, has been based on the anthropological concept of culture. This is a concept about the utility of which I continue to have many doubts. These doubts have been strengthened by recent criticisms of the concept by the anthropologist G.P. Murdock (1971) and, specifically in relationship to archaeology, by Colin Renfrew (1977). Like Renfrew and like many social anthropologists I find the concept of society far less mystical and dangerous.

Also, while I accepted the New Archaeology's insistence on maximizing the explanatory potential of archaeological data as methodologically stimulating, its emphasis on archaeology as a self-sufficient branch of anthropology conflicted with my British-derived concept of prehistory as a discipline that integrated both archaeological and non-archaeological data to achieve a better understanding of the past. My faith in prehistory was reaffirmed in Chapter VIII, which reflects the influence of Daniel McCall's (1964) *Africa in Time-Perspective* and of the still earlier work of Edward Sapir (1916).

Lurking behind this difference in emphasis is the further question whether archaeology is primarily an historical discipline, that seeks to explain the record of human development, or a generalizing one that sees its main task as being to establish universally-valid laws concerning human behaviour, either as part of the discipline of anthropology or as the nucleus of a new science of material culture. My own somewhat polemical efforts to draw the attention of New Archaeologists to an historical option are reprinted in Chapters II and III. Chapter I, which considers recent trends in New Archaeology, also may provide American readers with additional contextual background for these papers.

Finally, I have been disturbed by the New Archaeology's adulation of ethnographically-inspired unilinear evolutionary sequences, although as is evident in Chapter XII, I do not entirely eschew them as an heuristic device. While the emphasis of recently-proposed sequences is primarily socio-political rather than technological, they seem to share many of the conceptual problems of nineteenth century ones and appear simplistic and regressive by comparison with the multilinear schemes of Childe and Steward. As Kroeber (1952) foresaw, the ambiguity of the term *evolution*, as it is used by anthropologists, has helped to produce the confusion between history and science to which I already have alluded. Most archaeologists would agree that explanations must be concerned with processes and not products. Yet if this is so, a necessary belief in uniformitarianism drives us to conclude that most of these processes can be studied best in the contemporary world. In this respect, studying the processes of societal evolution is an integral part of the nomothetic social sciences. Generalizations about the nature of various stages of societal development are like generalizations about the characteristics of mammals and reptiles; they are part of science but do not constitute its explanatory core. I would agree with Murdock (1959b) that the course of evolution, as distinguished from its processes, must be identified with what actually has happened in the past, not with highly abstract generalizations about what is believed to have taken place. The former cannot be predicted in detail and therefore cannot fully be explained, but the evidence can be understood to some degree in terms of what we know or can learn about contemporary human behaviour. The study of this aspect of evolution is identical with the study of history. By providing even imperfect explanations of actual processes, historical studies complement sociological generalizations, which account for limited relationships studied in isolation from the broader context in which they occur.

The concise format of an essay may compel an author to express his key ideas with a clarity that is often lacking in longer works. This is particularly likely when essays deal with theoretical issues that arise as part of an extended programme of research. Yet the lack of nuance that results from brevity sometimes can be mistaken for lack of thorough or subtle

Introduction

insight. I hope that to some extent this has been averted by the cross-cutting subject-matter of many of the papers. The main theme that animates these essays is the conviction that a better understanding of the past, as distinguished from formulating timeless laws about human behaviour, is itself of value and therefore a worthy goal for archaeologists. Equally important, however, is my conviction that such an understanding of prehistory is an integral aspect of the scientific investigation of human behaviour. In sustaining this thesis the following essays, new and revised, must now stand on their own.

PART ONE

═══════════

Archaeology: Science or History?

═══════════

I

Current Trends
in American Archaeology

Old and New

THE MOST IMPORTANT DEVELOPMENT in American archaeology in the mid-1970s is that the New Archaeology has ceased to be controversial. For most archaeologists it has become, in fact if not yet in name, a new orthodoxy. Except where old beliefs are totally invalidated, such rapid acceptance rarely can be achieved without a significant amount of compromise and accommodation between old and new, as occurred when Christianity became the official religion of the Roman Empire. This paper will consider how the success of the New Archaeology has influenced its own nature as well as American archaeology generally.

Part of the success of the New Archaeology might cynically be attributed to its founders and their first disciples now being middle-aged and well entrenched in influential academic posts. Yet this explanation does not account for its widespread, though often tacit, acceptance by older archaeologists, and it gravely underrates the positive attractions of the movement (Martin 1971, 1974). It is generally acknowledged, even by those critical of many aspects of the New Archaeology, that it has greatly benefited archaeology and has moved the discipline in a direction in which most American archaeologists feel they can take pride.

As a result, there has been a damping down of the polemical, programmatic literature that characterized its early phases. Some New Archaeologists have adopted a conciliatory, if patronizing, attitude towards older workers (Flannery 1976). There is also growing dispute and criticism within the New Archaeology; the objects of attack now being the ideas of other

2

New Archaeologists rather than of those who can be labelled Traditional. New Archaeologists are also paying increasing attention to the practical implications of their programmes.

One of the reasons why it has been accepted so rapidly is that many of its innovations have occurred within a framework of assumptions that antedates New Archaeology and therefore is shared by Traditional Archaeologists. Thus, while it would be wrong to claim that New Archaeology does not constitute a break with many aspects of the past, it is equally true that it has been built upon a set of deeply-rooted concepts that are part of a continuing tradition of American archaeology (cf. Taylor 1969; L. Binford 1968b: 27).

Two related themes serve to distinguish this tradition from most European archaeology. The first is the conviction that archaeology, along with ethnology or social anthropology, physical anthropology, and comparative linguistics, is an integral part of a broader discipline of anthropology. R. S. MacNeish (1974) is one of the few American archaeologists who maintains that archaeology could flourish outside the institutional framework of anthropology; he has also founded one of the few separate departments of prehistoric archaeology in North America. The belief that archaeology must be part of anthropology has resulted from the various anthropological disciplines developing in America as different aspects of a holistic study of the American Indian. By contrast, most European archaeologists, at least during the twentieth century, have viewed their discipline as an extension of European history into prehistoric times.

American prehistoric archaeologists have little contact with historians and do not view their work as being relevant to archaeology. History is seen as dealing with Whites, and anthropology with Indians; and Whites and Indians are held to have little in common. This has reinforced among archaeologists the low esteem in which history is held by American scholars generally; Henry Ford was merely reflecting a widespread opinion when he maintained that 'history is bunk'. Archaeologists tend to view historical studies not as a branch of science but as being antithetical to the aims of science. History is labelled as idiographic, which is wrongly construed to mean nothing more than narrative or descriptive, and it is alleged to

Current Trends in American Archaeology

rely mainly on common sense to explain events (Spaulding 1968).

This view has helped to produce the second contrast between American and European archaeology. American archaeology generally, and the New Archaeology in particular, has seen its goal as being to explain archaeological data. There is little sense of archaeology being part of a wider discipline of pre-history, in which the findings of archaeology, ethnography, linguistics, physical anthropology, folklore, and history are utilized together in an effort to interpret and understand the past. Insofar as this sort of work is done within the Americanist tradition, it is done mainly as part of ethnohistory, which is separate from archaeology and has rather weak connections with it.

From another point of view, American archaeologists view the discipline of history as doing the same thing they do when they establish cultural chronologies, which makes history and chronology synonymous in their minds (e.g. Bennett 1943 : 208–209). Science, by contrast, is viewed as nomothetic, that is, as seeking to establish general laws that are at least potentially of predictive value and hence may be relevant to the problems of the modern world. Just as Aristotle rated the timeless verities of poetry as superior to the temporal concerns of history, so American social scientists rate the search for general laws ahead of the contextual accounting for specific events. Many of them can conceive of the goal of explanation as being only the formulation of general laws. These are not concepts that began with or are limited to the New Archaeology.

In the following sections, special attention will be paid to the manner in which the tenets of the New Archaeology concur with or represent a break away from an older American tradition. Mine is a less integrated view of the postulates of the New Archaeology than has been presented by Willey and Sabloff (1974 : 178–211). The reason for this will be explained below.

Tenets of the New Archaeology

1) *General Laws of Human Behaviour*. The most attractive feature of the New Archaeology in the eyes of most American archaeologists is that it has enhanced the status of prehistoric archaeology within the social sciences. Since the 1930s,

4

American archaeologists had been concerned mainly with defining archaeological cultures in terms of their formal content, delimiting them geographically and chronologically, and accounting for their interrelationships in terms of concepts such as migration and diffusion. These operations constitute what American archaeologists have chosen to call and conceive of as an 'historical' approach, although this bears little relationship to English usage. This approach perhaps realized its inherent strengths and limitations most fully in Martin, Quimby, and Collier's (1947) *Indians Before Columbus*, a factual compendium almost wholly devoid of interpretive ambition and of no interest or relevance beyond the discipline of archaeology. Nevertheless, the 'historical' approach remained widely popular into the 1960s. It was little wonder, in view of archaeology's almost exclusive concern with cultural chronology and formal description, that ethnologists came to view it condescendingly as the 'lesser part' of anthropology (Willey and Sabloff 1974 : 134). Indeed, most archaeologists came to be viewed as persons who were not intelligent enough to do any other sort of anthropology.

Beginning in the 1930s, ethnologists such as Clyde Kluckhohn (1940) argued that the only way for archaeologists to escape from this impasse was for them to do well what ethnologists claimed to be doing already: to explain how and why culture changes, by discovering the laws that govern human actions. Under the heading of explanation, Walter Taylor (1948 : 156–167) embraced the establishment of general laws as being the supreme goal of archaeology and viewed archaeology and ethnology as converging to constitute a unified discipline of anthropology at this level. He saw his own functional (conjunctive) approach as being an intermediate step towards this goal. Willey and Phillips (1958 : 5–6) likewise viewed explanation as the highest goal of archaeology, although they believed that, as of 1958, nothing of importance had been achieved at that level. Thus the adoption of explicitly nomothetic goals by the New Archaeologists and the rejection of idiographic ones did not represent a major break with the past. It was the culmination of American archaeology's commitment to anthropology and to the latter's search for generalizations that explain human behaviour.

It was believed in America, as it was in Europe, that the incomplete nature of archaeological data severely limited their usefulness for generalizing about human behaviour. L.R. Binford (1962) argued that the archaeological record had been shaped by the entire cultural system and that, through the development of new analytic techniques and the application of fresh concepts, archaeological data could yield significant information not only about technological and economic matters but also about social organization and ideology. While this initial statement stimulated much valuable research, it is now increasingly being realized that archaeological data differ from ethnological data and that the questions asked must be appropriate to each. It is also argued that the archaeological record of changes in specific cultural systems over long periods of time is data unique in the social sciences (Tuggle 1971 : 131).

Generalizations seek to explain regularities that recur in a variety of situations. In comparative investigations in anthropology only common factors tend to be regarded as worthy of explanation; differences are treated as accidents that are of little importance. Julian Steward (1955 : 179) formally sanctioned this methodology when he contrasted a scientific concern with the regularities of a cultural core with an unscientific one directed towards 'cultural differences, particulars, and peculiarities'. This view comes close to identifying a concern with recurrent factors as Science and a concern with the factors specific to particular instances of the same phenomena as History. There is no concept of scientific history, such as Childe (1958c : 6–7) outlined in his *Valediction*, where he wrote not only of showing phenomena as instances of general principles but also of explaining the individual and unique in terms of the specific conjunction of general and familiar processes. The latter operation is no more than a simple extension of the New Archaeology, but the limited understanding of scientific history among American archaeologists makes progress in this direction unlikely in the near future.

2) *Deductive Reasoning.* A second major tenet of New Archaeology has been that all explanations must assume the form of an hypothesis or an absolute or statistical covering law which is then tested by the evidence (Watson *et al.* 1971 : 3–19). A.C. Spaulding (1968 : 34) has asserted that 'there is only one kind of serious explanation, the nomological or covering-law

6

explanation'. Yet, in spite of widespread support for this positivist approach at least for structuring reports on research, little effort has been made to assess the relative significance of proposed covering laws or to interrelate them in a logical and hierarchical manner. Recently, appalling trivialities have been dignified as laws (Schiffer 1975); an operation that scarcely can enhance the scientific status of archaeology.

Most archaeologists would agree that any explanation involves assumptions and is not simply self-evident from the data. They would also agree that the New Archaeology has benefited archaeology by insisting that in every possible instance these assumptions should be made explicit and subjected to careful scrutiny. Yet there is less agreement about the specific value of the deductive approach, both from a practical and a theoretical point of view, than there is about any other tenet of the New Archaeology. It is observed that in the conduct of research inductive and deductive procedures always are interrelated. The collection of facts with broad problems rather than specific hypotheses in mind often has resulted in the production of extremely important theories, including Darwin's concept of Natural Selection. An unwarranted stressing of the formulation of deductive hypotheses as a pre-condition for research indeed may constrain and limit research to an unwarranted degree.

Many archaeologists also doubt that the covering law format alone will produce explanations. A variety of other explanatory procedures, such as statistical-probabilistic ones, have been proposed as alternative or supplementary to a logico-deductive one (Willey and Sabloff 1974 : 194–196). At the present time, many archaeologists do not view a deductive approach as a necessary part of the New Archaeology (pp. 196–197). It is the only major tenet the acceptance of which seems in doubt.

3) *Cultural Ecology.* By the 1950s, American archaeologists were deeply committed to reconstructing prehistoric environments and studying the utilization of them by different cultures. They were influenced to a large degree by Julian Steward's concept of cultural ecology and more remotely by the work of Grahame Clark and other British archaeologists. Increasing interest in the processes of plant and animal domestication and in the role of irrigation in the rise of civilization also drew

attention to cultural ecology. It was quickly recognized as an approach that permitted much to be learned from archaeological data. It is not surprising that in his initial formulation of the New Archaeology L.R.Binford (1962 : 218) stressed the importance of cultural ecology as a 'valuable means of increasing our understanding of cultural processes'.

More recently, archaeologists have been influenced by an ecosystemic view of culture. This sort of approach views human populations as parts of larger ecological systems and posits multiple reciprocal exchanges between a cultural system and its environment (Watson *et al.* 1971 : 88–107). In the opinion of Willey and Sabloff (1974 : 191) it offers unlimited possibilities for 'studying the processes involved in the evolution of ecosystems (with the focus on human populations)'.

The increasing emphasis on an ecological perspective in American archaeology has paralleled rising public interest in contemporary ecological problems in America. Concern about the ecological costs of technological development and with the limitations that ecological factors may impose upon such growth is reflected in the increasing pessimism about progress that has characterized recent ecological models in archaeology. Instead of being pictured as a hungry savage, the hunter and gatherer has tended to become again the leisured and noble savage (Lee and De Vore 1968). Likewise, those who subscribe to the ideas of E.Boserup tend to view the development of civilization as a form of cultural pathology, much as it was viewed by Grafton Elliot Smith and W.J.Perry (Spooner 1972). In the long run much good cannot help but come from the rethinking of archaeological problems from current ecological perspectives. Yet the direct manner in which this rethinking reflects the current mood of American society suggests a need for caution in evaluating the results obtained so far.

In two recent papers dealing with the evolution of political and religious systems, Flannery (1972) and Flannery and Marcus (1976) have argued that the whole of culture can be analysed profitably from an ecological perspective. If this is merely a restatement of the standard functionalist position that all aspects of a culture are interrelated, this argument is not particularly controversial. The implication of such a position would be that the whole of a culture profitably can be viewed

8

from any one part, as Malinowski analysed Trobriand culture in separate studies from the viewpoint of agriculture, trade, magic, and other features. There is no agreement among social scientists that any one of these viewpoints is of privileged causal importance. Therefore if Flannery and Marcus are claiming a determining role for ecological adaptation in shaping the overall configuration of a culture their position is interesting but certain to be controversial. There is also a danger that the concept of ecology will be weakened and trivialized by placing upon it too all-embracing an explanatory burden.

4) *Social Organization and Ideology*. Increasing interest in reconstructuring social organization and belief systems, in addition to material culture, also pre-dates the New Archaeology. The social implications of settlement patterns received much attention following the publication of G. R. Willey's *Prehistoric Settlement Patterns in the Virú Valley, Peru* (1953). Interest in prehistoric social organization and religious-intellectual behaviour reflects a new confidence in what can be done with archaeological data and also the training that American archaeologists receive within anthropology departments. This training is characterized by a heavy emphasis upon ethnology and often little emphasis on the physical and biological sciences. This may explain Maxine Kleindienst's (1976) observation that artefactual evidence often constitutes the most conventional and least interesting part of modern archaeological reports. In her opinion, American archaeologists wrongly fail to spend as much time analysing artefacts as they do studying environmental evidence or settlement patterns.

Recent studies are characterized by growing awareness that ethnological concepts, other than those directly related to material culture, may not be appropriate for archaeological investigation, but must be selected and adapted for this purpose. For example, while residence may be a valid subject for archaeological investigation, descent systems probably are not (Aberle 1968). While American archaeologists have experimented with the application of concepts of locational analysis currently popular in Britain (Clarke 1977; Hodder and Orton 1976), they seem to be more critical of the theoretical basis and applicability of these concepts than are European archaeologists (R. Adams 1975 : 458). Settlement archaeology in America seems to achieve its most important results by making what in Europe are traditional studies of the microdistributions of artefacts within sites.

There is also a burgeoning interest in studying art styles (Donnan 1976), iconography (Bernal *et al.* 1973), and settlement data (Marcus 1973) in terms of what they may reveal about the belief systems, behavioural patterns, and social organization of prehistoric societies. These studies often have strong ethnographic, ethnohistorical, or in the case of Mesoamerica epigraphic components; hence they diverge furthest from the purely archaeological interests of the New Archaeology and have the strongest humanist orientation of any work currently being done in American archaeology. They are also the studies least constrained by a materialist bias. For this reason, they are of considerable theoretical interest.

5) *A Systems Approach*. The adoption of a systemic viewpoint by American archaeology is an innovation that has proved important for anthropology as a whole (Watson *et al.* 1971 : 61–87; Willey and Sabloff 1974 : 198–192). L.R.Binford's (1962) initial view of culture as a system made up of major technological, social, and ideological subsystems did not carry archaeology beyond the structural-functional view of societies or cultures proposed by social anthropologists decades earlier. What the New Archaeology has done since is to stress the importance of studying archaeological cultures as systems changing through time. Social anthropologists recognized to some degree long ago that functional relationships within a socio-cultural system can be demonstrated (as opposed to posited) only by showing how the system changes through time (Harris 1968 : 618), but archaeologists now make systematic use of this concept. Taking a longer view, they visualize cultural change as a series of evolving trajectories, rather than in terms of the mechanical, clock-like permutations favoured by most social anthropologists who are interested in change.

More specifically, archaeologists increasingly are viewing cultures as complex systems for the exchange of matter, energy, and information, and, by virtue of being systems, as sharing important properties with all physical and biological systems. Attempts have been made to account for cultural change in terms of General Systems Theory, a growing body of concepts

10

that purports to account for the properties common to all systems regardless of their physical nature. The most familiar of these concepts at present are those of positive and negative feedback, which are used to conceptualize many aspects of cultural stability and change (Watson *et al.* 1971 : 73–83). Flannery (1967) sums up the most important claim of General Systems Theory when he suggests that even culture may be powerless to influence the properties of systems.

General Systems Theory has produced an awareness of hitherto largely unsuspected constraints on the variability of individual cultures. This has helped archaeological theory to move abreast and even ahead of much of the work going on in social anthropology. It also has provided various models that are useful for analysing and interpreting specific bodies of archaeological data. As yet, however, archaeologists have tended to use General Systems concepts in a piecemeal fashion, rather than seeking to construct an integrated body of theory. Mathematicians express doubts that archaeological data are sufficiently complete to permit the application of General Systems analysis in more than an analogical fashion (Steiger 1971). The detailed quantifying of energy flows even in ethnographic contexts is very difficult and it is questionable whether the scientific pay-off would justify the complete application of such an approach.

6) *Evolutionism.* The influence on archaeology of evolutionists such as Leslie White and Julian Steward antedates by many years the New Archaeology. By the early 1960s support for an evolutionary view of human development was widespread in the discipline. Hence there was little difficulty in establishing evolutionism as one of the key concepts of the New Archaeology (Willey and Sabloff 1974 : 178–189). Nevertheless, evolutionism now stands at the heart of a controversy that is beginning to develop within the New Archaeology. Evolution is an amorphous word that means many things to different people. In American archaeology, the concept is equated with the idea that there is a relatively small number of sociocultural types, such as bands, tribes, chiefdoms, and states (Service 1971), representatives of which share basically similar structural features. These types do not necessarily constitute a unilineal series and the similar features are not viewed as analogies but as

structural regularities that are valuable for interpreting archaeological data. Much evolutionary theorizing is based on Leslie White's (1949) assumption that technology determines culture. This is a way of saying that the forces which shape cultures are relatively constant and can be comprehended easily (Harris 1968 : 242). This faith in determinism constitutes the essence of American evolutionism.

Those who hold this point of view tend to regard a systems approach as being inherently inductive and as begging the problem of causality, which to the evolutionist is a matter of crucial importance (Leone 1975 : 197). It may be true that to a considerable degree those who are most interested in a systems approach view causality as complex and regularities as not easily discoverable. If this is so, the tension which underlies the seeming complementarity of the evolutionary and systemic approaches may augur a continuation of the controversy between Boasian particularism and Whitean evolutionism within American archaeology.

It has also been objected that the current view of evolutionary processes, as being almost exclusively internal to societies and superorganic, has resulted in cultural development being interpreted in terms of gradually unfolding cycles of development and decline. This view does not account for the precipitous and drastic transformations that cultural systems sometimes experience (R. Adams 1974 : 248). It is perhaps significant in this respect that the one basic tenet of Marxism that is rejected by the American anthropologist Marvin Harris (1968 : 230) is the dialectic, which is concerned with radical transformation.

7) *Materialism*. British archaeologists long have recognized that their data encourage the adoption of a materialist perspective; they disagree, however, in their assessment of the degree to which social organization and ideology are responses to the economic base. Even in his explicitly Marxist writings, Childe (1947 : 75-76) saw these relations as being remote and by no means automatic. Much New Archaeology explicitly has been identified with a materialist position and to a large degree with Leslie White's technological determinism. White (1948) denounced Childe's assumption that in the long run the 'means of production' determine culture as an example of fuzzy-minded humanism and also opposed Childe's view that

through the development of social sciences man could hope to control his social environment. 'Culture changes and develops in accordance with laws of its own', White declared, 'not in obedience to man's desire or will' (p.218). Other New Archaeologists have been influenced by the more broadly-based materialist positions of Julian Steward and Marvin Harris. For some, adaptation to the environment has replaced technology or the economy as the core or base which determines the rest of a culture.

Many archaeologists seem to equate materialism with determinism. They argue that culture is an independent variable which determines human decisions or that, because it is impossible to obtain evidence about such decisions, it is best to study culture systemically and without reference to them. Other archaeologists do not view a materialist perspective as being incompatible with a concern for individual decisions. Robert M. Adams (1974) has argued, for example, that the precipitous rise and fall of many ancient states can be understood as resulting from political decisions made by their rulers in the absence of perfect knowledge of the risk-taking involved. Yet no current discussion of this problem seems as sophisticated as Childe's (1947 : 80) model of intersecting individual wills giving rise to an historical event no one has willed; what Childe termed 'a natural event'. It is not clear, however, how many American archaeologists concur with a materialist view of culture. Many maintain a more eclectic outlook; others assign a major determining role to religion or some other factor. Until archaeologists pay more attention to explaining differences as well as similarities among cultural systems, thereby attempting to account for the failure of specific societies to display the functional profile posited by materialist-evolutionary theories, materialism will remain a matter of faith for archaeologists, as it is for other social scientists. By grappling with these 'exceptions' archaeology might contribute better to an understanding of materialism as an analysis of human behaviour.

Practical Problems

Certain developments of New Archaeology pose problems of identity and purpose for the discipline, which resemble those

Current Trends in American Archaeology

raised for British archaeology by David Clarke (1968). It is generally assumed that whatever else archaeology may do, it is concerned with the study of the past. It is also evident that in recent decades social anthropologists and ethnologists have been negligent in the study of material culture. Thus the ethnologists' understanding of the domain of culture that is most relevant to archaeology is too weak to be of much use to archaeologists. There is also little sign among ethnologists of a revival of interest in material culture. Because of this, certain archaeologists, such as L.R.Binford, are studying living non-Western peoples in the expectation that their findings will facilitate the interpretation of archaeological data. Others are studying material culture in the context of modern American society. These studies include investigations of waste disposal which aim to define more precisely the relationship between the archaeological record and the rest of society (Rathje 1974). At least some of the archaeologists involved in such work insist that research of this kind constitutes archaeology; archaeology being what archaeologists do (Reid *et al.* 1975). Some, as David Clarke did, see archaeology as the core of a new nomothetic science of material culture.

This attempt to redefine the scope of archaeology raises a series of questions that have important implications for the New Archaeology. To what degree does work of this sort constitute an admission that data from contemporary societies are a better basis for generalization than are archaeological data? Can the diversion of archaeological effort to the study of contemporary material culture be justified and does it not mean that in fact ethnology and social anthropology grow at the expense of archaeology? The latter is a serious consideration in view of the present numerical weakness of archaeologists within the anthropological establishment. Is it also not possible that the view that archaeology should become the core of a new science of material culture sells archaeology short? Are there not other things that archaeology might better remain or become? And does not the idea of a science of material culture paralleling social anthropology tend to emphasize the synchronic investigation of a limited aspect of culture, when it is claimed that the greatest asset of archaeology is its 'holistic diachronic perspective?'

We must also consider what effect the New Archaeology, as

14

distinguished from new techniques of physical or biological analysis, has had upon field work. It clearly has stimulated a desire to derive a broader spectrum of information from sites, which makes excavation and analysis slower, more painstaking, and more expensive. Archaeologists also have become more interested in the investigation of sites within regional contexts, which require the study of more sites. Taken together, these developments push the archaeologists' requirements for new data far beyond their human and financial resources for recovering these data. The rapid development of rescue archaeology has augmented these resources considerably and has given rise to debates about how programmes of rescue archaeology best can contribute to the investigation of theoretical problems while discharging their particular institutional responsibilities (King 1971). The development of scientific sampling techniques represents a significant effort to adjust research objectives to resources in a rational manner. An emphasis on sampling conflicts, however, with the desire of some archaeologists to recover whole settlement plans for purposes of societal interpretation.

James A. Brown and Stuart Struever (1973) have opened a major debate about the responsibility of excavators to their sites by challenging the old principle that, since excavation is destruction, archaeologists have an obligation to record as much information as possible for posterity. They argue that sites are excavated to solve problems and the data collected are determined by the problems that the archaeologist has in mind; moreover, this is not only what is done but also what should be done. Brown and Struever's position may not have won widespread explicit acceptance and it has not affected adversely the quality of Struever's own field work. It is, however, a logical application of a deductive approach to archaeological research that less capable archaeologists could use as an excuse to justify gross negligence and self-indulgence in their recording. This raises the question of whether, in addition to the data that are required by an archaeologist's own research, there is not a minimum corpus of data that must be recorded for every excavation. The responsibility for providing these data is not lessened by the fact that an understanding of what is required will alter and grow through time.

Much of the problem-orientated research of the New Archaeology has developed in areas, such as the American Southwest, where cultural chronologies were highly developed and provided an indispensable background for the investigation of processual problems. It is perhaps because of this that most New Archaeologists have tended to regard chronological investigations as being of little theoretical interest and, with the conspicuous exception of Fred Plog (1973, 1974), have not been particularly concerned with specifically temporal problems (Sterud 1976). Yet it is surely erroneous to assume that the study of chronology ever reaches a stage where it can be regarded as complete or carried out independently of other problems.

Some New Archaeologists have argued that data collected to study cultural chronology largely are useless for processual research (Flannery 1973 : 49). Yet it is possible that the conduct of archaeological research and reporting exclusively along problem-orientated lines may result in a breakdown of any uniform treatment of archaeological data, such as in the past facilitated regional culture-historical synthesis. This has been offset to some degree by the SARG project in the southwestern United States, which attempts to computer-record data for a large number of sites according to a common format (SARG 1974). Yet even this project is of limited geographical extent and the data processed are limited by its own particular research objectives. Many of the New Archaeologists who are wholly committed to nomothetic research may regard regional comparability as being of no particular importance, just as social anthropologists tend to view their research as a series of specific, self-contained studies. Yet it has been my own experience working with the *Handbook of North American Indians* that it is now very difficult for archaeologists to draw current research for the eastern United States together even in the form of a systematic cultural chronology. This is regrettable since American Indian history is now of great interest to the Indians themselves and prehistory has a vital role to play in promoting public awareness of the Indians' history and accomplishments. Such history is potentially far stronger rather than weaker because of the New Archaeology. It is not impossible that the concern of native people for their own history may be the principal means by which a European-type of understanding of the past ultimately is introduced into American archaeology.

16

Finally, it must be observed that nothing has happened to upset the traditional view of American prehistory to a degree remotely comparable to that of the impact of bristlecone pine calibrations upon European prehistory (Renfrew 1973a). In Europe a dating process firmly situated within the context of the physical and biological sciences has called into question the validity of a reconstruction of European prehistory that has been accepted generally for several generations and with it the validity of the concepts upon which this reconstruction was based. This imparts a personal quality and a striking focus to the current upheaval in European prehistory.

By contrast, the New Archaeologists in America have been less concerned with revealing specific errors in the study of the past than with demonstrating how fresh perspectives can permit that past to be studied more adequately and more completely. This circumstance has cushioned the generational conflict produced by the new paradigm by reducing it to a matter not of right and wrong but of not-so-good and better. Such a point of view provides a broad basis of accommodation between the old and the new.

The lack of a burning substantive issue also helps to explain the unfocused nature of the New Archaeology, which consists of widely scattered individuals and groups of individuals innovating along many lines and in respect of problems that are very different from one another. They are united by certain common perspectives, but as an act of conviction or faith rather than from having to cope with common problems. In Durkheimian terms, the unity of the New Archaeology is mechanical not organic. Because of this, it is not difficult for a New Archaeologist to be disinterested in the accomplishments of vast numbers of his colleagues.

CONCLUSION

As European and American archaeology grow more sophisticated, each stands to profit more from the accumulated experience of the other. Fruitful exchanges are taking place with increasing frequency and ease, and with results that suggest that a transatlantic, if not an international, tradition of archaeology may be evolving. Such exchanges can occur more easily if it is accepted that British and American archaeology are products of different historical traditions. These traditions are characterized by much convergence in practical matters related to the analysis of archaeological data but view archaeology within different academic and social contexts. Such differences often prevent a straightforward understanding and evaluation of what is going on in the other tradition and contribute to a needless and harmful sense of alienation. There is also the danger that enthusiasm for the New Archaeology among younger British archaeologists (Spriggs 1977) may lead them to reject the British approach without considering its merits. An effort to understand the peculiarities of both of these traditions seems justified if it permits archaeologists on both sides to recognize what is culturally-specific in their own thinking and facilitates a two-way transmission of ideas which allows them to handle their data better.

II

Aims in Prehistoric Archaeology

NOT LONG AGO THE THEORETICAL literature in archaeology dealt mainly with excavation techniques and the processing of archaeological data. In recent years, the successful realization of many of these empirical objectives, plus a rapidly increasing corpus of data, have motivated a younger generation of archaeologists to investigate more carefully the problems that are involved in the explanation of the data and the study of prehistory in general. This concern has produced a spate of publications which, although they often disagree radically about particular issues, are attempting a) to investigate the theoretical structure of prehistoric archaeology, b) to formulate a more rigorous canon for the interpretation of archaeological data, and c) to pioneer new methods of analysis (S. and L. Binford 1968; Chang 1967b, 1968; Clarke 1968).

One has to be conservative indeed to fail to appreciate the positive value of these studies. However sectarian and polemical some of them are, and however much they may bristle with an often superfluous terminology, they promise a better understanding of the significance of archaeological data. One cannot justly regard these studies as an aberration that serves only to divert professional interest from more important objectives (cf. J. Hawkes 1968). On the contrary, whether their authors admit it or not, most of these studies are based very solidly upon the previous achievements of prehistoric archaeology. The fact that they are compelling archaeologists to become increasingly explicit and self-conscious about their goals is surely evidence of the maturation of the discipline.

The most vital problems that these studies pose for the profession as a whole concern the general orientation of prehistoric archaeology. Until recently, it generally was taken for granted that prehistoric archaeology was an historical

19

discipline that aimed to investigate man's past for those periods for which written records are absent or scarce. Lacking the tools of history proper, prehistorians attempted to learn about the past from the artefacts and other traces of human activity that survive in the archaeological record, much as palaeontologists strive to extract information from fossils, and historical geologists search for it amongst geological strata. It is no accident that the links between these historicizing disciplines have been close, and that they have shared much the same conceptual basis for their methodology.

It is fashionable today to say that archaeology has three aims: to reconstruct culture history, to reconstruct prehistoric patterns of culture, and to explain cultural processes (S. and L. Binford 1968 : 8–16). However, most of the 'New Archaeology' has tended to place considerably more emphasis on the second and third of these goals than on the first; and, in some circles, this has given rise to a divergent view of the aims of archaeology. L. R. Binford (1967a : 234–5; 1962) for example, considers that archaeology should be 'an objective comparative science involved in the explication and explanation of cultural differences and similarities'. In an address to the American Anthropological Association, F. Plog (1968) advocated a similar role for archaeology, as an 'experimental social science' capable of testing hypotheses that are relevant to the theories of the social sciences and therefore contributing to the explanation of human behaviour. In what is undoubtedly the most rigorous and systematic single programme for archaeological interpretation outlined to date, D. L. Clarke (1968 : 20–24) defines the primary aim of archaeology as being to explain the regularities that the archaeologist observes in the archaeological record. He argues that this will make archaeology a generalizing discipline studying material culture, structurally similar and substantively complementary to social anthropology.

Each of these scholars seems to view archaeology as being ideally a nomothetic or generalizing discipline having goals identical to those of ethnology and cultural anthropology. These goals, like those of the social sciences in general, are to formulate laws that will explain socio-cultural processes and associated human behaviour.

It is no surprise that these same archaeologists express varying degrees of hostility towards the traditional, particularizing view of prehistory, which they stigmatize as being descriptive and lacking theoretical content. L.R.Binford (1967a : 235) denies that 'reconstruction of the past' can be the ultimate aim of archaeology. If it were, archaeology would be 'doomed to be a particularistic, non-generalizing field'. The 'reconstruction and characterization of the past' is viewed as mainly having a 'role in the general education of the public'. Binford, apparently, does not believe that historical objectives have scholarly value in their own right, although here his stand may be polemical. He has himself produced historical work of high quality (1967b) and elsewhere has expressed more moderate views on historical objectives. Plog (1968) draws a similar distinction between 'processual as opposed to strictly historical analysis' and champions the use of the past 'as a laboratory for testing hypotheses concerning social and cultural process'. Clarke (1968 : 635–64) appears to entertain a more modest view of archaeology's scientific goals and to be more sympathetic to particularizing than is either Binford or Plog. There are, however, few references to historical objectives in Clarke's *Analytical Archaeology*, and it is clear that in this book at least, Clarke's interest in cultural process greatly exceeds his interest in history.

Most British archaeologists still appear to believe that such views about the aims of prehistoric archaeology lack adequate foundations or motives. This is especially so among archaeologists whose work brings them into close contact with professional historians and who share with them, consciously or unconsciously, many of the same views about the general nature and goals of their respective disciplines. By contrast, the views of the New Archaeology have substantial roots in the American anthropological tradition. In his *A Study of Archeology*, W.W.Taylor viewed 'synthesis and content' (palaeo-ethnology and historiography) 'as middle range objectives which logically precede a study of the nature and working of culture'. Of this final level he wrote 'When the archaeologist collects his data, constructs his cultural contexts and...proceeds to make a comparative study of the nature of culture in its formal, functional and/or developmental aspects, then he is doing cultural anthropology' (1948 : 41). Likewise, in *Method and Theory in American Archaeology*, Willey and

Aims in Prehistoric Archaeology

Phillips (1958 : 9) classified culture-historical integration as a descriptive operation preceding explanation, which in turn they equated with processual interpretation. In both these works, as in the writings of the anthropologist Leslie White (1945b), historical activities tend to be viewed as essentially descriptive, while the ultimate aims of archaeology are characterized as being processual, that is to say, concerned with the formulation of general rules of cultural behaviour. In addition to reflecting the prestige of nomothetic or generalizing activities in contemporary American social science, this insistence upon generalizing as the ultimate goal of archaeology reflects the strength of the American commitment to the idea that prehistoric archaeology and ethnology are branches of anthropology and therefore should share common goals.

The lip-service paid to these common goals was of little importance so long as American archaeology was interested primarily in the recovery of data (Taylor 1948 : 13; Willey 1968; Schwartz 1968). The main thrust of the theorizing we have been discussing was clearly at the level of 'culture-historical integration'. It is significant that neither Taylor nor Willey and Phillips bothered to examine the ultimate objectives of archaeology in any detail. A comfortable degree of ambiguity persisted between the concepts of historical and processual explanation at this level and the distinction between generalizing and particularizing was not seen as being of great importance. These distinctions only became so as archaeologists paid increasing attention to problems of explanation in archaeology, which in turn has required that the goals of explanation be considered more carefully. Archaeologists are now faced with demands that they should use their findings, alongside ethnological data, as building blocks in a single generalizing science of culture. I see this not as an erratic demand, but rather as the logical culmination of one line of thought that long has been implicit in American archaeology. Unfortunately, the objections that have been raised against this point of view have not succeeded so far in coming to grips with the main issues. Instead, they have revealed that a great lack of clear thinking about major theoretical issues lies behind the facade of much traditional archaeology.

In an article in *Antiquity*, Jacquetta Hawkes (1968 : 255) reaffirmed her faith that the final aim of archaeology is 'the reconstruction of individual events in time', but in so doing she unfortunately adopted the very phraseology that exponents of the New Archaeology use when they wish to imply that the traditional aims of archaeology are purely descriptive. Further-more, as we shall see below, her identification of history with a vaguely defined humanist approach seriously misrepresents the nature of historical enquiry as it is understood by most modern historians and implicitly by many archaeologists. Indeed, her view of history is not dissimilar from the views that are held of it by the most violent anti-historicists in archaeology. Her condemnation of natural science methods has to be interpreted as a criticism not only of current developments but of all prehistoric archaeology since the days of Christian Thomsen.

Another paper that exemplifies the limited view of the nature of historical enquiry that is held by many archaeologists is Sabloff and Willey's 'Collapse of Maya Civilization in the Southern Lowlands' (1967). In that paper, the authors defend an historical approach in archaeology by attempting to show that a single event may explain the collapse of Maya civilization better than do current 'processual theories' that attribute it to ecological or social factors. The event which they choose is an hypothesized invasion of the Maya lowlands from the highlands of Mesoamerica. Following the interpretative procedure already outlined by Willey and Phillips in their book *Method and Theory in American Archaeology*, they argue that 'by first gaining control of the historical variables, we will then be in an excellent position to gain control of the processual ones'.

This identification of history with events but not with process has provoked a well-merited response from Erasmus (1968) and L.R.Binford (1968a). Both point out that historical events cannot be understood apart from their processual contexts, and that the mere demonstration of a sequential relationship does not constitute a meaningful explanation of that relationship. Even if Maya civilization did collapse following an invasion, the reasons for its collapse must be sought in the social and economic conditions that permitted such an invasion to occur and to have such far-reaching consequences. Erasmus concludes that historical events should not be given priority over process, but has nothing to say about the implications of this conclusion for an understanding of the structure of historical explanation.

Aims in Prehistoric Archaeology

Binford comes close to eliminating the dichotomy between history and process by defining a proper historical approach as one that embraces a concern with process. He claims that his main disagreement with Sabloff and Willey, and with other traditional archaeologists, is over method. According to Binford, traditional archaeologists are content to use an inductive methodology, which means they formulate propositions which they believe explain the past. Binford argues that, instead, archaeologists must employ a deductive approach whereby these propositions are tested. Binford's apparent sympathy for an historical approach that embraces a concern for process is offset, however, by a tendency to characterize inductive approaches as being particularizing and deductive ones as generalizing. The deductive method is seen as leading, through a knowledge of the operation of past cultural systems, to the formulation of laws of cultural dynamics and cultural evolution. Rather than being explicitly rejected, the concept of history is lost sight of within Binford's general theoretical framework.

We are thus presented with the unhappy spectacle of the supporters and foes of an historical archaeology in seeming agreement that historical objectives can be satisfied at the descriptive level. This is not the first time that such a conclusion has been arrived at in American anthropology. Kroeber once accused Leslie White of having appropriated for his concept of evolution all that was significant in history while refusing to accept the rest. 'It will not do', Kroeber wrote, 'to gut history and leave its empty shell standing around; there might be the embarrassment of no one's claiming it' (1952 : 96). The current emphasis on processual studies in archaeology again seems to be threatening historical approaches with such a fate.

Here it is necessary to pose a few hard questions. The first is: granting that archaeology traditionally has conceived of itself as an historical discipline, is it true that archaeologists have sought only to reconstruct and describe the past ? Or have they also sought to explain it ? Secondly, is any attempt to justify an historical approach merely a semantic exercise, or is the concept one of vital significance for prehistoric archaeology and for understanding the relationship between it and other disciplines ?

To begin to answer these questions it is obviously necessary to clarify what is meant by historical investigation and to do this the archaeologist needs to look beyond his own discipline. In this and in the following section I have restricted my observations to the fields of archaeology and history proper (i.e. documentary history), although similar observations could have been made with reference to historical geology, palaeontology, and cosmogony. Historical analysis is not limited to the study of human behaviour but also is an integral part of the physical and biological sciences (Kroeber 1952 : 66–78).

It is simply not true that historical disciplines have only descriptive objectives or are interested only in determining matters of fact and discussing chronological relationships. In the last century, partly as a protest against the moralizing interpretations of history that were popular prior to that time, historians tended to conceive of facts as constituting the hard core of history, while interpretations were regarded as little different from personal opinion. According to the great historian L. von Ranke, the aim of history was simply 'to show how it was', ('*wie es eigentlich gewesen*'). Objectivity of this sort was a congenial goal during the later nineteenth century, which E. H. Carr (1962 : 2–3) has described as 'a great age for facts'. Unfortunately, the image that history developed of itself at this time has influenced the view that other disciplines have held of it ever since. Yet, even then, it was scarcely an accurate reflection of what was going on in history. Most historians were aware that interpretation played a vital role in the writing of history, even if this was based on some commonly-held view of man or society masquerading as the historian's own philosophy. Works such as Mommsen's *History of Rome* clearly derive much of their value from the manner in which their authors were able to use their personal insights into current social and political problems to explain the past (Carr 1962 : 29–38).

For a long time now, most historians explicitly have rejected the empiricist dichotomy between fact and explanation. It is generally recognized that pure description is not only a

Aims in Prehistoric Archaeology

grotesque goal, but also impossible of attainment. Ideally, a purely descriptive history would aim to recount in the most minute detail what happened to every person living at a particular period. Every particle of information would have to be judged as being as important as every other, and no attempt could be made to suggest the overall significance of what was happening. Such a caricature is the very antithesis of all real historical investigation, which is based upon a selection of those facts which the historian deems are significant (Carr 1962 : 4–14). The selection of these facts is influenced by the opinions or theoretical orientation of the historian. In earlier times, as we have already suggested, this orientation was preferably implicit and frequently unconscious.

In an otherwise admirable discussion of explanation in archaeology, Spaulding (1968 : 33–9) sees the chief difference between science and history as being the latter's dependence on commonsense explanations, but this clearly does injustice to the work of many modern historians. In the 20th century the tendency has been for this sort of history to be replaced by one in which explanations are based not on personal impressions of human behaviour but on solid bodies of social science theory. This development has led to the emergence of social and economic history as flourishing sub-disciplines, closely linked with sociology and economics. G.R.Elton, in his *The Practice of History* (1969 : 38–56) gives a stimulating, if not always optimistic, assessment of these developments. Likewise, the findings of psychology are being used with growing effectiveness to interpret the behaviour of particular historical figures (Erikson 1959). While the significance of chance and determinism for history is still a subject for debate, it is accepted that individual behaviour is not random and must be viewed in terms of a social and cultural matrix which is itself subject to orderly development, that is, which can be explained, if not predicted, by general rules (Carr 1962 : 81–102).

History differs from the generalizing social sciences only in that its primary aim is to explain individual situations in all their complexity rather than to formulate general laws for indefinitely repeatable events and processes. That is what is meant by saying that history is idiographic, the social sciences nomothetic (Nagel 1961 : 547; Elton 1969 : 22–24, 41). This does not mean that historians deny the existence of general rules; rather they seek to employ them to gain an understanding of individual (i.e. unique and non-recurrent) situations. The generalizing social sciences, on the other hand, extract recurrent variables from their socio-cultural matrix so that relationships of general validity can be established between them. As Kroeber (1952 : 63) has pointed out, in history process is treated as a 'nexus' among phenomena, not as a thing to be extracted from them.

The use of general rules to explain a concrete situation is no less an act of creative skill than is the formulation of such rules to explain repeated correlations. Because the aim is to explain a particular situation in all its complexity, the application of such rules serves as a test of theory, and, because a variety of different bodies of theory may have to be applied in conjunction with one another, historical interpretation serves as an inter-disciplinary arena in which the explanatory power of different theoretical approaches may be ascertained. As Carr (1962 : 84) has said 'Every historical argument revolves round the question of the priority of causes'.

Moreover, the fact that historians set as their goal the detailed explanation of particular historical events does not mean that they do not perceive regularities that occur repeatedly in their data or attempt to formulate general rules to explain these regularities. Such efforts are the primary motives underlying the work of historians such as Spengler and Toynbee, which, however, not all historians recognize as history (Elton 1969 : 83). For the most part, professional historians tend to regard attempts to discover 'historical laws' as contributions to socio-logy or to one of the other social sciences, rather than to history proper (Nagel 1961 : 551). This in no way denies the right of an historian simultaneously to pursue generalizing and particularizing objectives.

Current trends in history proper thus reveal the irrelevance of the traditional dichotomy between history and science. Historians use social science theories to interpret their data while social scientists, in turn, use the findings of historians as one means of formulating and testing general theories. History and the generalizing social sciences are like the two sides of a coin – complementary rather than antithetical. Under these circumstances it is difficult to maintain that the apparent

Aims in Prehistoric Archaeology

distinction between science and history is equivalent to that between the sciences and the humanities. In *The Structure of Science* Nagel (1961) broadly has defined science as those activities concerned with determining and explaining relationships between objective phenomena, as opposed to those concerned with making aesthetic or moral judgements. The term humanities is best used to refer to the latter disciplines. With a definition of science that includes both idiographic and nomothetic goals, a growing number of historians are willing to regard themselves as scientists and to make use of the findings of the other social sciences.

Archaeology as History

Especially in recent times the development of prehistoric archaeology has been characterized by growing interest in using explicit models borrowed from the social sciences and by insisting upon theories whose validity is subject to verification through further testing. One important breakthrough in this direction came early in the history of archaeology when Christian Thomsen rejected the antiquarian conviction that had been current prior to that time, that the ruins of the past could be 'explained' adequately only by determining which historically-known tribes had produced them. In place of this, Thomsen, and later Worsaae, posed the question: from what point of view can man's past best be explained, given the nature of the archaeological record? The current demand for interpretations of prehistory that are susceptible to further testing stands squarely in the Thomsen-Worsaae tradition and should not be construed as an attack upon established principles of archaeology. Value judgments and aesthetics have a place in both history and prehistory, but should be distinguished for what they are. In both of these disciplines the search for new methods to understand the past better and the constant endeavour to distinguish fact from fiction are not professional virtues: they are duties (Carr 1962 : 5).

G. M. Trevelyan (1949, I : xii) recalled Thomas Carlyle's observation that the smallest real fact about the human past is more poetical than the best of poems and more romantic than the best novel. I endorse this view and am in full agreement with the criticisms that have been levelled against archaeologists

28

who seek to round out their data with unwarranted speculations in a desperate effort to produce something resembling narrative history. Whatever qualities of imagination or literary skill such works possess and however much they may appeal to the public, they no more qualify as serious works of prehistory than historical fiction qualifies as history. Long term respect must be reserved for the scholar who distinguishes between his interpretations and the evidence on which they are based and thereby makes clear the limits of his knowledge.

Moreover, by using explicit models and by formulating testable hypotheses, archaeologists are helping to make archaeology an experimental, albeit idiographic, discipline. Every scrap of new data that is recovered not only permits a more detailed reconstruction of the past but also serves to test earlier expectations. When a particular mode of explanation is found to generate explanations that fail to stand up under repeated testing of this sort, the chances are that it will be abandoned or at least used with an awareness of its limitations. The declining favour with which archaeologists view migration as an over-all explanation of change in the archaeological record is one example of this (Rouse 1958). While personal prejudice or a scientific understanding of the nature of culture will influence an archaeologist's sense of problem and his preference for particular types of explanation, no wrong, or wrongly-applied, theory can forever survive repeated testing against new archaeological data. In this sense, W.Y. Adams (1968 : 213) is right (but looking at only one aspect of the data-interpretation problem) when he states that 'only solid evidence can ultimately serve as the building blocks of history'.

Drawing an analogy between the development of history and prehistory, one can foresee the latter profitably continuing to evolve as a particularizing discipline that seeks to determine and explain the course of cultural development in prehistoric times in all its detail and local colour. By its very nature, this endeavour embraces the first two goals of prehistoric archaeology that were enumerated at the beginning of this study. No historian can hope to explain events in a satisfactory manner without a detailed understanding of the socio-economic milieu in which these events took place. Rebels and great men are no longer viewed by historians as operating apart from this

Aims in Prehistoric Archaeology

setting, but rather as acquiring their noteworthy characteristics in terms of it (Carr 1962 : 47). In a similar manner, if a prehistorian wishes to provide an explanation of the development of any culture, it is necessary for him to determine, as far as possible, the nature of the social and political system at successive phases in that culture's development. Only in this manner is it possible to understand the changes that take place within such systems.

Specialized techniques are now being developed for the reconstruction of various features of prehistoric cultures. While the resulting cultural profiles are essential for historical purposes, it is clear that they may also be of non-historical value, particularly for structural comparison in social anthropology and ethnology. Despite this, the interpretative 'reconstruction' of prehistoric cultures remains as integral a part of prehistory as the reconstruction of the anatomy of a dinosaur does of palaeontology.

Archaeology in Relationship to the Social Sciences

I have been arguing that a discipline of prehistoric archaeology that is idiographic, but not merely descriptive, not only is possible but has been developing successfully during the past hundred years. Generally speaking, the goal of reconstruction always has implied explanation, and, as more evidence has accumulated and the basic cultural chronology for different parts of the world has been worked out, growing attention has been paid to it. The question we must now ask is whether prehistoric archaeology, as a discipline, must choose between concentrating on historical explanation or developing a nomothetic approach in which archaeological data are used in the same manner as ethnological data to generalize about the nature of culture. Or are both of these legitimate and profitable activities within archaeology?

It is at this point, I believe, that those who support historical objectives can take the offensive. Only when these objectives are recognized as being the very core of prehistory will it be possible to establish the productive working relationship between archaeology and anthropology which many archaeologists are seeking. Insofar as archaeology is searching to define a productive role for itself as part of a broader science of man,

30

the question we must consider is fundamentally a heuristic one: in what way can the study of the past serve best to advance a general understanding of human behaviour?

In the biological sciences evolution long has been recognized as the key unifying concept, as many argue it should be in anthropology (Harris 1968). Yet, in biology, the success of evolution seems to lie in its being more broadly defined than in anthropology, the latter having tended to equate it with ideas about progress and increasing cultural complexity. In biology, the term is used in two conceptually distinct ways to refer to differing, but clearly interrelated, approaches or fields of interest (Mayr 1963 : 9).

In the first place, evolution is used to denote all the processes that effect hereditary changes in life forms, the main ones being mutation and selection. The study of evolutionary processes clearly is nomothetic, that is, it aims to formulate general laws that explain hereditary change regardless of the particular environment, period, or life form that is involved. For obvious reasons, most of the research on such processes of change is carried out on living plants and animals.

Secondly, biologists use the term evolution to refer to the actual development of life forms, as distinct from the processes which explain this development. The study of this constitutes the discipline of palaeontology, which most biologists would characterize as being idiographic and historical. Palaeontology studies extinct species of plants and animals and seeks by understanding them and their geological context to reconstruct and explain the lines of development that link them together.

Charles Darwin made evolution the key concept in biology when he proposed an explanation for processes of change observed among contemporary plants and animals which, if extended to the past, was also capable of explaining more adequately than any previous theory the changes that were apparent in the fossil record. The concept that linked his two lines of argument together was that of uniformitarianism: the assumption that the products of processes that went on in the past (in this case fossils) can be interpreted in terms of processes that can be observed at work at the present time. Uniformitarianism does not necessarily imply Lyell's further assumption that these processes need go on at the same rate at all times.

The application of uniformitarianism in the field of geology had already effected a major revolution in that discipline prior to the development of Darwin's theory. Without the mechanism that Darwin formulated to explain his observations of contemporary life, the fossil record could not adequately have been explained; on the other hand, without the fossil record, the significant changes wrought over long periods of time by Darwin's evolutionary mechanism – including the formation of species and higher taxa – almost certainly would not have been appreciated. Both approaches had to be interrelated to generate a full-blown theory of biological evolution and they have remained interrelated ever since.

Moreover, palaeontology has not ceased to be an historical discipline since Darwin's time, in spite of a growing understanding of evolutionary mechanisms. Even if detailed comparative studies of living species may be able to suggest with a considerable degree of accuracy the historical relationships between these species (Sokal 1966), proof of such relationships has to be sought in the fossil record. It is impossible, on the basis of the present conditions and biological processes alone, to retrodict in detail the nature of species that are now extinct or the particular sequence of development that these species passed through. That this is so does not reflect any specific weakness in current biological theories of process, although there are large gaps in understanding, particularly about mutation. Instead, the situation arises because the factors influencing the evolution of any species are so varied and so difficult to control that any substantial 'prediction' of developments in the past from present-day circumstances alone is impossible. To do this, not only would numerous biological variables have to be controlled, but the biologist would also have to have at his disposal detailed information about geological, climatic, and solar conditions in the past that exceeds anything that the disciplines dealing with these phenomena are able to provide. Some day enough may be known about processes in all of these fields so that it will be possible to reconstruct the past on the basis of contemporary circumstances alone. Until that day arrives, the justification of palaeontology, or of any other historical discipline, remains the same: these disciplines alone can determine and explain what actually has happened in the past. The biologist Ernst Mayr (1963 : 11) has assessed the importance of palaeontology in the following terms: 'If the fossil record were not available, many evolutionary problems could not be solved: indeed many of them would not even be apparent'.

The structure of biology provides a model for integrating idiographic and nomothetic objectives that the archaeologist would do well to consider. I do not advocate that anthropologists borrow ideas about process uncritically from the biological sciences; only that they consider their overall scheme of organization. The study of process in biology may be viewed as roughly analogous to the study of innovation and adaptation in the social sciences; processes that in a broad sense embrace all of the generalizing studies of structure and function undertaken by these disciplines. By means of the generalizations arrived at in their various branches, the social sciences hopefully are advancing towards an overall understanding of socio-cultural processes, and of the behaviour patterns underlying them, that is valid regardless of time and place.

As in biology, it is impossible to 'forecast' the past retrospectively from a knowledge of the present. Even the most general trends in cultural development have been demonstrated solely on the basis of archaeological evidence. All sorts of speculations about progress were indulged in prior to the middle of the last century, yet without archaeological evidence it would have been impossible for anthropologists to have demonstrated that the most striking tendency in human development had not been one of degeneration from a higher state or a cyclical process characterized by no overall progression. An understanding of what has happened in prehistory requires the detailed recovery and explanation of the archaeological record in every part of the world. Because such an understanding only can be obtained from the archaeological record, a serious responsibility is placed upon archaeologists not to abandon historical objectives. Pursuing the analogy with palaeontology, it is possible to view the study of prehistory for its own sake as one important facet of the overall study of socio-cultural evolution.

The desire to make nomothetic objectives the primary goal of archaeology is rather like a biologist attempting to use the fossilized remains of *Merychippus* to study the circulation of the

Aims in Prehistoric Archaeology

blood, or the skulls of juvenile and adult australopithecines to work out general principles of bone development. Both of these problems clearly are studied best on living animals in the laboratory, although the general understanding that results, will no doubt be useful for interpreting fossil evidence. The logic of this has long been recognized (perhaps too dogmatically) by social anthropologists, who, wishing to generalize about the nature of society, have tended to reject all but living societies as suitable objects of study. The archaeologist who is interested primarily in formulating laws about socio-cultural processes might better become a social anthropologist or an ethnologist and work with living or historically well-documented peoples rather than with the more refractory material of archaeology.

Recent developments in prehistoric archaeology do not dissuade me from this opinion. Most studies aimed at explaining archaeological data employ a direct historical approach, in which ethnographic data are projected into the past by tracing continuities and slow changes in the archaeological record (Deetz 1965; L. Binford 1967c; Longacre 1968), or else ethnological examples are used to formulate relationships that it is hoped later can be applied to archaeological evidence (Dethlefsen and Deetz 1966; Clarke 1968). Even where the problem being tackled is wholly prehistoric, the terminology and the conceptual apparatus are derived from the study of contemporary societies (L. and S. Binford 1966; S. Binford 1968), the application of which to the past appears to be primarily a process of particularization, not one that leads to the formulation of general principles.

Nor am I impressed by another argument in favour of nomothetic goals, which states that certain types of society no longer exist and our understanding of cultural variation is incomplete without them. This argument rests on the questionable assumption that all types of society that have ever existed need to be known before adequate generalizations can be made concerning human behaviour. This is clearly a confusion of nomothetic and idiographic objectives. To understand the specific conditions under which various state-organized societies evolved, archaeological data obviously are required, and the more data we have the better are our opportunities for understanding concrete sequences of development. Yet understanding these sequences is clearly different from

34

determining the general conditions that give rise to states. The latter requires a detailed understanding of structure and function that is derived best from the thorough study of living societies, not from an interpretation of the remains of societies preserved in the archaeological record. If one's sole aim is to generalize about states, the information contained in E.R. Leach's *Political Systems of Highland Burma* clearly is more useful than volumes of speculation about social organization in the ancient civilizations. It is illusory to regard the study of these ancient civilizations as being primarily nomothetic: although of extreme interest and importance these studies are fundamentally idiographic.

The acceptance that tracing and explaining the actual course of cultural development in all its complexity is the fundamental aim of archaeology does not prevent the individual prehistorian from pursuing nomothetic as well as idiographic goals. Indeed, the more interested a prehistorian is in process, the better he is likely to be able to explain the past. In biology, the comparative study of the palaeontological record has resulted in important questions being asked about rates of development and related matters, which in turn have stimulated important lines of research in genetics and other nomothetic branches of biology. We have already noted this 'feedback' between nomothetic and idiographic approaches as being characteristic of the study of man.

Many archaeologists are interested in learning more about the past for its own sake; others wish their work to be not only of antiquarian interest but also relevant for understanding the modern world and its problems. The idea that the latter objectives best can be attained by using archaeological data to repeat the work of the nomothetic social sciences reflects a simplistic view of the social utility of scholarship which unhappily is all too common these days. By attempting to understand and explain the past, archaeologists are contributing to human self-awareness. By demonstrating that man and culture evolved from humble beginnings, the archaeologists of the last century effected as revolutionary a change in man's view of himself and of his place in nature as have Copernicus, Darwin, or Freud.

CONCLUSIONS

Prehistoric archaeology has an important role to play as an historical discipline within the larger framework of the sciences of man. To understand its role, however, archaeologists must cease to think in terms of narrow, straw-man definitions of history. Historical research embraces an interest in process as well as in events and chronology. The aim of any historical discipline is not only to describe but also to interpret specific events. For the present at least, archaeology best fulfils its potential not by trying to duplicate work being done in the nomothetic social sciences but by providing detailed information about the actual course of socio-cultural development. The particularizing nature of such a task does not imply a lack of concern with theory, but indicates that within prehistory theoretical formulations should be sought in order to explain events, rather than as ends in themselves. It is highly unlikely that archaeologists will not make comparisons and formulate general theories about process. These theories should be recognized, however, as part of the general domain of social science rather than of prehistoric archaeology as an organized discipline.

III

The Future of Archaeology
is the Past

Aims

THIS CHAPTER AIMS TO DEVELOP certain arguments
originally presented by me in *Antiquity* (1970a) [Chapter 2,
above] concerning the role of so-called scientific and historical
goals in prehistoric archaeology. More generally, I wish to
demonstrate that both idiographic (particularizing or historical)
and nomothetic (or generalizing) disciplines are vital components of a scientific study of human behaviour. This kind of
argument must involve some consideration of the role of
idiographic and nomothetic approaches in the biological and
physical sciences, although references to these will be limited to
a few analogies.

In recent years the preference for nomothetic goals has
become particularly strong in the social sciences. It is argued
that progress toward science is made whenever variables are
substituted for proper names – sites, artefact types, or cultures
– and that whenever a researcher finds that a generalization
holds for one period, region, or culture and not for another, his
duty is to look for additional variables to explain the difference
instead of being content with merely citing it (Przeworski and
Teune 1970). This has led certain archaeologists to advocate
that the principal goal of archaeology should be to formulate
and test hypotheses regarding social and cultural processes
(L. Binford 1962) or, alternatively, that archaeology should be
viewed as constituting the basis of a nomothetic study of
material culture (Clarke 1968 : 20–24).

Particularly in North America, this position has been
reinforced by historical as well as institutional factors. Archaeology and ethnology share a common interest in the American

Indian and, at least until the recent development of ethnohistory, have been sharply differentiated from history, which concerns itself with the activities of European settlers. It is worth asking what has been lost through the absence of ties between archaeology and history, and to what degree current arguments concerning the goals of archaeology are merely an attempt to rationalize the unity of archaeology and ethnology within the established discipline of anthropology.

Erroneous Views of History

Among American archaeologists, the estrangement of archaeology from history has led to serious misconceptions about modern historical research, and indeed about idiographic studies in general. One very common point of view is summarized in the following quotation from *Current Anthropology*:

> The focus of interest is not only on the two traditional 'goals' of archaeology – culture history and the reconstruction of past lifeways – but also on a third goal – the study of cultural process. That is, investigation now not only aims at chronology and description, but also attempts to *explain* under what conditions an adaptive shift...will occur (Wright 1971 : 449).

Far from expressing a novel position, this statement reflects the longstanding tendency of American archaeologists to equate historical research with chronology and description (Taylor 1948 : 45; Willey and Phillips 1958 : 9). The quotation illustrates how easily a switch from description to nomothetic explanation can obscure the existence of a third type of study – that has both idiographic and explanatory goals. Chronology and description are basic to both nomothetic and idiographic explanation but, by themselves, they do not constitute history. The goals of historical research are as explanatory as the goals of the nomothetic social sciences.

The principal misconceptions that archaeologists hold about the nature of history are:

1) *The principal aim of historians is to describe rather than to explain.*

2) *Historians depend on common sense to explain their data, unlike social scientists, who rely on testable theories of human behaviour.*

38

3) *Historians depend on a type of explanation that they claim is different from scientific explanation, while in fact no separate form of historical explanation exists (Spaulding 1968 : 35).*

Scientific explanation generally means using the covering law model, that is, accounting for the occurrence of a particular event (E) by demonstrating that a specific set of determining conditions (C_1, C_2...Cn) was present and that whenever these determining conditions are present, an event of that kind will take place (Hempel 1949 : 459–460). Those who support this model consider explanations that do not conform with it to be false or incomplete and to fall short of scientific precision.

The problem of historical explanation deserves more careful consideration by American archaeologists than it has received so far. If historical explanation means either a separate body of theory pertaining specifically to the analysis of historical data, or assumptions about the nature of human behaviour that are different from, or contrary to, those assumptions found in the generalizing social sciences, most historians would deny the existence of historical explanation. The explanations that historians give, insofar as they are reputable, also must be scientific. Most historians agree that the explanations of human behaviour that they use to interpret historical events and those formulated by social scientists ideally should be the same, since both are explaining the same thing. On the other hand, if historical explanation means that to explain historical data, special techniques are required that lie outside the normally accepted logical structure of covering law theory, then many historians and philosophers of science would agree that historical explanation does exist. Even more historians would maintain that in practice special modes of explanation are required, although they are uncertain whether these modes should be accorded more than heuristic status.

Idiographic Aspects of Historical Interpretation

Problems of historical interpretation apply equally to the work of prehistorians and historians. The aim of any idiographic discipline is to explain specific events or situations. The ideal in each case is to account for a particular development or event by isolating the determining conditions and showing how these

The Future of Archaeology is the Past

were sufficient to cause it to take place. Such an explanation cannot be differentiated from a social anthropologist's account of how the introduction of steel axes among a people who previously had only stone ones affected their way of life. Almost invariably, the explanation of such an event involves setting forth a number of testable generalizations about human behaviour. On this basis it might be argued that the interpretation of historical, as well as ethnological, evidence can form the basis for significant generalizations about human behaviour. This, in turn, supports the view that history is, or can be, a generalizing discipline like most of the social sciences. If there is a difference between history and the other social sciences, it is generally assumed that this is because historical data are less complete than are those that form the basis of other social sciences. Because of this, the historian tends to use already formulated laws, instead of formulating his own (Dray 1957 : 7).

Such an interpretation is based, however, on a false assessment of the nature of explanations offered by social anthropologists and sociologists when they attempt to account for specific complex situations. The claim that such studies are basically nomothetic is of limited validity. Generalizations may emerge from, or be tested by, such studies, but the situation being explained invariably contains many elements that are not covered in any way by the theoretical propositions being advanced. Insofar as these explanations of specific ethnographic situations claim to be adequate, they share far more in common with historical explanations than with nomothetic generalizations.

The resemblances between history and the generalizing social sciences diminish only when viewed in terms of other activities of the latter disciplines. In the generalizing social sciences, the principal emphasis is said to be on the study of regularities and the formulation of explanations to account for them. Most observed regularities of human behaviour are established between a limited number of cultural variables, often only two. Ideally, relationships between such variables are studied in many specific cases of behaviour, which occur in total contexts that frequently differ considerably from one another. It is assumed that, given a sufficient variety of total contexts, the parameters of the variables being studied can be

40

treated as if all things were equal. In this way, it is believed that valid relationships can be established between these variables. Generally, however, because of the complexity and inter-relatedness of human behaviour, the result is the establishment of explanations to account for correlations that have a low to medium range of statistical significance. It is assumed that these middle-range generalizations ultimately can be subsumed under, and accounted for in terms of, broader generalizations about human behaviour, social structure, or cultural process. At present, however, most higher level generalizations tend to be trivial, not generally accepted, or both. More important, the relationship of these higher level generalizations to middle level ones generally is obscure. From the point of view of explaining real situations, the main difference is that historians attempt to provide partial explanations for total situations, whereas social scientists with a nomothetic orientation aim to provide total explanations for selected aspects of these situations (Kroeber 1952 : 63).

Systems Theory

Many archaeologists have become concerned with the complexity of social systems and have sought to develop models to help them explain the variability that underlies these systems and the changes they undergo (Watson *et al.* 1971 : 61–87). This has led to an increasing interest in applying the techniques, or at least the general ideas, of General Systems Theory to the explanation of archaeological problems. This type of approach is interesting because it seems to approximate, on the one hand, the ideal of historical explanation and, on the other, the nomothetic goal of generalization. If the aim of the historian is to explain a specific situation or cultural transformation in its entirety, the explanation might be viewed ideally as taking the form of a complex system. It is inevitable, however, that the more complex a system becomes, the fewer examples of such a system are likely to be encountered. In principle, the systems designed by historians would be so complex that they would manifest themselves only once. Yet, to be of cross-cultural significance, systems must be more general. It may be argued that systems constructed to explain specific situations will contain relationships of more general applicability and that

The Future of Archaeology is the Past

various models, or parts of models, can be combined organically to provide more detailed explanations of specific circumstances than otherwise would be possible.

Yet the mathematician William Steiger (1971) has pointed out that except where a system's components, as well as their properties and linkages, are known in advance, or the analyst has the liberty to ask unlimited questions of those parts of the system that cannot be analyzed directly, the analytical value of systems theory may be very limited. Because of the nature of archaeological data, these strictures may well apply to generalizing types of analysis in archaeology that employs systems theory. If this is so, the most significant contributions of the latter approach to archaeology may come, not through the nomothetically orientated analysis of archaeological data, but through a) the application of this approach in generalizing social sciences and b) the greater rigour with which the archaeologist is led to formulate his explanations of specific events.

It also seems that, whatever may be the value of systems theory to prehistoric archaeology or to the social sciences in general, its application will neither eliminate nor bridge the divergent tendencies of idiographic and nomothetic explanation. On the contrary, these opposing, but inextricably linked, modes of explanation will maintain the same interrelationship within the context of a systems theory approach as they have had within all other approaches.

Evolutionism

Anthropologists, including archaeologists, who want to use a crude form of the covering law model to explain specific events generally are determinists. The basic assumption on which their explanations are based is that the totality of human behaviour, or of cultural process, is determined by a limited number of factors that constitute the core or substratum of a culture. This reduces the number of conditions that are required to be accounted for in order to explain a particular culture. Opinions differ concerning what factors, or how extensive a range of them, constitute the cultural core. In general, the theories predicating the minimum number of factors are those of the so-called unilineal or universal evolutionary type (White 1959). By contrast, multilinear theories

42

admit a larger range of factors to take account of environmental variations (Steward 1955). Even with multilinear evolution, however, the number of cultural types requiring explanation is strictly limited.

The problem with all deterministic explanations of the evolutionary variety is that they tend to be overly general and trivial. By their very nature, they are unable to explain the total configurations of specific cultures; instead, they attempt to account for a limited number of features that a particular class of cultures may have in common. The broader the class of cultures being considered, the fewer are the features that they have in common and that need to be explained. All of these explanations suffer from the general weakness of proposed generalizations that ascend too far into generality and therefore lose their methodological interest. In Dray's (1957 : 29) words: 'Their triviality lies in the fact that the farther the generalizing process is taken, the harder it becomes to conceive of anything which the truth of the law would rule out'.

The reason for this is that social processes are complex, and the events they give rise to are even more so. In physics, the lawful explanation of a relatively few conditions accounts for any particular type of event, and these events tend to be repeated a vast number of times. In order to explain any event in the social sciences, it is necessary to account for many more conditions. This notion is implicit in the basic proposition that all elements of a cultural system are interrelated and that alterations in any one component will result in changes of varying degree throughout the whole system. The number of variables is also considerably increased by the need to consider additional relationships between the natural and cultural systems, as well as by biopsychological factors influencing human behaviour. The complexity of the variables involved in concrete socio-cultural relationships explains the often claimed uniqueness of historical events, which is the basis of much historiographic theorizing.

It may be argued that the limited nature of archaeological data conforms better to a deterministic or evolutionary model than does purely historical data, because it automatically reduces the amount of detail to be explained. The assumption underlying this claim is that the segments of culture that are

The Future of Archaeology is the Past

represented in the archaeological record, particularly those that concern technological and economic patterns, are ones that constitute the core of a culture, whereas those areas that are more imperfectly represented are mainly random epiphenomena of minimal importance. While it may be argued, also along functionalist lines, that all aspects of human behaviour in some way influence material culture, and therefore are available for study by the archaeologist, insofar as material culture is preserved in the archaeological record, the fact remains that large domains of individual actions, oral culture, and belief systems are represented very imperfectly, or not at all in the archaeological record. Nevertheless, if one accepts even a modified version of the functionalist view that all aspects of culture are in some way interrelated, then the more partial nature of archaeological data does not signify that the explanation of these data in reality is any less complex than is the explanation of a contemporary situation.

Both archaeologists and historians also can argue that the problems posed by the complexity of historical data can be minimized by concentrating on the features that classes of events have in common. It can be argued, for example, that all revolutions can be studied as examples of revolution and explained by accounting for the features that they have in common. This, of course, is what Steward (1955) has done in his so-called multilinear evolutionary approach, when he attempted to account for unilineal and composite bands, or early civilizations. It is, however, erroneous to identify this particular kind of generalizing as the only kind of explanation. Historians, while not denying the importance of features that events, such as revolutions, have in common, are also interested in explaining those features that are not common to all of them. They justify such an interest by pointing out that each revolution is different from any other and that these differences are not less worthy of explanation than are the features common to revolutions.

Theoretical Justification of Particularizing

The historians' position, as outlined above, could be dismissed as merely being an unscientific refusal to generalize. Some more conservative historians would accept this characterization and

44

deny that their aim was to generalize or, indeed, that generalization was possible. This is largely, however, an antiquated position. The major proof that the explanation of an individual event, as it is attempted by historians, is a valid act of explanation is that this level of specificity cannot be predicted from more general levels. It could be argued that the difference between individual events belonging to the same class (such as revolutions x, y, and z) is so small that these differences are of little or no theoretical interest. However, insofar as social scientists are concerned with explaining similarities and differences in human behaviour, there is no obvious theoretical justification for such a position. It is possible for social scientists to make fairly accurate statistical predictions concerning complex phenomena, such as election results or national weekend accident rates, but these predictions for the most part are made on the basis not of general theories, but of empirical evidence. Likewise, it is not possible to predict the specific features of one particular revolution from revolutions in general. The armchair prehistorian, no matter how much general theory he knows, is unable to produce a detailed reconstruction of the course of human prehistory on the basis of what he knows about man at the present time. He is even less able, using theory alone, to rule out the possibility that alternative developments took place and thereby to demonstrate the accuracy of his reconstruction without making an appeal to outside evidence, namely to the archaeological record. Predictions about human behaviour tend to be either statistical or of a very high order of generality, and usually cannot be used to reconstruct the past from a knowledge of the present alone. The inability to 'predict' (i.e. retrodict) past events is of considerable theoretical significance. There is general agreement that the use of a theory to predict a specific event is merely another aspect of its use to explain that event (Dray 1957 : 2). It therefore becomes evident that existing theories of human behaviour are inadequate to explain the past if explanation is used only in this sense. The question remains, however, whether this is merely an indication of the immaturity of social science theory or is more significant.

If complex situations involving human behaviour tend to be unique, they evidently cannot be accounted for on an individual level by explaining the features that they have in common with

The Future of Archaeology is the Past

other similar events. This does not mean, however, as certain determinists on the one hand and some antiscientific historians on the other have suggested, that specific events cannot be accounted for in detail in terms of general laws. There is no logical reason to believe that the most apparently trivial feature of an event is any more accidental or, in an ultimate sense, free or nondetermined than are the most significant regularities. Obviously, what is required is a different perspective on the mechanisms for explaining human behaviour.

A comparison with biology may be enlightening. Just as each event in human history appears to be unique, so every genotype (with the exception of that of identical twins) is different from every other. The reason for this variation is the large variety of genes that can combine to give rise to any single genotype. Because of the number of genes involved, the chances of precisely the same combination coming together in any two individuals are vanishingly small. Nevertheless, in spite of this natural variation, processes of mutation, recombination, dominance, and selection have been formulated that explain what is happening to these genetic components. One can assume that the variation in human behaviour that makes each event unique must be a product of many factors, each subject to its own covering laws. These factors are part of complex chains of causality that involve interaction between a wide variety of cultural subsystems, each with its own determining conditions. In the case of human behaviour, the complexity of the situation is increased because more than one type of entity (equivalent to the gene) is involved and because the socio-cultural system interacts with the natural one and with a series of factors that are part of man's biological nature. In specific situations, individual factors either reinforce or oppose one another, and by their combination shape the course of events. The involvement of factors derived from such a variety of systems in any specific historical event accounts, in large part, for the complex causality and hence the uniqueness of such events.

Indeterminacy in Explaining Historical Events

In practice, the multiplicity of determining conditions that account for any one event means that historians usually lack sufficient theory to predict all the conditions required to explain that event and therefore may be unaware of significant, and even key, elements in a particular situation. In addition, social science explanations may be lacking for many elements known to be present, which means that their function remains uncertain. Because the determining conditions of any particular event go well beyond the range of any one discipline and often beyond the range of the social sciences, the researcher rapidly reaches the point at which an attempt to account for the parameters in a specific situation becomes of trivial theoretical interest and transcends his ability to control the necessary data. Indeed, it is questionable whether a 'total' explanation of an event can be given in the social sciences, in which at least some residual aspects will not ultimately have to be accounted for in terms of chemistry and physics.

This situation long has been encountered in biology, where the understanding of process, as represented by the synthetic theory of evolution, is considerably more advanced than it is in the social sciences (Rouse 1964). Yet in biology it is generally recognized that it is impossible, on the basis of a knowledge of present life forms and of biological processes alone, to retrodict in detail the nature of species that are now extinct or the particular sequence of development that these species have passed through. If this could be done, it would be possible to 'predict' with equal confidence the detailed 'palaeontological' record for future as well as past times. This deficiency does not result fully, or even in large part, from specific weaknesses in current biological theories of process. Instead, the situation arises because the parameters influencing the evolution of any species are extremely varied and difficult to control. To do this, not only would numerous biological variables have to be explained, but also the biologist would have to have at his disposal information about geological, climatic, and cosmological conditions in the past that exceeds what the disciplines dealing with these phenomena are able to provide. The possibility cannot be ruled out that some day enough will be known about process that the detailed prediction of the past and future will become possible in the biological and social sciences. Such a development would have to take place, however, within the framework of a unified general science of a complexity unimaginable at this time. The prerequisite for prediction of this sort would be

The Future of Archaeology is the Past

total, or almost total, knowledge of process, which would mean that by the time it was possible, no further advances could be made in the nomothetic sciences.

'How Possibly' Explanations

If, given the state of knowledge existing in the social sciences now, or in the foreseeable future, it remains impossible to be certain of the full range of conditions that are operative in any particular event, then it remains impossible to rule out the possibility that any event being predicted might turn out differently. Under these circumstances, the elucidation of historical events inevitably assumes the form of a 'how possibly' rather than a 'why necessarily' explanation (Dray 1957 : 158). As philosophers of history have pointed out, an important aspect of such explanations is having sufficient knowledge to see how x happened, rather than to be able to account for what made x happen. The latter implies that, given the explanatory conditions, it can be proved that nothing but x could have happened. An important characteristic of 'how possibly' explanations is the reconstruction of a chain of events, accompanied by an effort to account for these events and their sequence. The explanations ideally should be based on well-established social science laws, but frequently common sense must be used as a filler because of the lack of such theory. Many answers to questions that arise as part of 'how possibly' explanations take the form of additional data that eliminate one or more alternative possibilities (Dray 1957 : 156–169). The now venerable concept of archaeological explanation taking the form of alternative possibilities may be viewed as a corollary of this approach (Chamberlain 1944). The same is true of the idea that archaeological explanations represent approximations of truth that cannot be proved and can only be disproved when shown not to explain the data they were meant to cover.

By providing new evidence about an event, or series of events, the archaeological record offers a test of the adequacy of the reconstruction, and also of the interpretation, of the event. This is inevitable because, in explaining the evidence, certain tentative hypotheses will have been advanced concerning aspects of what happened not covered by the archaeological

48

evidence that originally was available. This too is an old view of archaeological method. It is, however, one that fits very comfortably into a 'how possibly' structure of explanation, as opposed to attempts to apply a more rigid covering law model. This mode of explanation also attaches special significance to the archaeological record. Instead of being seen as only another source of data for generalizing about cultural processes, the archaeological record becomes the most important means by which the prehistory of man can be reconstructed and explained. An understanding of the past can be derived only by explaining the evidence of the past as it has survived in the archaeological record. If archaeological evidence can be used as a basis for generalizing about the nature of culture, the reverse is not true – generalizations and a knowledge of present conditions alone do not permit the reconstruction and study of the past. Because of this, it becomes both expedient and reasonable to view the primary aim of archaeology as being the explanation of the archaeological record rather than the nature of material culture.

A Final Objection Countered

It frequently is argued that certain generalizations about human behaviour can be based only on historical or archaeological data (Tuggle 1971 : 131). In particular, it is suggested that only these latter disciplines may be able to produce the data concerning a variety of slow, long-term processes about which general explanations should be formulated and tested. A second argument draws attention to the long periods of human development to which modern behavioural data may not apply. More specifically, it is argued that only archaeological evidence ever can be used to test theories about the behaviour of early hominids, which certainly must have been different from that of modern man.

I do not disagree with the suggestion that archaeological evidence can be used profitably to test theories about certain very significant categories of human behaviour. I am convinced, however, that one of the weaknesses of much of the current theorizing in archaeology can be traced to the tendency of some archaeologists to treat their discipline as simply the 'past tense

The Future of Archaeology is the Past

of ethnology' or a kind of 'palaeoanthropology,' instead of defining its goals in terms of the potentialities of its data and asking the kinds of questions with which the data of archaeology are equipped best to deal.

I share the traditional social anthropological view that long-term studies of the past are irrelevant for understanding the processes that underlie human behaviour and account for the functioning and changes that take place in all social systems, irrespective of age or degree of socio-cultural complexity. Biologists are able to explain the palaeontological record as the outcome, over long periods, of processes, such as mutation and natural selection, that are best studied as they occur at the present time. I believe that the same kind of uniformitarianism applies to studies of human behaviour and that ultimately archaeologists should be able to explain the archaeological record in terms of processes such as innovation, diffusion, and adaptation, which can be studied fully and completely in any contemporary society. I do not share the view of some social anthropologists that the past can live in the present only as myth and that therefore any objective understanding of the past is impossible. Nor do I wish to deny that the study of the past, either through written documents or the remains of material culture, can contribute to the formulation and testing of rules about human behaviour. I would argue, however, that archaeological evidence is a far more intractable source of information about many, if not all, areas of human behaviour, than are studies of contemporary man. I would also argue that, since there are no generalizations about human behaviour that one can expect to gain from archaeological data that could not be gained far more efficiently from studies of contemporary societies, the use of archaeological data for this purpose tends to be wasteful and inefficient. Explaining the behaviour of early hominids is largely an idiographic objective and, in any case, many more general principles for doing this are likely to be derived from the comparative study of living primates than from the analysis of archaeological data.

SUMMARY

In light of the preceding discussion, it is possible to view prehistoric archaeology as having four principal goals:

1) *To generalize about the nature of culture or human behaviour.* It has not been my aim to deny that archaeological evidence can be used as a basis for generalizing, in the same manner as other data used by social scientists. However, in comparison with studies of living peoples, such evidence is more difficult to collect and the range of variables available for observations tends to be limited, as does the behavioural context of the data.

2) *To test existing theories.* The complexity of historical events is such that the generalizations of the social sciences cannot be used to retrodict, or therefore to explain, the past without reference to archaeological evidence. To explain the past, archaeological evidence is essential. In spite of this, the explanation of these data requires the application of social science theory, particularly as derived from ethnology. Such explanations use theory and, in this sense, serve as a test of theory.

3) *To explore interconnections between existing bodies of theory.* From a theoretical point of view, the 'how possibly' explanations of history and prehistory do more than merely test theory. By attempting to explain specific complex events, historical explanation facilitates the exploration of interconnections between bodies of theory associated with the various established nomothetic disciplines. This facilitates the discovery of unsuspected correlations requiring explanation and of interdisciplinary areas of considerable potential interest. This function, being a more particular property of prehistoric archaeology than are the first two, in this sense may be regarded as a more important one.

4) *To explain the past.* If the social sciences possessed an almost total understanding of socio-cultural process and were able to control for the effects of a sufficient number of parameters, it might be possible to predict past or future on the basis of the present and to demonstrate that no other past or future was possible. Until such feats can be done, the study of prehistory must be essentially an explanation of the archaeological record. Insofar as an understanding of past development is an important aspect of understanding current variations in behaviour and culture, such a study, while idiographic, is a vital part of a scientific study of man. Moreover, since the formulation and testing of generalizations about human behaviour can be based

The Future of Archaeology is the Past

on contemporary, as well as archaeological, data, while the past can be explained only with the help of archaeological data, the explanation of past events must be regarded as the most important goal of archaeological research.

PART TWO

Progress, Culture, and Society

IV

Archaeology and the Idea of Progress

The Concept of Progress

IT IS WIDELY ACKNOWLEDGED THAT the concept of progress has been of crucial importance in the development of archaeology and that during the nineteenth century it enabled archaeologists to play an important role in shaping influential views about the nature of man. I will go further and suggest that varying views of progress have dominated all archaeological interpretation; that archaeology as a discipline came into existence at least partly as a result of a growing fascination with technological and social change; and that many of the more far-reaching transformations of archaeological theory can be correlated with major shifts in attitudes toward progress in the social sciences and in society generally. Most of my discussion will be about American and British archaeology.

Although the archaeological record is acknowledged to reflect many different aspects of a social or cultural system, material culture and technology generally are believed to be represented most clearly. The record thus is seen largely as documenting technological progress and stability and therefore as having a strongly materialistic bias. Archaeologists disagree, however, about the significance of this bias. Christopher Hawkes (1954) argues that archaeology makes available for study mainly those aspects of human behaviour that man shares with other animals, while excluding or making extremely difficult the study of those aspects that are most distinctly human. Other archaeologists deny that technological development is paralleled to any significant degree by social or ethical progress and some have argued that material progress is accompanied by moral degeneration. By contrast, archaeologists who

54

hold a materialist view of causality maintain that archaeology has at its disposal a significant amount of information concerning the principal determinants of all socio-cultural systems. Childe (1956a : 160) and others after him have argued that in this respect archaeologists are fortunate, since for them the investigation of cultural systems is not distracted from essentials by a superabundance of largely irrelevant detail concerning social behaviour and belief systems. Even without an explicitly materialist bias, by assuming that there was a strictly limited number of combinations of technology, social organization, and beliefs, the so-called unilineal evolutionists of the nineteenth century were able to assume that knowledge of material culture permitted reconstruction of other areas of culture. Yet today few archaeologists would maintain that social organization and ideology are determined so directly by material culture that they can be predicted in detail from material culture alone.

The Origins of Archaeology

Priests and scholars in many of the early civilizations appear to have been curious about human origins, but satisfied their curiosity with a mixture of history, legends and mythology. The ancient Egyptians and Mesopotamians exhibited a passing interest in their own antiquities and the Chinese developed antiquarian studies to a high degree (Rouse 1972 : 29–30). Yet these activities were not the basis for a new science of man. It is impossible to explain the development of archaeology as resulting merely from curiosity about the past, since such curiosity is itself a social product and in most instances is satisfied by speculation and mythology.

O. G. S. Crawford (1932) saw the development of archaeology as being stimulated by the evidence collected as a by-product of the vastly-expanded engineering activities of the early Industrial Revolution. He was extending to archaeology the better-documented link between the extensive cutting of canals in Britain in the late eighteenth century and the development of geology, especially through the field studies of William (Strata) Smith (Casson 1939 : 185–186). Many archaeologists have espoused the view that their discipline developed when

Archaeology and the Idea of Progress

technological and social change began to occur rapidly enough to become obvious in the course of a single lifetime.

Such explanations, while not devoid of merit, are too simple. It is impossible to account for the development of archaeology in isolation from broader intellectual fashions, which in turn are, at least in part, complex reactions to changing social and economic conditions. These relationships are so complex that it may be impossible to isolate all of the factors that have shaped the development of archaeology or even to say which of them have been the most influential. Stuart Piggott (1976 : vi) sees archaeology beginning as 'an episode in the history of taste'. Many archaeologists, however, view the beginnings of their discipline as being related to issues of more far-reaching social importance.

S. Toulmin and J. Goodfield (1966 : 103) claim that about AD 1400 some men in Western society first became aware that social structures were changing over time. This probably was related to the breakdown of feudalism (Slotkin 1965 : x–xi). Their date corresponds closely with the activities of Cyriac of Ancona, who has been labelled the 'Father of Archaeology'. He visited Greece for 25 years, collecting inscriptions, coins, art, and manuscripts (Casson 1939 : 93–99). The revival of Classical scholarship associated with the Renaissance created a new awareness of contradictory teachings about man and his place in nature. This provided the plurality of competing traditions that J. Pocock (1962) sees as promoting a concern with historical explanation.

In Classical literature Renaissance scholars found a variety of differing views concerning the development of society. Hesiod's successive ages of Gold, Silver, Bronze, and Iron constituted a degenerative scheme, while Lucretius set out an explicitly materialist and evolutionary sequence. The Platonists adopted a static and transcendental view of eternal principles embracing the universe, including the social and moral order, while the Stoics held a cyclical view. On the whole, many Greeks and Romans seem to have accepted the idea of material progress, but tended to link it with moral decline. Some of these speculations may have embodied historical knowledge of the transition from the Bronze to the Iron Age in the Mediterranean region. Yet no one in the Classical world thought of searching for a means by which these ideas empirically might be tested.

It was believed generally that rational knowledge of the past was impossible for periods to which surviving documents and legends failed to apply (Toulmin and Goodfield 1966 : 49).

The traditional Christian teachings to which these views offered an alternative had sought to understand man within an historical context. Yet society was viewed as being of supernatural origin, and change was equated with successive divine interventions in the course of history; hence there was no sense of developmental continuity (Ibid. p.56). Christianity had absorbed Aristotle's idea of a *scala naturae* which ordered plants, animals, social classes, and the various ranks of the supernatural in a sequence of increasing complexity and spiritualization. The *scala naturae* implied a fixed order of nature in which each entity was assigned a definite place. The maintenance of tradition was viewed as good, change as decay, and increasing variety as evidence of degeneration. Change was brought about mainly by diffusion, which represented a falling away from the perfect state in which the world had been created. The physical and moral decay of the world was believed by most Christians to be in an advanced state and its end imminent (Ibid. p.76).

The interest of Renaissance scholars in antiquity enhanced literary and historical studies, encouraged the recovery of antiquities, and increased an awareness of alternatives to the Christian tradition, but in some respects it did not mark a major break with the past. Indeed, a preoccupation with the greatness of Greece and Rome and a belief that their cultures were superior to those of modern times reinforced the belief in degeneration (Hodgen 1964 : 269).

Beginning in the sixteenth century, the development of national states in northern and western Europe encouraged the compilation of historical and geographical data for patriotic purposes. National origins were sought in myths, legends, and outright fabrications, as well as in early writings, and prehistoric as well as historic monuments were recorded as evidence of past greatness. In England, scholars who saw the destruction of the monasteries and their libraries were moved to record their vanished glories (K. Clark 1962 : 23). In general, these national antiquaries belonged to the leisured, but not rich, middle classes, while the nobility collected Greek and Roman antiquities (Casson 1939 : 141–143).

Growing knowledge about the American Indians encouraged an awareness of European prehistory. Comparison suggested that the stone arrowheads and axe blades being found in Europe were of human rather than natural origin. This idea was first recorded by Michele Mercati in the sixteenth century and in print by William Dugdale in 1656, although it was not wholly accepted until the eighteenth century (Slotkin 1965 : x). Early in the seventeenth century the poet Samuel Daniel suggested that the life of the early Briton might have resembled that of the American Indian, and, soon after, the antiquarian John Aubrey estimated that the ancient Britons were '2 or 3 degrees' less savage than the Indians (Piggott 1976 : 67, 112). Dugdale maintained that stone tools were manufactured before the art of making arms from brass or iron was known. In this fashion, antiquaries began to think about an implicitly evolutionary scale of cultures that was different in its emphasis from the older class-conscious *scala naturae*.

In the seventeenth century, René Descartes formulated his view of nature as a vast machine governed by laws that were universal and eternal in their application. God had created the universe, but stood apart from its clock-like operation. Descartes's views helped to promote an understanding of human nature as something that was fixed rather than declining as part of a deteriorating world. In England, the struggle between Crown and Parliament promoted a keen interest in history as each side searched for precedents to bolster its claims. Every age was seen as having its own characteristics. Yet historical development still was not conceived of; instead history was viewed as a series of variations within a framework that was fixed by an unalterable human nature (Toulmin and Goodfield 1966 : 111–115). From this it was but a small step to a belief in psychic unity, as expounded in the writings of William Temple and Benedictus de Spinoza (Slotkin 1965 : 109, 170). Cultural differences generally were attributed to environmental factors.

Francis Bacon was among those who opposed the idea that the thoughts of antiquity were superior to those of modern times. By the second half of the seventeenth century, the belief that the world was nearing its demise was replaced by one full of hope for the future (Toulmin and Goodfield 1966 : 109). Increasing faith in the reality of progress encouraged scholars to treat contemporary cultural gradations as illustrating a temporal sequence of development (Hodgen 1964 : 390). Savages were transformed into primitives. Some scholars, following the opinion of Tacitus, imagined these primitives to be noble savages, whose lives were uncorrupted by the vices of civilization. Others, more impressed with the benefits of civilization, pictured primitive life as being solitary, poor, nasty, brutish, and short.

In Britain, by the end of the seventeenth century the development of the physical sciences and the empirical approach of Bacon and Descartes, particularly as transmitted through the Royal Society, were encouraging the objective, though still largely descriptive, study of antiquities (Lynch and Lynch 1968). Stuart Piggott (1976 : 20) sees this as initiating the liberation of archaeological interpretation from a dependence on literary sources. Yet, whatever potential there was in the work of this period was lost as antiquaries began to elaborate sterile fantasies based on an ill-matched mixture of archaeological and historical data. This aberration, which was paralleled in contemporary historical studies in England, reached its climax in William Stukeley's efforts to link the religion of the Druids with Christianity through an alleged shared belief in the Holy Trinity (Piggott 1950).

The most important studies of prehistory in the eighteenth century were made, not by antiquaries, but by the French *philosophes* and by Scottish scholars such as William Robertson Smith, John Millar, Adam Ferguson, and James Burnett, later Lord Monboddo. These savants were interested in what Dugald Stewart called 'theoretic or conjectural history'. This involved the comparative study of living peoples, arranging them into logical developmental sequences, usually unilineal in nature, and projecting these sequences into prehistoric times. While most of their studies were based on ethnographic data, some of the Scottish Primitivists cited archaeological evidence in support of their theories (Harris 1968 : 34).

These and other philosophers of the Enlightenment promoted a belief in progress as being desirable, and at least some of them, such as Anne Robert Jacques Turgot, viewed it as being

Archaeology and the Idea of Progress

an inevitable law of nature (Slotkin 1965 : 357). Progress was seen as following a single course in technology and science and also (depending on individual views about human nature) in society and morals. Yet, in accordance with a Cartesian point of view, progress was seen not as transforming human nature, but as perfecting it by eliminating passion and superstition (Toulmin and Goodfield 1966 : 123). Philosophers of the Enlightenment also viewed change as continuous and as proceeding from natural causes rather than resulting from supernatural intervention. While John Locke and others thought of the mind as an empty cabinet and education as determining human behaviour, this did not prevent other philosophers, including Adam Ferguson, from regarding a desire for improvement as being innate in mankind (Slotkin 1965 : 440). Progress was viewed as a natural result of rational thought being applied to existing circumstances. In keeping with the assumption of psychic unity, cultural evolution was interpreted as germs of thought unfolding by a process of inner logic. Environmental factors continued to be assigned a prominent role in accounting for cultural differences; sometimes by means of the effects they were alleged to produce on human physique and temperament. The native peoples of the New World generally were supposed to have developed their ways of life independently from those of the Old World. Similarities between cultural development in the two hemispheres were attributed to the effects of psychic unity.

By the end of the eighteenth century Kant had envisaged cosmological evolution but rejected biological or moral evolution. Vico had conceived of social change but saw no progress in nature. Herder combined both to produce a 'philosophical vision' of historical processes embracing the universe, nature, and society but he did not foresee that higher forms were derived from lower ones. For him history was a progression not a transformation (Toulmin and Goodfield 1966 : 136). Nevertheless, by 1800 scholars in many fields were in a position to appreciate the concept of development and to see its relevance for the interpretation of their data. Yet in middle-class society a Cartesian view of the universe remained popular in the clockwork analogy of William Paley's *Natural Theology*. This view saw the world as being perfect, changeless, and good and man as the special creation of God (Daniel 1950 : 27).

Evolutionary Archaeology

During the eighteenth century, antiquaries such as Erik Pontoppidan and Kilian Stobaeus in Scandinavia (Klindt-Jensen 1975 : 35–37) and Bishop Lyttelton and John Frere in England (Daniel 1950 : 26–27) continued to assert that a Stone Age had preceded the manufacture of metal tools in Europe. In 1793, James Douglas in his *Nenia Britannica* assumed that barrows containing only stone tools were older than ones which also contained metal tools (Lynch and Lynch 1968 : 47). The innovations of the Danish prehistorian Christian Thomsen must be understood against this background and in terms of the instinctive knowledge of typology that he had acquired from his intensive investigations of numismatics. Thomsen was familiar with the conjectural history of the Enlightenment, probably as embodied in the works of Skuli Thorlacius and Vedel-Simonsen (Clarke 1968 : 10), and it was this which led him to use Lucretius's model of successive ages of Stone, Bronze, and Iron as a basis for organizing the prehistoric antiquities of Denmark. The novelty of his approach did not lie in the concept of technological development or his assumption of a sequence of stone, bronze, and iron tools. Instead it lay in Thomsen's use of seriational principles to work evidence concerning technology, grave goods, and the shapes and decoration of artefacts into an internally-consistent developmental sequence. Stylistic criteria allowed him to distinguish bronze artefacts manufactured in the Bronze Age from bronze ones manufactured in the Iron Age (Heizer 1969 : 24–29). By doing this, Thomsen freed archaeology from dependence upon written documents to date and explain its material; thereby establishing it as an independent science.

The main accomplishment of archaeology at this period was to document that technological progress, rather than degeneration or cyclical processes was the most prominent feature of human history (Daniel 1950 : 57–121). This constituted an important and in many quarters a welcome vindication of the evolutionary assumptions of the Enlightment and represented a major advance towards an objective understanding of human development.

Yet at the same time Thomsen was inventing scientific archaeology, historical events were leading many influential thinkers to reject the ideals of the Enlightenment on which his work was based. The French Revolution and the subsequent resistance to Napoleon encouraged the development of nationalism throughout Europe, while the reaction against the French Revolution led many academics to reject rationalism and universal ideals of liberty and equality in favour of a romantic belief that history was moulded by the unconscious habits and special ways of thought and behaviour that were implanted in people as members of particular ethnic groups (Kohn 1961).

The early stages of this reaction reinforced Paley's Natural Theology, as expressed in the *Bridgewater Treatises*, and also won widespread support for Georges Cuvier's theory of geological catastrophism, which was pre-Cartesian in its intimation of divine intervention in the workings of the universe. Near Eastern archaeology evolved around a concern to vindicate the Bible, and many of its practitioners manifested considerable prejudice against a scientific approach (Casson 1939 : 207–208). Yet prehistoric archaeology continued to develop within the perspectives of Enlightenment philosophy.

Prehistoric archaeology took on new significance as Charles Lyell's uniformitarian approach in geology and Charles Darwin's formulation of successful arguments in favour of biological transformation pushed human origins beyond the Biblical date of 4004 BC, and made man's physical origins a subject for archaeological investigation. Before then, most archaeologists who had espoused the Three Age theory were content to work within the Biblical chronology, while in 1843 Sven Nilsson (1868 : LXI) had maintained that it was never possible to learn about human origins. Archaeologists clearly had inherited the idea of cultural evolution from the speculative history of the eighteenth century and were working within an evolutionary framework that antedated the development of evolutionary frameworks in geology and biology. Nevertheless, Marvin Harris (1968 : 53) is right when he maintains that the concept of evolution was saved in archaeology by advances in geology and biology, inasmuch as these advances posed important new problems for archaeological investigation. After 1859, archaeology, geology, and biology were brought together by a common interest in human origins and archaeology became more clearly than ever before the paramount science of human progress.

Evolutionary archaeology reached its high point with Gabriel de Mortillet's formulation of his laws of similar development, which made archaeology seem more than ever to vindicate the speculations of the Enlightenment (Daniel 1950 : 119–120). Cultural development was viewed as inevitable and as following a parallel course everywhere in the world, even in the absence of genetic or historical ties. Only the rate of progress differed, largely for environmental reasons. De Mortillet evoked the operation of migration and diffusion in this treatment of specific cultural development, but he regarded these processes as being of relatively minor importance compared to the effects of psychic unity. John Lubbock (1882; 1913) argued forcefully against the idea that cultural degradation had played a major role in human history and, to emphasize the significance of evolution in every sphere of human life, he went out of his way to portray primitive peoples as inevitably few in numbers, wretched, and depraved. The notion of the noble savage was not popular at this period among archaeologists.

Normal human beings were viewed as having a natural desire to progress. Archaeologists such as Augustus Pitt-Rivers (1906) agreed with Charles Darwin and many ethnologists that man's mind was perfected by means of natural selection – a doctrine which implied that primitive peoples were biologically less intelligent than civilized ones (Harris 1968 : 121). Sven Nilsson (1868 : LXVII), like James Burnett (Piggott 1976 : 153) and William Temple (Slotkin 1965 : 111) still earlier, had posited population increase as an important factor producing economic and cultural changes. Yet for the most part cultural change continued to be regarded as resulting from the exercise of reason to utilize the environment more effectively and thereby to promote human happiness and well-being. Pitt-Rivers (1906 : 23) observed that 'It is the mind [archaeologists] study' and 'the psychology of the material arts'. The proofs which archaeology offered that European society had developed from primitive Stone Age beginnings stimulated a revival of speculative history in the period 1860 to 1890, this time among ethnologists such as Johann Bachofen, Henry James Sumner

Maine, John Ferguson McLennan, Edward B. Tylor, and Lewis H. Morgan, to name only a few. Indeed, ethnology, far more than archaeology, was dominated during these years by a simplistic unilineal approach (Harris 1968 : 144).

In the second half of the nineteenth century the concept of evolution played a major role in the study of ethnology in America, but was of far less practical importance in archaeology. This was because the American Indians, who were the exclusive focus of archaeological investigation, widely were believed to be incapable of progress. This view was reinforced by the archaeological observation that no Indians living within the borders of the United States in prehistoric times had advanced significantly beyond the conditions of the Stone Age. Insofar as the Moundbuilders were believed to have possessed advanced skills, such as the ability to work iron, they were thought not to be Indians; those who believed them to be Indians denied that they had such skills (Silverberg 1968). This view of the Indians as being savages who lacked history and whose cultures were unchanging inhibited archaeologists from attaching significance to small-scale changes in the archaeological record and led them to support a short chronology for the Indian occupation of America.

The Reaction against Evolution

Towards the middle of the nineteenth century, the increasing idealization of national and ethnic characteristics promoted the development of intellectualized racism, as embodied in the writings of Count Joseph Arthur de Gobineau (1856). Racial explanations of human behaviour gained further prestige from Charles Darwin's assertion that natural selection had made civilized peoples biologically as well as culturally more advanced than primitive ones. The explanation of human behavioural differences in terms of allegedly unalterable biological differences eventually coloured the thinking of prehistorians as well as ethnologists. To see this, one has only to compare the racially-preoccupied late Victorian writings of John Lubbock (1882; 1913) or Augustus Pitt-Rivers (1906) with the relatively non-racial approach of Daniel Wilson (1851) a few decades earlier. Racial thinking continued to intensify into the 1920s. The ideals of the Enlightenment were clung to most strongly

64

by those who hoped for revolutionary social change and therefore valued the plasticity of human nature. By contrast, conservatives and ameliorationists found comfort in believing human nature to be unchangeable and hence supportive of traditional values.

The economic problems and growing class conflicts of the late nineteenth century eroded further the idealism of the Enlightenment and began to produce serious doubts about the desirability of material progress. G. M. Trevelyan (1949, IV : 119), for example, notes that John Ruskin was able to fill a rising generation of writers with disgust for an industrial civilization in which a previous generation had taken pride. Concepts of national and racial identity were invoked increasingly to counteract growing class conflicts within nation states, while scholars came to view society from a consciously antimaterialist point of view (Harris 1968 : 271). Archaeologists had increasing doubts about the validity of progress. Ancient civilizations were found to have fallen into ruins and the validation of the antiquity of Western European cave art was interpreted as ruling out aesthetic progress. Even Pitt-Rivers came to speak of sequence rather than progress as being the main rule of human development (Daniel 1950 : 181–82). He further stressed that innovation was the result of accident rather than of premeditation or design (Pitt-Rivers 1906 : 96).

Archaeologists also were becoming uneasy that a single sequence of stages did not account for much of the geographical and temporal variation that could be observed in the archaeological record. This interest in the complexity of the archaeological record was part of a general concern with indeterminacy and unpredictability that was coming to dominate the study of man. It produced a growing preoccupation with the subjective and idiosyncratic and with the study of particular phenomena by inductive means. Leopold von Ranke convinced his fellow historians that their main duty was to deal with facts; the geographer Friedrich Ratzel stressed the importance and unpredictability of diffusion; and Franz Boas introduced a similar particularist view into American ethnology. The work of all these men was coloured by strong doubts that human behaviour was governed by regularities that could be discovered easily or expressed in comprehensible formulations.

Archaeology and the Idea of Progress

Within this intellectual milieu, archaeologists became increasingly interested in uncovering the prehistory of specific peoples and showing that ethnic characteristics that were valued in modern times were of maximum antiquity. Cultures were idealized as natural possessions suited to particular peoples. In keeping with this romantic outlook, human beings came to be viewed as conservative, resistant to change, and generally uninventive. While the capacity for innovation was seen as varying racially, it was considered to be sufficiently restricted and quixotic that basic discoveries, such as pottery or bronze working, were unlikely to have been made twice. Hence cultures tended to be viewed as static and cultural change was attributed to changes in population. This is exemplified in the work of W. M. F. Petrie (1939) who explained almost all cultural change in terms of migrations of whole peoples or transfers of small groups of artisans from one society to another. As Marvin Harris (1968 : 174) has pointed out, it was diffusionists who denied the possibility of multiple independent inventions; not evolutionists who denied diffusion.

This trend reached its most exaggerated development in the formulations of the British hyperdiffusionists and the Austrian *Kulturkreise* anthropologists. Both of these were schools of ethnology that had important implications for archaeology. They admitted that cultural evolution had taken place but maintained that each successive stage had evolved only once and accounted for present cultural complexity throughout the world by assuming cultural mixing and loss as this single sequence had diffused from its source. Both schools also interpreted resemblances between Old and New World cultures as resulting from interhemispheric connections. Grafton Elliot Smith (1923; 1933) and W. J. Perry (1923; 1924) sought to trace all but the simplest cultures in the world back to a single origin, but stressed that individual instances of diffusion depended upon idiosyncratic factors and were wholly unpredictable. Their work was suffused by an idealism that saw almost all cultural development as a byproduct of religious concerns. Primitive cultures were idealized as being wholly in harmony with human nature, while cultural evolution was portrayed as an accident which produced societies that were unstable and largely contrary to human nature. The Kulturkreise school similarly idealized early man and equated technological evolution with moral decline. The concept of degeneration was revived to play an important role in the thought of both schools. Childe (1946b : 245) saw in their view of diffusion a revival of the old concept of catastrophism and equated their idea of evolution with the Biblical concept of the fall of man.

While many archaeologists were familiar with the ideas of these extreme diffusionists, they were also aware of the insuperable problems that were involved in using these ideas to explain the archaeological record. Most British archaeologists preferred to adopt a middle position, as represented by the work of Childe. Although Childe's theoretical formulations often are misunderstood as being those of a nineteenth-century-style unilineal evolutionist, in reality they embody the sombre view of man that dominated the social sciences early in the twentieth century. While Childe (1956a : 167) regarded claims that savages never invent anything as nonsensical, he nevertheless viewed mankind as a whole as being intensely reluctant to modify old traditions and as having a distaste for real thinking. Even when cultural changes correspond to the altered needs of a society, Childe thought that it often required a shock from outside for them to be accepted (Childe 1950a : 10). Because of this, Childe believed that an archaeologist should assume that major technological innovations were made but once and diffused from a common centre, unless the archaeological evidence indicated otherwise. Yet he did not believe that similarities in pottery styles in the Old and New Worlds necessarily constituted evidence of an historical connection. Ultimately, proof of historical connections depended upon archaeological evidence (p.9). Childe did not view progress as being either inevitable or automatic and saw change in many societies as leading to dead ends or annihilation (Childe 1947 : 66, 75). Among the factors that Childe believed might inhibit or prevent cultural change were environments that were too harsh (1946a : 24), specialized economic political or class interests (1947 : 16), too great a preoccupation with religion (1936 : 46), or an obsolete ideology (1942 : 11). Because of the operation of these factors, Childe was reluctant to interpret archaeological data by means of ethnographic parallels.

In spite of this, Childe viewed cultural evolution as being characterized in the long run by progress. Hunting and

Archaeology and the Idea of Progress

gathering societies were not only poor but also brutish and nasty; in reply to the *Kulturkreise* vision of moral decline, Childe (1956a : 166) pointed out that the archaeological evidence suggested that cannibalism had existed already in the Palaeolithic era. Progress was defined as being the more successful adaptation of a culture to its environment or, in later stages, the more effective adaptation of an environment to the needs of a culture (Childe 1944 : 109). Progress could be measured by improved health and longevity, and hence by an expanding population. The benefits of progress were believed to be sufficiently obvious that the diffusion of useful innovations by means of trade and other forms of contact could be explained in terms of the exercise of human reason alone (Childe 1929 : VII). Childe (1958a : 76) sometimes saw increasing population as an independent variable influencing social change, but even in his attribution of the origin of oriental civilization to desiccation, he stressed increased human contact rather than a higher population density as the main cause of cultural change (Childe 1928 : 42). While Childe, more so than most of his early contemporaries, rejected racist interpretations of human behaviour, he did not become, like the Boasians, a cultural relativist. He saw societies that rejected technological progress for religious or other reasons as dooming themselves in the long run to destruction at the hands of technologically more progressive cultures. He also argued that the knowledge possessed by technologically advanced societies not only is more comprehensive and coherent than that of small-scale societies but also works better and provides more reliable rules for a greater number of actions (Childe 1956b : 111–112).

American archaeologists, partly for emotional reasons but mainly because of the evidence at their disposal, were unwilling to attribute the cultural development of the New World to influences from the eastern hemisphere. Beginning late in the nineteenth century, Franz Boas and his students started to counteract the myths of Indian inferiority and of their incapacity for progress. After 1914, American archaeologists manifested a growing interest in stratigraphy and seriation and soon were documenting cultural change in the archaeological record. Under the influence of the historical particularism being expounded by Franz Boas, this led to an approach that was concerned almost exclusively with defining archaeological cultures and working out regional cultural chronologies. Boas's influence encouraged an anti-evolutionary bias in American ethnology, but he cannot be accused of having destroyed an interest in evolution amongst archaeologists, since little in the way of such an interest had existed prior to 1914 (Willey and Sabloff 1974 : 86–87).

Perhaps as a reflection of their distaste for interhemispheric diffusion, American archaeologists also tended to play down the importance of diffusion for hemispheric cultural development. Important schemes for classifying archaeological cultures, such as those of the Gladwins and the Midwestern Taxonomic Method tended to ignore the role of diffusion and viewed cultural evolution as being primarily a process of differentiation. This weakness also seems to reflect the priority that they accorded to biological models of species evolution. The American approach to archaeological data in the 1930s resembled that of Childe in its concern with cultural chronology, but lacked Childe's interest in questions of how and why culture had developed. These interests were derived to a large degree from the older European evolutionary tradition. Childe kept these processual concerns alive and adapted them for interpreting the archaeological record in terms of a matrix of cultures rather than of developmental stages. Childe's prolonged and tortuous efforts to square his new cultural mosaic with the traditional system of ages is probably a concrete expression of his desire to infuse an evolutionary concern with progress into a culture-based paradigm.

In Britain the later writings of Childe (1951) and the ecological and economic approaches of Grahame Clark (1952) reflect a growing concern with individual cultures as functioning systems. Both Childe and Clark shared a strong materialist bias in their approach to archaeology. Childe seems to have derived his tripartite division of cultures into economic, social, and ideological spheres directly from Karl Marx, while Clark adopted a similar analysis from Emile Durkheim through A. R. Radcliffe-Brown. Childe and Clark both stressed the complexity of the relationship between these different segments of cultures and the impossibility of predicting the detail of the superstructure from the economic base.

Archaeology and the Idea of Progress

While not wholly losing sight of an evolutionary perspective, both of them also exhibited a Boasian-like interest in the detail and individuality of specific archaeological cultures, although this ideal was never fully realized by Childe and Clark (1974) does not feel that he realized it in his early work. Moreover, although Clark (1970 : 105–106) has stressed that man is a product of the same processes of natural selection that have molded other forms of life, there is in his work and that of most British archaeologists a strongly human-centred approach to the analysis of archaeological data. In particular this has been made manifest in recent years by a strong emphasis on the concept of society as a mode for interpreting archaeological findings (Renfrew 1973c). It is worth noting that the term 'social archaeology' was coined as early as 1921 by O.G.S. Crawford (p. 100).

Neo-Evolution

In the United States the rebellion against Boasian particularism, both from within and from outside the movement, took the form of a growing interest in evolution and ecology. Leslie White, like Childe, stressed progress as a characteristic of culture in general, though not of every individual culture. Unlike Childe, White denied a significant role to human actors in the processes of cultural development; to him – as to the sociologist Robert Ezra Park – culture, and more specifically technological development, was the independent variable, and man the dependent one (White 1948). White's position was a materialist one with a strong antipathy towards psychological or mentalist explanations. Julian Steward's (1953) self-styled multilineal evolution did not fail to recognize developmental stages, but his theoretical concerns were directed mainly towards questions of ecological adaptation.

Although White and Steward both were ethnologists their concern with regularities was grounded in material conditions which were at least partially recoverable in the archaeological record. They therefore have exerted perhaps even more influence among archaeologists than among ethnologists. Sahlins and Service (1960) attempted to reconcile the approaches of White and Steward by differentiating between general and specific evolution, which were characterized as

70

being concerned with progress and adaptation respectively. The concept of evolution was thereby dissociated from automatically implying progress. In spite of this, American anthropologists, including Sahlins (1968) and Service (1971), increasingly have used ethnological data to construct speculative and highly abstract sequences of unilinear development. The most popular of these have as levels: band, tribe, chiefdom, and state. These sequences have provided many generalizations which archaeologists have attempted to use to interpret their data. Implicit in these models is the belief that technological progress is not inevitable in specific cultures, but that at least to date the greater selective fitness of technologically-advanced cultures ensures that progress is an overall characteristic of cultural development (Segraves 1974).

Into the 1960s, larger-scale societies generally were believed to cope more efficiently with their environments and to provide a richer, more secure, and more leisured life for their members than did primitive ones. Soon after, however, American optimism was dampened by a series of political and economic crises that were accompanied by growing anxiety about industrial pollution, exhaustion of energy supplies, and nuclear proliferation. Even the accelerating expansion of population which Childe had accepted as the key index of progress came to be viewed as a menace, while the increasing rate of change was interpreted as producing dysfunctional 'future shock'. These conditions led many anthropologists to reconsider the concept of progress in a more sombre light.

Ethnologists re-examined the economies of hunting and gathering peoples and found that their way of life often was able to support a low population density with less effort than was required by food production. Hunters and gatherers thus tended once more to be viewed as leisured and noble savages (Lee and De Vore 1968). Anthropologists also were intrigued by the arguments of the economist Ester Boserup to the effect that while increasingly intensive modes of agriculture produce more food per unit of land, they also require a greater labour input for the amount of food produced (Spooner 1972). Both of these views have led archaeologists to reject the notion that technological innovation is an autonomous process of rational self-improvement and the driving force behind cultural

Archaeology and the Idea of Progress

evolution. It is now generally accepted as being necessary to determine why specific innovations are accepted and what factors encourage or retard innovation. More specifically, it is believed that inventions are unlikely to be made or accepted unless changing conditions threaten the stability of the cultural system. Population increase, which formerly tended to be viewed as resulting from technological change, now is treated as an important independent variable promoting cultural change (Cohen 1977). The breakdown of traditional controls against population increase frequently is seen as compelling major irreversible changes in the cultural system until a new stable adjustment has been achieved. Much of this is expressed in the terminology of General Systems Theory, with a particular emphasis on positive and negative feedback.

Thus once again disillusionment about present day affairs has led many archaeologists to reject the view that cultural progress is inevitable or even desirable. Archaeologists used to believe that the greater security of a technologically-advanced way of life would induce less advanced peoples to adopt it, if it were possible for them to acquire the necessary skills. It is now widely assumed that most human beings seek to preserve rather than to change familiar styles of living and that to do this at least the more egalitarian prehistoric peoples consciously sought to be 'conserving societies' (e.g. Cunliffe 1974 : 27). This constitutes a striking reversal of middle class Anglo-American attitudes toward technological change. It also is maintained that individuals and groups are unable to foresee the consequences of what often begins as minor modifications of traditional behaviour and that most cultural change therefore cannot be the result of conscious planning. Instead, cultural development is attributed to pressures that compel men and women to work harder in order to survive in an increasingly complex social setting.

This pessimistic and even tragic view of cultural evolution is not differentiated from older views merely in that change is not regarded as inevitable, since Childe and White both realized that. Rather, while avoiding imponderable questions about human nature such as complicated the work of the extreme diffusionists, many modern archaeologists agree with the latter in viewing change and progress as undesirable. Man is seen as being the victim of forces that lie beyond his under-

72

standing and control. In keeping with the longstanding traditions of evolutionary thought in American anthropology, the creative role of people either as individuals or as aggregates is played down and a strong emphasis is placed on ecological and cultural systems rather than on society (Flannery 1967).

Not all Americans subscribe to these pessimistic views. Bennett Bronson (1972) has called into question much of the evidence on which Boserup's views are based and has suggested that, in the long term, intensive agriculture may produce food more efficiently than slash and burn methods. George Cowgill (1975) has reviewed the problem of population growth in broader perspective and suggests that innovation may result in part from a conscious desire for change, while Robert M. Adams (1974) has reminded archaeologists of the need to consider planning and decision-making as part of understanding cultural change. There may be a place for game theory in archaeology as well as systems theory.

CONCLUSIONS

Older theories of cultural evolution were based largely on contradictory psychological assumptions that human beings were or were not predisposed to change their way of life. These assumptions tended to be implicit and none has proved susceptible of rigorous demonstration. Archaeologists also tended to be naive in not taking a systemic view of factors that promoted and impeded technological change, although some older archaeologists, such as Childe (1947 : 11–14), saw the need for such a view. Recent developments have encouraged archaeologists to adopt a systemic view of innovation and to escape from what had become a psychological impasse.

Yet, current views appear to strip man of volition in the process of cultural change and to take an unwarrantedly pessimistic view of human achievements. Increasing longevity, improved control of disease, and the expansion of communication and education must be set alongside the problems of the moment if we are to evaluate mankind's achievements within a sufficiently broad framework. Does the technological progress documented in the archaeological record suggest that man should be able to cope successfully with future problems of

Archaeology and the Idea of Progress

adaptation, as the nineteenth century evolutionists believed? Is the fate of our own civilization to be read in the ruins of those of antiquity, as G. Elliot Smith maintained? Is the development of a technologically-advanced civilization a pathological development leading to planetary annihilation? Or are archaeological data irrelevant for understanding the future? Only time may tell. Yet Childe (1946b) saw some measure of prediction as being the ultimate value and validation of any science. With its control over data concerning various aspects of human development over long periods of time, archaeology should be able to play a significant role in assessing the future of mankind – if for no other reason than because it alone can provide accurate information about what has happened in prehistory. To assess these data the study of progress and stability must be shifted from the realm of subjective opinion to that of scientific investigation.

V

The Development of the Archaeological Culture in Europe and America

Culture

IT IS FREQUENTLY AND OFTEN condescendingly suggested that the interpretation of archaeological data, like that of data in all of the social sciences, tends wittingly or not to mirror little more than contemporary social concerns and prejudices (Leone 1975). Yet archaeologists would like to believe that their discipline possesses a cumulative body of theory that in the long run allows deeper and more accurate insights into the significance of archaeological data and of human behaviour generally. In order to distinguish concepts that are related intrinsically to the analysis of archaeological data from mere social prejudices, it may be useful to apply to the history of archaeological theory the traditional archaeological technique of the controlled comparison of independent or nearly independent sequences of development. For this purpose, I will examine the early development of the concept of the archaeological culture in Europe and America, paying attention both to the social contexts and to the specific archaeological traditions within which this concept evolved.

Kroeber and Kluckhohn (1952) have documented how in the course of the eighteenth century French and German philosophers began to use the French word *culture*, which originally was applied to agricultural pursuits, to designate human progress or enlightenment. In Germany the word was altered further to denote the customs of individual societies and, after 1782, works on *Kulturgeschichte* (cultural history) began to proliferate. Beginning in 1843, Gustav Klemm published ethnographic data under the headings of *Culturgeschichte* (1843–52) and *Culturwissenschaft* (1854–55). E.B. Tylor was aware of Klemm's usage as early as 1865, but he continued to call his subject matter *civilization* until 1871, when in *Primitive Culture* he adopted the word culture and provided it with its first and still classic definition: 'Culture or Civilization, taken in its wide ethnographic sense, is that complex whole which includes knowledge, belief, art, morals, law, custom, and other capabilities and habits acquired by man as a member of society' (p.1). From this holistic or processual view of culture it was an easy step to a partitive one of individual cultures as ways of life transmitted by specific peoples from generation to generation. It was this view of culture that in the 1920s was to constitute a 'new starting-point' for prehistoric archaeology in Britain and America. In T.S.Kuhn's (1970) terminology, it permitted the replacement of an evolutionary paradigm by an historical one.

An archaeological culture may be defined as a geographically contiguous set of artefact types that may occur in differing combinations in different functional contexts and that together form the surviving material expression of a distinctive way of life sufficiently comprehensive to permit its bearers to perpetuate themselves and their behavioural patterns over successive generations. It generally has been assumed that archaeological and ethnographic cultures are alike, in that the former are in some sense the remains of once living cultures. There has been more debate about the formal relationship between the two. Some archaeologists view archaeological cultures as being only remnants of material culture; others see them as reflecting facets of every aspect of an ethnographic culture (L.Binford 1962). Especially important for the archaeologist was the realization that the entire archaeological record was a mosaic of archaeological cultures, each occupying a specific geographical area and lasting for a length of time that had to be determined empirically. At least in Europe, the implementation of this concept also required the realization that cultures in every instance had to be built up from assemblages of artefact types rather than created by subdividing ages or evolutionary stages (Daniel 1943 : 52). Equally important was the belief that all recoverable aspects of the archaeological record, not merely a few classes of artefacts that had been assigned evolutionary significance, were valuable for understanding the past.

76

Europeans generally have viewed archaeology as providing an account of their own cultural development, even if they live in areas where it is clear that shifts in population have made most of the archaeological record irrelevant to their own ethnic past. Prehistory has been valued as providing an extension of European history into preliterate times. Glyn Daniel (1950 : 57–121) amply has demonstrated that the scientific archaeology which emerged following the pioneering work of Christian Thomsen was concerned primarily with documenting the evolution of material culture through stages of development that were characterized by increasing sophistication and complexity. Its evidence that cultural evolution, as opposed to cycles or degeneration, had been a significant feature of human history made archaeology pre-eminently a science of progress. Much of the popular appeal of archaeology in early Victorian times lay in its seeming demonstration that the contemporary technological advancement, which intrigued and delighted the middle class, was not an accident but the acceleration of a tendency for progress that was innate in mankind. Yet the intellectual roots of evolutionary archaeology lay not in the nineteenth century but in the Enlightenment of the previous one. The French *philosophes* and the Scottish primitivists had cultivated a belief in progress as a desirable and prominent if not an inevitable aspect of human history, in cultural evolution as proceeding from natural causes, and in improvement as being a result of the application of rational thought to the human condition. The Enlightenment also encouraged a belief in psychic unity. This posited that mankind's talents and disposition everywhere were similar, hence their responses to specific problems could be expected to be much the same.

Yet even before evolutionary archaeology had won acceptance, historical events were undermining faith in the beliefs that had helped to give rise to it. The reaction against the French Revolution encouraged a host of nationalisms and also prompted many thinkers to reject the rationalism and universalism of the Enlightenment, which were blamed for having engendered the revolution. Both of these developments encouraged many people to believe that history cannot be understood without reference to unconscious habits and ways of thinking implanted in people as members of ethnic groups. This accorded with an increasing tendency to account for behavioural differences in terms of biological differences, culminating in the racism of men such as the French diplomat Count Joseph Arthur de Gobineau (1856).

In the latter part of the nineteenth century, this concern with human biological differences coloured the thinking of many archaeologists and tended to supplant the idea of psychic unity. John Lubbock (1882; 1913) saw technologically less-advanced peoples as being not only culturally but also mentally and emotionally more primitive than civilized ones, and followed Charles Darwin in attributing this to the operation of natural selection. Augustus Pitt-Rivers (1906 : 8) drew learnedly upon psychological theories and Lamarckian notions of heredity to argue that the ease with which anyone could learn a specific set of concepts depended upon how long his ancestors had exercised their minds about them. For Pitt-Rivers, this explained within a single framework the superior abilities not only of civilized man as compared with savages but also of the upper classes of his own society as compared with the lower ones.

The growing economic problems and social conflicts of the late Victorian period further eroded the ideals of the Enlightenment as concepts of national and racial identity were invoked to counteract increasing class conflict within nation states. Among artists and intellectuals growing disillusionment with the negative social and aesthetic consequences of technological development sapped further a belief in the value of reason and progress (Harris 1968 : 271). Competition and struggle continued to be valued but were viewed as contests between races or nations having unequal biological endowments. As change came to be viewed as undesirable, human beings were seen as being naturally conservative and resistant to change. Evolutionary archaeologists, including J. J. A. Worsaae and even the redoubtable Gabriel de Mortillet, had conceived of diffusion and migration as processes operating alongside of independent development. As belief in psychic unity and human inventiveness waned, migration and diffusion were relied upon more heavily to explain cultural change. Archaeologists such as W. M. F. Petrie (1939) attributed almost all change to migrations of whole peoples or the transfer of smaller groups from one society to another; he thereby equated cultural change with ethnic change. Klemm had drawn a distinction between culturally creative and passive races, while Pitt-Rivers (1906 : 48–49) was not alone in believing that it was the duty of culturally and biologically superior peoples to eliminate groups whose low state of development rendered them biologically incapable of further progress. Moderate diffusionists allowed for the ability of one group of people to learn from another. Increasingly, however, cultures were romanticized as being natural possessions suited to particular peoples, while creativity was explained in terms of the biological, the accidental, or even the supernatural. Extreme diffusionists, such as G. Elliot Smith (1933) and W. J. Perry (1923; 1924) regarded man as naturally suited to a primitive life, and civilization as an unstable product, accidental in its origins, and pathological in character. Degeneration was once again countenanced as playing a major role in human history. How did archaeology adjust its analytical schemes to accord better with this revised concept of man?

Archaeologists also were experiencing increasing difficulty in trying to arrange their data within the evolutionary framework of a series of successive epochs. These epochs frequently were maintained to be universal stages through which each society must evolve, although as Glyn Daniel (1943 : 22) points out, in practice they were defined for specific areas. Because of this, problems of regional comparability increased as the Scandinavian Three-Age System was extended to cover all of Europe. Already in 1851, when Daniel Wilson (1851 : 353, 559) applied the system to Scotland, he noted that the late Iron Age there and in Scandinavia differed greatly in detail. These problems were only compounded as Christian Thomsen's three ages increasingly were subdivided to try to take account of proliferating data. Even de Mortillet never could have been serious about the universality of his highly specific western European Bronze and Iron Age periods (Childe 1956a : 27). E. Chantre (1875–76) was among the first who formally acknowledged geographical variation, when in his

The Development of the Archaeological Culture

L'Age du Bronze he divided Europe into three archaeological provinces: Uralian, Danubian, and Mediterranean. In Germany and England growing attention also was paid to mapping the geographical distributions of specific artefact types.

Although most archaeologists of the late Victorian period continued to pay lipservice to the idea that all cultures had developed through a fixed series of stages, important divergent trends can be recognized in their work. At least some of these trends suggest the approaching exhaustion of the evolutionary paradigm. Pitt-Rivers (1906) anticipated the concept of universal evolution by studying the development of specific classes of artefacts as logical sequences of ideas and without reference to geographical divisions. Other archaeologists followed Sven Nilsson (1868) in emphasizing a functional interpretation of the remains of prehistoric cultures (Brown 1887). Still others, such as W. Boyd Dawkins (1880), began to treat the archaeological record as a source of historical information. Significantly, Dawkins was one of those who criticized Montelius for ignoring geographical variation in the archaeological record (Daniel 1950 : 125). It was this view of archaeology as offering a history of the peoples of Europe that was to provide a basis for the most significant new developments in archaeology.

Christian Thomsen had made a science out of archaeology by demonstrating that the archaeological record could be interpreted without reference to written sources. Yet the success of his method did not wholly suppress an interest in relating the known peoples of antiquity to the archaeological record. Glyn Daniel (1950 : 130) is right when he states that prior to 1900 there was little awareness that there could be different contemporary archaeological assemblages in the same region or that these might be viewed as the material culture of distinct groups that had lived side by side in prehistoric times. Instead, attempts were made to identify local manifestations of epochs with historical or hypothetical groups, such as the Iberians, Celts, and Teutons. Nevertheless, the French excavations at Alesia in 1862 to 1865 clearly illustrated the nature of Celtic culture at the time of the Roman conquest. This enabled E. Desor and F. Keller to recognize a collection of iron tools and weapons from La Tène on Lake Neuchatel as similar, and therefore putatively Celtic, and by 1871 de

Mortillet attributed still other similar weapons in northern Italy to a Celtic invasion (Childe 1953 : 8). By 1890, A. J. Evans had no difficulty in attributing the late Celtic urnfield at Aylesford to Belgic invaders.

By the beginning of the twentieth century, many archaeologists had come to view the prehistoric archaeological record as the product of many contemporary peoples. In the Aegean region, the strong historical orientation of classical archaeology encouraged the recognition of a number of contemporary Bronze Age cultural traditions that were assigned arbitrary historical or geographical labels, such as Minoan, Mycenaean, or Cycladic. In Childe's (1935 : 3) view, the concept of the archaeological culture was forced upon Scandinavian, Central European, and Italian archaeologists by the contrasting, juxtaposed, and coeval remains that their excavations were revealing. In 1898, Sophus Müller argued that the 'separate graves' and megaliths of Denmark were contemporary, yet the weapons, pottery, and ornaments they contained were wholly different and hence must represent two different groups of people. By 1901, J. Abercromby had identified the 'Beaker-folk' as an element in British prehistory.

Nationalism was strong in Germany after 1870 and most archaeological finds there were post-Palaeolithic (Childe 1956a : 28). In the 1880s, the German ethnologist and geographer Friedrich Ratzel (1882–91; 1885–88) was elaborating his influential views about cultural complexes. This provided the background for the work of Gustaf Kossinna (1911; 1926), a German historical linguist turned archaeologist whose political aberrations have resulted in his important contributions to the development of archaeology being ignored or greatly underrated by most English-speaking archaeologists. Kossinna was a fanatical nationalist who sought to use archaeological evidence to prove that Germany was the original home of all the Indo-European speaking peoples, along with the allegedly related Finns and Sumerians, all of whom he derived from the Maglemosian culture. By inflating the archaeological chronology of Germany in relationship to that of the rest of Europe, Kossinna sought to attribute almost all inventions to its inhabitants and to explain the spread of these innovations as resulting from the domination of other peoples by Germanic

81   *The Development of the Archaeological Culture*

conquerors. Kossinna's writings increasingly became tainted by a virulent racism, which asserted that the Germans were biologically superior to other Indo-Europeans, since they alone had remained in their homeland and hence had avoided cultural and racial mixing with inferior peoples. Kossinna regarded his archaeological research as a patriotic exercise and was prone to urge archaeological precedents as a justification for Germany's expansion (Klejn 1974).

While these ideas invalidated Kossinna's historical writings, what he called his *Siedlungsarchäologie* (settlement archaeology) or *Kulturarchäologie* (cultural archaeology) embodied certain methodological principles of lasting importance. Kossinna was one of the earliest exponents of what American archaeologists call the direct historical approach, which means that archaeological data are used to trace a known historical group sequentially back into prehistoric times. In this he saw himself as guided by Oscar Montelius's principle that cultural continuity in the archaeological record denotes ethnic continuity (Kossinna 1911 : 8). More importantly, his interest in ethnicity led him to organize the archaeological record in terms of recurrent assemblages which the Germans already called *Kulturen* and which, at least when sharply defined, he equated with specific peoples. Indeed Kossinna preferred the expression *Kulturgruppe*, because it emphasized the explicitly ethnic nature of his units. Archaeological cultures sharing numerous features were grouped to form cultural provinces which were believed to correspond with a broader ethnic concept, such as 'German', as opposed to a particular German tribe. Kossinna undertook to trace the extent of each culture both temporally and geographically – this constituting his settlement archaeology.

From German usage and ethnology the archaeological term culture began to gain currency in Britain early in the twentieth century. Its rise paralleled the demise of the evolutionary approach. The terms 'culture-period' (from Montelius's [1903] *Kulturperioden*) and 'culture-phase', which were popular at this time, expressed the ambiguities of the transition from an evolutionary to an historical viewpoint. In 1908, the American R. Pumpelly (p.xxxv) used the term culture as a synonym for civilization in the influential report on the excavations carried out at Anau by himself and the German archaeologist Hubert Schmidt. By the 1920s, the term archaeological culture

82

as well as its general significance were understood widely though used only intermittently in Britain. Cyril Fox (1923) in *The Archaeology of the Cambridge Region* dealt with cultural entities but referred only to 'culture phases' and organized his material in terms of 'cultural periods'. Harold Peake (1922), on the other hand, referred to the Maglemose, Tripolje, and other cultures, evidently confident that the term did not require explanation to his readers. O.G.S.Crawford (1921 : 79) in *Man and his Past* discussed the need to discover the origins, extent, and frontiers of archaeological cultures in a manner which assumed widespread familiarity with the concept. In 1923 M.C.Burkitt (p.18) offered a curiously elliptical definition of an archaeological culture.

This may explain why Childe (1925) felt no need to define the archaeological culture in his *The Dawn of European Civilization*, even though this book now is regarded as the first major demonstration of the potential of the new culture-historical approach (Clark 1957 : 34–35; 1976 : 5). In it Childe provided an account of European prehistory to the Middle Bronze Age in which the traditional periodization was enriched by the systematic organization of data into archaeological cultures. Because these were constructed from primary archaeological data, Childe's cultures existed independently from his periodization. Childe's book was recognized immediately as being valuable not only for its bold historical synthesis but also for its novel approach to handling data (Crawford 1926).

Although Childe did not acknowledge it at the time, he later made it clear that he had borrowed his conceptualization of the archaeological culture from Kossinna, purging it of its racist and Germanic connotations but retaining Kossinna's idea that an archaeological culture corresponds with a particular people or society (Childe 1929 : IV–V; 1956a : 28). Like Kossinna, Childe preferred the term 'cultural group' to 'culture' because of its emphasis on ethnicity. For the sake of simplicity, however, he agreed to use the shorter and in his words 'less happy' term. In so doing, he ignored the criticisms that E.Meyer and others already had made of Kossinna's equating of tribes and cultures.

In the *Dawn* and similar works of historical synthesis, Childe often established archaeological cultures on the basis of only a few traits and posited major synchronisms and inter-relationships using only a small number of general similarities. Later in his life he was to regret some of his conclusions (Childe 1958c : 6); yet it is unlikely that he could have synthesized such a large body of material to such general advantage had he been less uninhibited. On the other hand, in some of his more detailed studies Childe developed and applied a more exacting view of the archaeological culture which it is worth examining in detail, since in spite of the slowness with which Childe (1935 : 3) felt it was adopted, this was the view of the archaeological culture that most archaeologists shared until the 1960s.

Childe never attempted to provide a formal definition of an archaeological culture; what pass for definitions are incomplete and in some respects misleading (see, for example, Dyson's [1957] review of Childe's *Piecing Together the Past*). In *The Danube in Prehistory* Childe (1929 : IV–V) stated that a culture was 'certain types of remains – pots, implements, ornaments, burial rites, house forms – constantly recurring together . . . We assume that such a complex is the material expression of what would to-day be called a "people"'. Cultures had a distinctive content, occupied a specific geographical area, and were sufficiently limited in time that their remains can be regarded as representing a synchronous phase of a society's existence. Childe (1935 : 3) maintained that cultures were the distinctive creations of real peoples and therefore observed facts rather than constructs of the archaeologist.

Childe (1951 : 31) also believed that archaeological cultures did not differ in kind from those of the ethnologist, although they were much less comprehensive. In 1933, Childe (p.417) complained that prehistoric archaeologists, himself included, spent almost all of their time trying to isolate cultural groups and trace their differentiations and wanderings. This corresponds to Grahame Clark's (1975 : 6) observation that the early cultural archaeologists relied on 'a closed circle' of pots and stones to define assemblages, contacts, and chronologies. Yet it is clear that from the beginning Childe had a functional view of culture. He argued that hand-made domestic pottery was unlikely to be traded, hence it could be treated as probably diagnostic of specific cultures; while elaborate bronze swords were traded over wide areas, hence were not necessarily

84

characteristic of the cultures in which they were found (Childe 1929 : VII). Another example of Childe's functional outlook is his effort to classify and determine the behavioural significance of different types of bronze hoards (Childe 1930 : 43–45). Later he stressed a holistic view of archaeological cultures. Archaeological data were viewed as 'constituents [once] interrelated as elements in a functioning whole' (Childe 1951 : 16). He described a culture as 'an adjustment to environment approved by collective experience' and as 'a co-operative organization for producing means to satisfy its needs . . . and for producing new needs' (Childe 1942 : 11). He also advocated an ecosystemic view in which culture and environment were seen as mutually influencing one another (Childe 1944 : 109).

While Childe agreed that cultures might be defined in terms of a small number of distinctive artefact-types (as geological periods were defined by type-fossils), he noted that the criteria most useful for this purpose usually were arbitrary stylistic and behavioural details that had little importance for understanding a culture as a functioning system (Childe 1956a : 37–38). Cultures might be defined by diagnostic types but could only be described in terms of the whole assemblage of 'types and traits' associated with them (p. 121). Even in enumerating a culture's traits, Childe went beyond a simple listing of the artefacts and features associated with it. His inventory also included inferences about technical processes, social life, knowledge, and beliefs (p. 128–131). This view of an archaeological culture as a living entity and his rapid leap from archaeological data to cultural inference sharply distinguished Childe's treatment of archaeological data from the trait lists that characterized contemporary American archaeology. Childe (1956a : 80) also noted that the cultural significance of artefacts was not necessarily proportionate to their numerical representation; in his example, a single quern in a site might indicate food production. Hence the application of statistical analysis to the description of cultures was likely to be misleading.

In keeping with his functional view of archaeological cultures, Childe (1956a : 33) regarded them as polythetic sets (in David Clarke's usage), and not normatively, as American archaeologists use that term. Childe stressed that not all of the artefact-types assigned to a culture need recur in every assemblage belonging to that culture. Types found in houses may not normally be found in graves and artefacts typical of peasants' houses may not be found in palaces.

Childe saw a culture transmitted as a changing and cumulative (hence adaptive) social tradition which was the possession of a specific people or society. Even in his earliest works, he stressed that the correlation of archaeological cultures with known ethnic and linguistic groups was a speculative and hazardous undertaking (Childe 1926 : XII). Later he became increasingly nebulous about what peoples or societies might be; in fact he defined 'people' as a deliberately 'non-committal' term (Childe 1956a : 133). Peoples did not necessarily belong to a particular race, speak a single language, or act as a political unit (Childe 1951 : 40). The precise nature of societies was equally hard to determine from purely archaeological data (Childe 1956c : 19).

Childe concurred with most of the anthropologists of his day in viewing individual cultures as a system of ideas. He stressed that archaeologists should remember that the objects they studied embodied the thoughts and intentions of human beings and societies (Childe 1944 : 2). Yet he rejected an idealist position; archaeologists cannot study ideas, intentions, or emotions, all they can study is behaviour (p.78; 1950b). Childe (1956a : 10) reconciled this paradox by suggesting that what the archaeologist could re-create in his own mind was not the 'subjective thought' of an individual but the 'objective thought' of a society.

In Europe the concept of the archaeological culture evolved spontaneously as archaeologists for various reasons became concerned about how their data varied in space as well as in time. The particular formulation of this concept that Childe transmitted to England and developed as part of the British tradition of archaeology may not be sufficiently explicit and precise to bear modern computer or societal analysis (Cunliffe 1974 : 312). Nevertheless, it was able to support not only the asking of questions about diffusion and migration but also the development of the ecological and economic approaches that were such important aspects of the functionalist trend in British archaeology between 1920 and 1968.

86

While the early development of archaeology in Europe was concerned with progress, its development in the United States was preoccupied with the American Indian. Central to the folklore of White colonization was the notion that the Indian was a savage who was incapable of progress. In the opinion of the Puritan clergy of New England and of many later American settlers, the Indians' failure to develop their land justified their being dispossessed of it by the Whites. The archaeological remains of the Atlantic seaboard did little to challenge this view; however, as explorers and settlers penetrated the Midwest vast numbers of mounds and artefacts were discovered which suggested that there had once been a higher civilization in that area. The most popular explanations of these finds attributed them to a civilized race of Mound-builders who had either left the central United States or been exterminated by the Indians in prehistoric times. Hence White settlement could be interpreted as avenging the Moundbuilders who were variously identified as Israelites, Danes, Vikings, Welsh, and Toltecs. Even when Cyrus Thomas succeeded in demolishing the Moundbuilder hypothesis in 1894, he did this by refuting (and indeed over-refuting) the claims for their culturally advanced status and by trying to show them as typical American Indians (Silverberg 1968).

After 1860, the Palaeolithic discoveries being made in Europe stimulated some American archaeologists to seek to demonstrate a similar great antiquity for man in the New World. William H. Holmes and Aleš Hrdlička failed to confirm any of the evidence brought forth in support of such claims. This, together with the evidence that no North American Indian group had evolved beyond Thomsen's Stone Age, seemed to support the popular belief that the Indian lacked any significant prehistory, either in a chronological or a developmental sense (Willey and Sabloff 1974 : 58–59). In accordance with this attitude, almost no attempt was made to work out local chronologies, nor was there even an awareness of methods that might encourage such a development (p.43). This can be accounted for only in part by the relative infrequence of stratified sites in North America. As Rowe (1962 : 399–400) has observed in respect of the early Kroeber, most American archaeologists were unable to appreciate cultural change in terms of anything less than major transformations of technology.

In 1887, Franz Boas argued that the ethnological material from across the United States which was accumulating in the collections of major museums should be exhibited according to geographical area and tribe rather than in terms of typological classification. The ethnologist Otis T. Mason published the first detailed treatment of the culture areas of North America in 1896 and was followed in this approach by Clark Wissler (1914). Having to organize large collections of artefacts for which only geographical provenience was documented, museum archaeologists responded in the same manner. North American lithic material (Moorehead 1910; Holmes 1919) and pottery (Holmes 1903) were examined in terms of their geographical distribution. These studies led archaeologists also to outline culture areas (Holmes 1914).

Lack of sufficient awareness of time depth and cultural change encouraged American archaeologists to interpret prehistoric remains in terms of what was known about historic tribes (Thomas 1898 : 22–23). William Beauchamp (1900) and A. C. Parker (1916) discussed prehistoric Iroquoian materials in upper New York State in terms of the historic tribes of that region and attributed earlier Woodland finds to neighbouring Algonkian peoples whom they believed the invading Iroquois had expelled (Ritchie 1932). In the south-western United States, archaeologists such as J. W. Fewkes (1896) compared prehistoric pueblos with the ethnography and traditional history of the modern Pueblo Indians. In 1913, R. B. Dixon asserted that archaeology could no longer be interested only in artefacts but had to approach the past from an ethnological viewpoint. This could be done best by means of what W. R. Wedel (1938) was later to call the Direct-Historical Approach. Dixon suggested that this approach could be applied quite easily in the west, where he believed there had been few population movements, but he was less optimistic about the east, where shifting historical events had made the archaeological record a complex palimpsest.

Increasingly, archaeologists were recognizing blocks of pre-historic culture in the archaeological record. This was particularly so in areas where a concern with the Moundbuilders had accelerated archaeological activity. Early in the nineteenth century Whittlesey had attempted to distinguish two Mound-building groups in Ohio, but he had mistaken a chronological difference for an ethnic one (Willey and Sabloff 1974 : 44). F.W.Putnam clearly recognized the close relationship between sites in Tennessee, western Kentucky, and Missouri that are now identified as units of Middle Mississippi. He also re-cognized the strong cultural similarities of Hopewell, Mound City, and the Turner Mounds, as did W.K.Moorehead, H.I.Smith, and others who dealt with them. In 1890 G.P. Thruston defined a Stone Grave 'race' in Tennessee, by 1903 William C. Mills had distinguished and named the Fort Ancient and Hopewell cultures in Ohio, in 1909 W.K.Moore-head identified the Glacial Kame culture, and soon after H.C.Shetrone (1920) was identifying and systematizing more cultural units in the Ohio Valley.

By the latter part of the nineteenth century archaeologists were familiar with the concept of culture as a result of their close association with ethnologists. Some used the term as Fewkes (1896) did when he titled one of his papers 'The Prehistoric Culture of Tusayan'. Yet most American arch-aeologists were not yet ready to transfer the ethnologist's concept of a specific culture to prehistory. Some of them tried to infer the culture of specific sites as illustrative of aspects of the life of prehistoric communities (H.I.Smith 1910). Others labelled the late prehistoric material from a specific area with the name of an historic tribe, but were unable or unwilling to work this material into precise developmental sequences or to define adequate geographical boundaries for it. The latter was a serious shortcoming, since historic and prehistoric boundaries often did not coincide. This confirmed B.Laufer's (1913 : 577) judgement that the main fault of American archaeology was its lack of chronological control.

Willey and Sabloff (1974 : 81) have stated that the principal concern of American archaeology between 1914 and 1940 was with chronology. Stratigraphic excavations had been under-taken occasionally in the United States since the 1860s but for a long time the method failed to attract widespread interest, even though important conclusions flowed from it, such as

The Development of the Archaeological Culture

Richard Wetherill's demonstration that Basketmaker culture preceeded Pueblo in the American Southwest (Kidder 1924 : 161). It was following his return from a visit to European sites in 1913 that N.C.Nelson's numerous and sophisticated stratigraphic excavations began to transform the archaeology of the Southwest. At the same time, A.L.Kroeber (1916) and Leslie Spier (1917) attempted to work out regional chronologies in the Southwest by means of seriation. These techniques gave precision to earlier vague notions of cultural change and began to transform the archaeology of the whole of the United States.

In his *Introduction to the Study of Southwestern Archaeology* A.V.Kidder (1924) attempted the first historical synthesis of the archaeology of any part of the United States. The material from nine river drainages was discussed in terms of four successive periods, or stages, of cultural development: Basket Maker, Post-Basket Maker, Pre-Pueblo, and Pueblo. Each period sometimes was called a culture, while the regional variants associated with the river drainages were also designated by names such as the Chihuahua Basin culture, Mimbres culture, or Lower Gila culture. While the term culture had not acquired a specific archaeological usage in this context, as a result of chronological studies something approaching the concept of an archaeological culture was now evolving.

H.S.Gladwin complained that, among its other short-comings, the Pecos Classification, which had embodied and refined Kidder's periodization, was better suited to the northern Pueblo area of the Southwest than to the more southerly Hohokam and Mogollon regions. In a paper titled 'A Method for the Designation of Cultures and their Variations' he and Winifred Gladwin (1934) proposed a hierarchical classification of cultural units in the Southwest, the oldest and most general of which were three roots called Basketmaker (later Pueblo), Hohokam, and Caddoan (Mogollon). These roots were subdivided into stems, which were named after regions, and these in turn into branches and phases labelled with more specific geographical names. Phases consisted of sites that shared a high degree of trait similarity. Willey and Sabloff (1974 : 111) note that while the Gladwin classification was based on relative degrees of trait similarities, its dendritic pattern also involved geographical considerations and was implicitly chronological. They also observe that the system implied that the cultures of the Southwest had become increasingly differentiated through time, which 'while a possibility was by no means demonstrated'.

An essentially similar scheme, that clearly was influenced by Shetrone's work, was first proposed by a group of Mid-western archaeologists in 1932, and soon under the designation of Midwestern Taxonomic Method was applied to the north-central and northeastern United States (McKern 1939). Faced with the need to classify large amounts of material collected, often with minimal provenience, by amateur archaeologists, the Midwestern Taxonomic Method proposed 'a classification based upon the cultural factor alone; temporal and distri-butional treatments will follow as accumulating data shall warrant' (p. 303). Materials representing a single phase of occupation in a site were called a *component*; components sharing an almost identical complex of artefact-types were designated as being a *focus*; foci sharing 'a preponderating majority of traits' were grouped to form an *aspect*; aspects sharing more general characteristics to form a *phase*; and phases sharing a small complex of broad, general traits to form a *pattern*. The traits used to define a pattern were 'a cultural reflection of the primary adjustments of peoples to environment, as modified by tradition'. Patterns in turn were assigned, rather tentatively, to *bases* that were characterized by a few fundamental traits relating to food production and to the possession of classes of products judged by archaeologists to be of outstanding cultural importance, such as pottery and basketry. Examples of bases were labelled Horticultural-Pottery and Nomadic-Hunting.

While any of these units might be described in terms of the totality of traits or artefact-types associated with it, each unit was defined by a smaller number of specific diagnostic traits or determinants. Proceeding from more general to more specific levels of this hierarchical system, determinants became more specialized and more numerous. The determinants of a particular focus were those of the aspect to which it belonged made richer in detail and augmented by additional traits specific to the focus (p. 307). It also was recognized that cemeteries and living sites belonging to the same culture might

The Development of the Archaeological Culture

contain different artefact inventories. Because of this, some archaeologists proposed to base foci on a range of sites representing the complete cultural manifestation of a local group or community rather than on components (p.310–311). It was believed that this and the incompleteness of data prevented absolute mathematical percentages from being used to establish degrees of relationship among different components. Nevertheless it was maintained that 'the quantitative similarity in culture indicators is decidedly serviceable in determining the classificatory place of a manifestation' (p.311).

Both the Gladwin classification and the Midwestern Taxonomic Method eschewed the term culture. McKern (1939 : 303) felt that culture was being used by American archaeologists to designate too broad a range of phenomena to have any precise significance. In essence, however, these two systems introduced the systematic use of cultural units for classifying archaeological data into America, and served the same purpose as did the concept of the archaeological culture in Europe. Their dendritic schemes implied that cultures, like biological species, developed along an irreversible course of differentiation, thereby ignoring the convergent effects of diffusion which are specific to cultural behaviour. In this respect, the American schemes, while striving for quantitative precision, were naive by comparison with the European concept of the archaeological culture. Yet in practice the weakness did not prove unduly harmful to American archaeology. As phases and foci were arranged into regional chronologies by means of stratigraphy and seriation, the higher levels of these schemes largely were abandoned. The result was that archaeological cultures (phases or foci) were viewed as a mosaic interrelated in time and space, much as Childe had studied them. Nevertheless it took time to realize that a single cultural tradition belonging to one people could evolve from the Woodland Pattern of the Midwestern Taxonomic Method to the Mississippian Pattern (Trigger 1970c).

The concern for cultural classification and chronology that was associated with the Midwestern Taxonomic Method and characterized most archaeological work that was done in the United States into the 1950s, came in for strong criticism in W. W. Taylor's (1948) *A Study of Archeology*. Taylor argued that the investigation of archaeological cultures consisted only of the elaboration and comparison of formal trait lists. Except in seriational studies, even quantitative comparison was neglected in favour of simply recording the presence or absence of traits. The prestige accorded to this formal approach resulted in the suppression of functional concerns even among archaeologists such as William A.Ritchie and W.S.Webb, who had formerly shown an interest in them (Taylor 1948 : 75–82). For most archaeologists, the 'reconstruction of cultural history' became, in the words of Willey and Sabloff (1974 : 116) 'little more than an ordering of the archaeological remains of a given area in a spatial-temporal framework'. The essence of this was a chronological chart on which foci or phases were aligned in terms of horizontal columns representing chronological periods and vertical columns representing geographical subdivisions. This kind of approach remained preponderant in American archaeology until the rebellion against it ushered in the New Archaeology with its emphasis on a functional and processual view of culture. Whether the explicit and programmatic introduction of functional concepts into American archaeology will prove more beneficial than the earlier, piecemeal penetration of such concepts into European archaeology remains to be determined.

Discussion

The concept of the archaeological culture evolved in very different milieus in Europe and America. In Europe archaeologists had been concerned with sequence and chronology as part of a broader interest in cultural evolution. The latter in turn had developed from a positive evaluation of technological development that had its roots in the early Industrial Revolution and the Enlightenment. By contrast, American archaeology developed in a context that regarded the American Indians as unwilling to change and perhaps incapable of it, hence as lacking in history.

In Europe, the concept of the archaeological culture developed and spread as increasing archaeological evidence, together with a growing preoccupation with national and ethnic differences, influenced archaeologists to take account of geographical as well as chronological variations in their data.

Interest in archaeological data as a source of information about the development of Europe encouraged archaeologists not only to trace migrations and diffusion but also to attempt to flesh out the remains of individual cultures with painstaking ecological and societal reconstructions. It was widely believed that these cultures were in some sense part of Europe's national or common past, embodying 'the achievements of our spiritual ancestors' which are still 'immanent in our lives' (Childe 1925 : xv).

In America, the lack of evidence of major technological change was interpreted as demonstrating that the Indian was indeed a savage who lacked any significant history. This led most American archaeologists of the nineteenth century to reject a high antiquity for man in the New World and to ascribe the seemingly more advanced culture of the Moundbuilders to vanished non-Indians. The resulting static view of Indian history encouraged archaeologists to project ethnographic differences among the Indian cultures of the United States into prehistoric times. This in turn promoted far greater awareness of geographical variations in the archaeological record than of chronological variation.

A growing appreciation of small-scale change eventually led to the application of stratigraphic and seriational methods to American archaeological data. Increasing chronological sophistication resulted in the conceptualization of American prehistory in terms of units approximating the European concept of the archaeological culture. Perhaps because of the vastness of the United States and the later start of archaeological research there, until the 1960s the principal emphasis remained on the ordering of archaeological data in terms of spatial-temporal frameworks.

It seems likely that the prolonged delay in coming to view archaeological cultures as functioning systems, as opposed to collections of traits, in part reflects the American archaeologist's detachment from the objects of his study and a continuing pejorative evaluation of Indians in White society. Even the New Archaeology's view that its data provide material for testing generalizations about human behaviour falls short of the sense of engagement with which Europeans view their prehistory or American Indians are coming to view theirs. As formerly, history seems to be for studying ourselves, anthropology for studying others.

The development of the concept of the archaeological culture clearly demonstrates that the questions archaeologists ask reflect in many important ways the outlook of the societies in which they live. In Europe, a fascination with technological progress encouraged an early interest in chronology, while in the United States contempt for the American Indian seems to have been an important factor inhibiting such interest.

Yet it is equally clear that the development of the archaeological culture was not the unilinear process that Leo Klejn (1973 : 695–696) claims it to have been. The concept evolved in Europe as a growing body of archaeological data, together with increasing nationalism, produced an interest in the geographical as well as the chronological parameters of artefact variation. In America, an analogous concept evolved largely independently when an early concern with geographical variation was complemented by a later concern with chronology. The ultimate results were formally, if not terminologically, very similar, although the greater emotional involvement of Europeans with their own past led them to view their data systemically more quickly than was the case in America.

Conclusions

That British and American archaeologists, working in relative isolation from one another, by different routes, and subject to radically different social influences, came to hold such similar views about the nature of the archaeological culture suggests that in the long run archaeologists are capable of devising concepts appropriate to their data. What happened seems to be a valid case of convergence, even though both groups of archaeologists had been influenced by the ethnological concept of a culture, which had a single German origin.

This observation does not mean that the development of archaeology is uninfluenced by the societies in which it takes place. Nevertheless, it offers hope that where archaeology is not directly controlled to serve political or religious purposes, it may overcome the errors and fads of the moment to develop a cumulative body of theory which makes possible a better understanding of man's past.

VI

Major Concepts of Archaeology in Historical Perspective

WHEN POPULAR WRITERS SPEAK about the history of archaeology, they frequently mean the development of new techniques of excavation and analysis, outstanding discoveries that have attracted public interest, or the gradual improvement of our understanding of the past. The present study is concerned with none of these. Instead, it will examine the evolution of some of the basic theoretical concepts that underlie the discipline and which constitute a sensitive measure of the progress and achievements of prehistoric archaeology at any given period.

The two concepts that will be examined are 'culture' and 'society'. The former, although it has been viewed differently at different periods, has been the key concept of prehistoric archaeology since the 1920s; the latter has become of interest to archaeologists only recently, and the importance accorded it here will require explanation. Both of these concepts are ones that prehistoric archaeology shares with social and cultural anthropology; hence an examination of their role in the former discipline must involve, at least to some degree, a consideration of the relationship between the major branches of anthropology.

Nineteenth Century Concepts

The development of prehistoric archaeology down to the end of the nineteenth century has been discussed in detail in a number of recent works (Bibby 1956; Daniel 1950; 1963; 1966; 1967; Lynch and Lynch 1968); hence it is necessary only to summarize the leading concepts that were developed at this time.

By general consent, the work of Christian Thomsen constitutes the birth of prehistoric archaeology. The theoretical significance of Thomsen's work lay in his decision to classify Danish antiquities not according to fanciful associations with various ancient peoples but instead in terms of three hypothesized stages of technological development. In so doing, he broke with the text-orientated, humanist approach to antiquity that had prevailed hitherto, and in its place adopted a natural history approach analogous to that being developed in palaeontology and historical geology. The natural history approach, whether applied to geological strata, fossils, or artefacts, is based on a principle of 'uniformitarianism', inasmuch as it is assumed that these inert products of processes that went on in the past can be interpreted in terms of processes that are at work at the present time. The prehistoric archaeologist's dependence upon the ethnologist's understanding of human behaviour thus was viewed as analogous to the palaeontologist's dependence on the zoologist for information about living animals that could be used to interpret the fossil record.

While the Victorians' concern with progress already may have been turning archaeologists towards interpreting their finds in terms of a unilineal sequence of development, this tendency was reinforced very much by the close ties that prehistoric archaeology developed with Pleistocene geology and palaeontology after 1859; the year which saw the publication of Charles Darwin's *On the Origin of Species* as well as the first undisputed evidence that stone tools had been manufactured in Pleistocene times (Gruber 1965). It is not inappropriate to refer to the archaeology of the period 1860 to 1890 as evolutionary archaeology. Just as palaeontologists divided the geological record into various periods and epochs, so archaeologists tended to view the record of man's development in terms of a series of stages, each of which was characterized by its own assemblage of artefacts (Bibby 1956 : 177–81). Little effort was made to view the various artefacts associated with any one stage of development as constituting a cultural system; instead, artefact types were treated as 'index fossils' that could be used to date particular archaeological finds. Cultural evolution was viewed largely as a continuation of biological evolution and, like the latter, was assumed to be universal and unilineal (i.e. characterized by progress). This attitude was

Major Concepts in Historical Perspective

reinforced by the fact that much of the early Palaeolithic material was found in Europe not in living sites but in glacial debris, that is, in geological contexts. The chief concession to the uniqueness of prehistory was the recognition that the rate of cultural development had varied in different parts of the world.

This unilineal approach to culture history made possible what seemed to be a mutually-beneficial rapprochement between archaeology and ethnology. If the most advanced societies in the world had evolved through a fixed developmental sequence, present day societies that were less advanced could be used to illustrate at least some of the stages that these societies had passed through in former times. Hence, living societies could provide evidence concerning all aspects of social and cultural evolution and thus supplement archaeological evidence concerning the development of material culture. In order to apply what was known about existing societies to the inter-pretation of the archaeological record, all the archaeologist needed to know about a prehistoric society was the stage of development it had reached. This was information that could be obtained easily through an examination of stage-diagnostic artefacts, i.e., 'index fossils'.

A psychological underpinning for this synthesis of arch-aeology and ethnology was provided by Adolf Bastian's theory of the psychic unity of man, which proposed that because of the uniformity of human nature, individuals or groups at the same level of development automatically would tend to evolve similar responses to the same problems (Lowie 1937 : 30–8). Aware as we are of the pitfalls and shortcomings of this theory, it behoves us to remember that much of the unity of the discipline of anthropology as we know it today (especially in North America) derives from the unifying effect that the theory of parallel unilineal evolution exerted upon the fields of ethnology and archaeology at this time. The unit-concept that dominated both fields was that of *stage*; cultures were seen as conforming to a limited number of types and those that could be assigned to the same stage were considered to be essentially equivalent, whether they existed at the present time or had existed at some remote period in the past.

Prehistorians were well aware, however, that there was much that unilineal evolution did not explain. Throughout the nineteenth century the concepts of migration and cultural diffusion were invoked with increasing frequency to account for the developmental patterns observed in the archaeological record. The principal exponents of unilineal evolution were not archaeologists, but ethnologists, who framed their explanations of cultural variations amongst living peoples in terms of pseudo-historical relationships. Bachofen, McLennan, Tylor, and Morgan did not have any direct experience of working with archaeological data (Daniel 1963 : 78–81). Instead, they sought to arrange the ethnological data they had at their disposal into a logical developmental sequence that would explain differences in institutions as points along a continuum of development from simple to complex. They were the precursors of modern ethnologists and social anthropologists and it was against their use of a pseudo-historical framework to study structural relationships that Radcliffe-Brown's (1958 : 3–38) attacks were to be directed.

The intense concern of this period with material progress encouraged archaeologists to seek general evolutionary trends in the archaeological record, rather than to note local variations in archaeological assemblages. This approach seemed the more natural in view of the tendency we have already noted – to view different classes of artefacts in isolation from each other and to treat each class, much as palaeontologists did fossil species, as undergoing progressive evolutionary development through time.

Thus a considerable amount of interest was focused on tracing the development of particular classes of artefacts in time and space, with little concern for the individual cultural contexts in which these artefacts were being found. In books of the period, individual chapters frequently were devoted to tracing the development of metallurgy, architecture, weapons, or the use of fire. The main purpose of most of these studies was to see a chronicle of universal human progress reflected in the development of material culture. While serious studies of this sort still are undertaken and are of recognised value for understanding the past, they now constitute only one of many approaches.

Cultural Archaeology

By the turn of the century many more archaeological data had been recovered and there was a growing awareness of regional differences in archaeological assemblages. Archaeologists began to look for new ideas that would permit them to perceive order in this variation. At the same time, the ties between palaeolithic archaeology and the natural sciences had begun to weaken and the new views that archaeologists were adopting about the nature of culture were influenced by the interest in cultural complexes that had been developing in cultural anthropology and human geography in the last decades of the nineteenth century (Daniel 1963 : 98). These developments suggested a new unit concept to replace the outworn concept of stage or epoch.

It soon became obvious to archaeologists that it was possible to group together components containing assemblages of artefacts that were identical or similar to one another, to form units that were analogous to ethnological cultures. Archaeological cultures clearly had to be defined in terms of similarities in material culture, but many archaeologists, including Gustaf Kossinna (1911) and Childe (1929 : v–vi), argued that close similarities in material culture were possible only if people shared a common way of life. Hence they concluded that the people who produced an archaeological culture must have spoken the same language, had a common sense of identity, and been bound together by social and political affiliations. Whatever the shortcomings of these initial ideas, the utilisation of the unit concept of culture, in place of stage, marks the birth of cultural, as distinguished from evolutionary, archaeology.

The full potentialities of the culture-unit concept were first realised by Childe in 1925 in *The Dawn of European Civilization*, a book that Glyn Daniel (1950 : 247) properly has described as 'a new starting-point for prehistoric archaeology'. The principal advantage of the culture-unit concept was that it allowed prehistory to free itself from a simplistic evolutionary bias and to take account of the complexity of the historical relationships that were apparent in the archaeological record. The evolutionary approach had been concerned with seeing a pattern of progress in this record; the new historical approach was interested in tracing the actual record of cultural development.

Within a very short time, Childe's approach was being followed throughout Europe, while a similar one had evolved independently in America. Everywhere, sites were being grouped together to form cultures and the temporal and geographical as well as the historical relationships between these cultures were being explored (Daniel 1963 : 98–103; Taylor 1948 : 43–92). In place of unilineal developmental schemes, the prehistorian's interests became fixed on studying the development of individual cultures and culture sequences. With this narrower focusing of interest, the concept of stages and even that of progress became less important, at least for the time being.

The archaeologists who used the culture-unit concept were at first far more interested in tracing historical relationships between cultures than in studying the internal organization of them. Their view of cultural processes continued to be dominated by the concepts of migration and diffusion that had developed prior to the adoption of the culture-unit concept. Both in Europe and in America, archaeological cultures were defined by listing those traits that either were associated with them in the archaeological record or could be assumed to have been present on the basis of archaeological evidence. Inferred traits, such as matrilineal clans or headhunting, sometimes were listed as additional items of 'social culture' or 'ideological culture', without any serious effort being made to explore the functional relationships between these various traits (Childe 1956a : 124–31). Thus, cultures tended to be conceived of in terms of trait lists.

Walter Taylor (1948 : 130–40) has noted many of the operational shortcomings of this atomistic view of culture. Often, no attempt was made to quantify finds; instead, traits were listed simply as being present or absent in a particular site or culture. The use of traits in this manner reflects a mechanical as opposed to an organic view of culture; one in which any and all traits are regarded as being equally representative of the culture with which they are associated. The sterility of this point of view becomes even more obvious when we note that while archaeological cultures nominally were defined

Major Concepts in Historical Perspective

in terms of total trait assemblages, in practice they were often delineated in terms of only one or at most a few classes of artefacts, usually pottery or lithic material (Kluckhohn 1962 : 76–6). The importance that was accorded the Midwestern Taxonomic Method in the United States (McKern 1939) is a further illustration of the nonfunctional view of culture that prevailed at this stage of development. This system now can be seen as a highly formalistic misapplication of the taxonomic approach to the classification of archaeological cultures.

Functionalism in Archaeology

To a considerable degree, the continuing concern with the external relationships between cultures was a reflection of a general anthropological concern with problems of diffusion. The latter part of the nineteenth century saw a growing disenchantment with the idea of evolution, a disenchantment that was accompanied in anthropology by growing pessimism concerning man's powers of inventiveness. By the beginning of the twentieth century it was a basic tenet of cultural anthropology that the nature of individual cultures could be explained by accounting for the origins of the various elements that made them up. A diffusionary approach was basic to all the schools of cultural anthropology: to the unscientific hyperdiffusionism of G. Elliot Smith and W. J. Perry, to the *Kulturkreise* theories of the Vienna School, and to the careful historical studies of the followers of Franz Boas.

The one-sidedness of this approach is now self-evident. Tracing historical connections may demonstrate that a trait actually diffused from one culture to another, and thus tell us something about its historical origins; yet only when the internal structure of the recipient culture is understood is it possible for the anthropologist to understand why the trait was adopted or how it came to play a role in that society. It was precisely the recognition of this weakness that prepared the way for the success of Malinowski's functional approach and Radcliffe-Brown's structural one, both of which, in spite of their differences, were concerned with the functional inter-dependence of variables within individual socio-cultural systems. These approaches not only permitted new insights into the significance of topics of long-standing interest, such as diffusion, but raised a host of other questions of major theoretical importance.

An implicit kind of functionalism had begun to manifest itself in prehistoric archaeology in the latter part of the nineteenth century, well before there was an open discussion of the concept in anthropology. For a long time, however, efforts to trace meaningful configurations in cultural patterns were restricted to the field of ecology (Daniel 1963 : 165–70). This is not surprising; while many archaeologists have realised that material culture is produced by, and reflects, the whole cultural pattern (Chang 1967a : 230), it generally has been maintained that the most detailed and reliable reconstructions that can be derived from this record are in the areas of technology and economic behaviour (C. Hawkes 1954). As early as 1898, scientists interested in prehistory began correlating distributions of archaeological remains with variations in their reconstructed environmental settings. Thereafter, the geographical approach became popular in Britain, culminating in Cyril Fox's (1932) magnificent ecological-positional study, *The Personality of Britain*. Among the advantages derived from this approach was the interest it generated in the careful and detailed reconstruction of the economic life of prehistoric cultures, as exemplified by Childe's (1931) report on the village of Skara Brae or Grahame Clark's (1954) study of Star Carr. Such reconstructions were part of an effort to understand relationships with the natural environment, but they also necessitated functional reconstructions of culture that are of considerable importance. Clark's (1952) *Prehistoric Europe: the Economic Basis* provides an illustration of what this approach has to offer. Still earlier, in *Archaeology and Society*, Clark (1939) outlined an implicitly functional approach to the study of prehistoric cultures, albeit one that was still heavily orientated towards the economic sub-structure.

Yet, however much an interest in ecology may have been turning British archaeologists towards a functional approach to the interpretation of their data, a thoroughgoing and explicit formulation of the functional approach was made not in Britain but in America; and there as a rebellion against a prolonged survival of the original version of the archaeological culture concept, which was concerned primarily with identifying arch-

Major Concepts in Historical Perspective

aeological cultures and tracing their external cultural connections (Taylor 1948 : 43–92). In *A Study of Archeology*, Taylor (1948) attacked the failure of his colleagues to consider artefacts within a functional context and saw this as related to their reluctance to use archaeological data to attempt to reconstruct the 'non-material' aspects of culture. Taylor (1948 : 98) carefully distinguished between culture as a system of ideas and the artefacts found in the archaeological record, which he defined as a product of culture. While the manufacture of these objects can be viewed as governed by norms about how they should be made and what they should look like, Taylor argued that it is not only possible, but also necessary, to treat these norms as being related to the broader cultural system. Even such basic items as tools may, through the material they are made of and their design and decoration, inform us about more aspects of a culture than simply its technology. L. Binford's (1962) tendency to equate an ideational view of culture with a crudely non-functional normative approach to the analysis of archaeological data seems to me to be erroneous and to deprive archaeology of a chance to benefit from recent developments in culture theory (Wallace 1961; Taylor 1967).

Taylor argued that by attempting to trace the functional relationships between the various kinds of evidence preserved in the archaeological record, not only were individual finds enhanced in significance, but also it should be possible to reconstruct at least the general outlines of prehistoric cultures as *systems*. By stressing the importance of studying the relationships within individual culture-units, Taylor was in effect introducing into archaeology a functional view of culture, comparable to that which Malinowski had already put forward for the study of contemporary peoples. Taylor's functionalism differed from the incipient functionalism of the British ecologists by being explicit and by extending to embrace the whole of culture. By viewing individual cultures not as collections of traits, but as systems, Taylor's approach has contributed significantly to the understanding of the cultural processes that underlie and have produced the archaeological record. Even traditional studies of the external relationships between cultures were enriched by the attention paid to the internal structures of the cultures that were interacting with one another.

The concept of the archaeological culture has played, and will continue to play, an important role in the structuring and interpretation of archaeological data. The introduction of this concept, as we have seen, permitted archaeologists to view prehistory in terms of the development and interaction of local cultural traditions and gradually led from studies of the external relationships between these cultures to an additional concern with their internal structure. These two aspects of the study of archaeological cultures provide a basis for understanding the processes that have shaped the cultural sequences observed in the archaeological record.

Societal Archaeology

In spite of the development I have just discussed, in recent years there has been a growing awareness of the limitations of the concept of the archaeological culture for the interpretation of archaeological evidence and the reconstruction of prehistory (MacWhite 1956). The complaints seem to fall into two main categories.

First, it appears that the concept of archaeological culture is suited best for studying the remains of small-scale, homogeneous, and relatively sedentary groups, that is of cultures at a 'mesolithic' or 'neolithic' stage of development. At this level, 'tribes' often are separated clearly from one another, each has artefacts or motifs that can be distinguished in the archaeological record, and the material culture of the group shows little or no variation along class lines (Sahlins 1968). Among less sedentary hunting peoples, such as the Eskimo, band composition often is less stable and casual contact between different groups more frequent. As a result, instead of finding geographically restricted and well-bounded cultures, the archaeologist is confronted with basic tool assemblages spread over vast distances and with stylistic variations that intergrade with one another. Under these circumstances, it may be impossible to distinguish individual cultures within a culture area. The concept of the archaeological culture likewise is inapplicable to the Lower Palaeolithic period, when the slowness of innovations permitted uniform stone-tool assemblages to cover vast areas. Here the concept of the archaeological culture is replaced by that of industries or assemblages (Braidwood 1967 : 33, 84).

Likewise, in complex cultures social and economic differences produce cultural heterogeneity both within and between communities. In these cases the archaeologist is compelled to discuss his 'culture' in terms of a number of subcultures (Rouse 1965 : 9–10). In such societies, linguistic, cultural, and political boundaries correspond even less than they do in non-sedentary ones, thereby rendering the concept of the archaeological culture of little value for the investigation of many of the problems that may interest the prehistorian.

A second source of dissatisfaction recalls the original aim of prehistoric archaeology: to discern regularities and general trends in the development of culture. The archaeological culture is a concept intimately related to studying relationships within, and between, particular archaeological assemblages and the development of culture in specific regions. The explanatory objectives of cultural archaeology, like those of history, are of a particularizing rather than a generalizing sort. While some prehistoric archaeologists, including many good ones, are happy to accept these particularizing goals, others feel compelled to generalize in some manner about the nature of cultural development and about culture itself.

This tension is well-illustrated in the work of Childe. His *Dawn of European Civilization* (1925) and *The Most Ancient East* (1928) are meticulous cultural syntheses of the archaeological data concerning two well-defined regions of the world. The concept of the archaeological culture is basic to both works and the explanations of cultural development that Childe offers are of a particularizing sort, dealing with the relationships among the various cultures that have been defined. Two of Childe's later works, *Man Makes Himself* (1936) and *What Happened in History* (1942) are very different. In these, the tracing of a detailed record of cultural development in any one region is subordinated to outlining a scheme for the development of civilization, which is then illustrated in terms of the cultures of the Near East and of Europe. Both works are dominated by a concern for progress, even if this progress is qualified as being discontinuous. Both of these books also have been viewed, probably wrongly, as being closer to the tradition of evolutionary pseudo-history that was popular in cultural anthropology prior to Boas, Malinowski, and Radcliffe-Brown than they are to the historical traditions of archaeology.

These two works are important because they laid the basis for the developments in Childe's thinking that are embodied in *Social Evolution* (1951) and *The Prehistory of European Society* (1958a). In the first of these books Childe adopted an explicitly functional approach to the analysis of archaeological cultures; every trait must be viewed as functionally related to every other trait (Childe 1951 : 167). Childe's concern with progress also led him to seek a new concept that could be used to generalize and bring order to the seemingly endless variations that were associated with individual archaeological cultures.

Although Childe devoted much of *Social Evolution* to an attempt to explain cultural similarities among adjacent cultures in terms of the operation of diffusion, it seems to have been clear to him that major similarities among unrelated cultures could not be accounted for in this manner. In spite of the restraints and selective pressures imposed by the functional configurations that are present in a culture, much of the detail of that culture is an historical accident, in the sense that it results from the culture's particular antecedents or the other groups with which it has been in contact. On the other hand, the range of variation in types of political systems and kinship is much more restricted; because, as Murdock (1959b : 134) has pointed out, only a few basic patterns of social relationships have enough coherence to give them a measure of relative stability. Thus, while because of historical accident the specific content of any one culture will be unique, its social system will tend to conform to a fairly well-understood and limited range of types.

Considerations of this sort seem to have prompted Childe to hypothesize that adjacent cultures at the same level of development might have essentially the same sort of social system and that by concentrating on patterns of social relations, instead of on the specific cultural detail that distinguishes one culture from the other, it would be possible to note important institutional regularities in the development of particular regions. Childe applied this approach in *The Prehistory of European Society* (1958a), where he traced certain general patterns in prehistoric European social structure and attempted to explain how and why these patterns differed from those in the Near East. A comparison of this book with *The Dawn of European Civilization* is highly instructive. *The Prehistory of European Society* is not merely a more general work than the earlier one; rather the two books are based upon entirely different concepts: in the first case culture; in the second, society. If Taylor can be credited with introducing a fully functional approach into archaeology, Childe can be credited with being the first to make considerable use of a socio-structural approach. Thus, having contributed so greatly to laying the foundations of cultural archaeology, Childe helped to create a new approach which, insofar as it attempts to interpret archaeological data in terms of social structure, we may label 'societal archaeology'. Through Taylor and Childe, the ideas of Malinowski and Radcliffe-Brown began to exert a belated influence on prehistoric archaeology.

Childe never argued the need to make a clear-cut conceptual distinction between culture and social structure. In spite of this, a growing interest in studying the significance of archaeological data in terms of their relationship to social systems is indicated by the more or less contemporary beginnings of the modern settlement approach in American archaeology. Prior to the publication of Gordon Willey's (1953) *Prehistoric Settlement Patterns in the Virú Valley*, the study of settlement patterns had been mainly ecologically-orientated; it was concerned with the relationship between site distributions and the natural environment. Willey (1953 : 1) chose to view settlement patterns as a 'strategic starting point for the functional interpretation of archaeological cultures' which reflect 'the natural environment, the level of technology on which the builders operated, and various institutions of social interaction and control which the culture maintained'. While Willey's definition explicitly refers to archaeological cultures and shows the influence of Taylor's concepts, it is clear from the text that the principal use that was made of the concept of culture was to distinguish successive phases in the cultural development of the Virú Valley and to group together sites that were known to belong to approximately the same point in time. Cemeteries, habitation sites, temples, forts, and irrigation systems belonging to the same period, in turn were used as the basis for attempting to reconstruct the social and political organization of the Virú Valley. Instead of viewing social and political systems as attributes of culture, Willey interpreted the cultural remains of the Virú Valley in terms of an evolving social system.

One of the most important consequences of Willey's settlement approach has been a growing interest in the ways in which archaeological data can be used to reconstruct social systems (Willey 1956a; Trigger 1967; Chang 1968). Some of this work, notably that of Chang (1958; 1962a) attempts to delineate cross-cultural regularities between material culture and social systems among living peoples, and to use these regularities in turn for the reconstruction of prehistoric social patterns. Most of the cross-cultural studies in this field have had to be done by archaeologists, because of the general lack of a theoretical interest in material culture among contemporary social and cultural anthropologists. Another approach, this time a purely archaeological one, attempts to reconstruct community organization through an analysis of the micro-distribution of artefacts within settlements (Hill 1966; Longacre 1966). For the most part, these studies have been attempted within the framework of a direct historical approach. Both of these approaches to the reconstruction of prehistoric social systems deal with individual sites and social relationships among them. Concepts such as community, social network, and political network tend to supersede that of culture (Willey & Phillips 1958 : 48–56; Caldwell 1966). Yet, in spite of this, it can be argued that any attempt to reconstruct prehistoric social systems inevitably contributes to a better understanding of the particular archaeological culture or cultures with which they are associated.

Equally importantly, however, the societal approach permits the archaeologist to investigate the development of social systems, unencumbered by the necessity of having to account for the cultural detail that as a result of historical accident becomes associated with any one culture. This permits the archaeologist to take an evolutionary view of the development of these systems; but an evolutionary view that is derived empirically and deals with the development of a single social system, or a group of related systems, rather than attempting to establish an ideal, often unilineal, scheme of social development.

This kind of approach was exemplified by a number of important studies during the 1960s. In his work on the development of Chinese civilization, Chang (1962b : 190, 191) draws a clear distinction between tracing 'the origin and history of the development of various and sundry objects' and 'studying the functional context of the development sequence itself'. It is clear that Chang (1963 : 138) regards this 'functional context' as being primarily an institutional one, since he traces the development of Chinese civilization mainly in terms of the increasing complexity of the social and political system. The significance of cultural traits, whether they originate inside the system or diffuse to it from abroad, is seen almost entirely in terms of the effect they have on the development of social institutions. Chang argues that, from a structural point of view, the origin of various cultural traits is of little importance, since alternative items of culture might have resulted in similar institutional developments, while the adoption of any one trait depends to a large degree on the development of the society at a given point in time.

A different, but equally important, use has been made of the societal approach by Robert M. Adams (1965) in *Land behind Baghdad*. In this study Adams examines the development of the irrigation systems in the Diyala Valley, Iraq, over a 6,000 year period. In so doing, he demonstrates the importance of social and political, as well as ecological, factors in shaping the history of agriculture in this region. In his more recent *The Evolution of Urban Society*, Adams (1966) has compared structural similarities in Mesopotamian and Mesoamerican civilizations, noting a variety of institutional similarities underlying vast differences in cultural detail. In his discussions of the development of an agricultural economy in the Tehuacán Valley in Mexico, MacNeish (1964) stresses the development of communities and of the political and economic ties that bind them together, rather than using a strictly cultural model.

Further evidence of the growing interest in a societal approach are attempts to explain changes in pottery decoration in terms of alterations in social organization or social relations. Deetz (1965) has attributed a reduction in the degree of regular association of design attributes in eighteenth century Arikara pottery to a shift in post-nuptial residence away from a former matrilocal pattern, the latter change being in turn the result of depopulation following epidemics and the attacks of horse nomads. McPherron (1967) explains shifts in the pottery styles found in certain Algonkian sites in northern Michigan in terms of variations in the marriage alliances effected among the patrilocal bands that presumably inhabited these sites and the women of different neighbouring groups. Both of these studies assume that 'stylistic traits have their primary meaning in sociological rather than technological contexts' (McPherron 1967 : 101).

I am not convinced that it is necessary, or even profitable, in every instance to draw a clear-cut distinction between the functional and societal approaches. Sometimes it seems to make little difference whether social structure is examined as a series of cultural traits or cultural traits are viewed in terms of their relationship to the social system. I would argue, however, that such a conceptual distinction always is theoretically possible and that in certain cases, particularly in the study of complex societies and non-sedentary or semi-sedentary groups, the structural approach permits the more elegant ordering and more penetrating interpretation of archaeological data. In a study of Predynastic Egypt, I have viewed the archaeological evidence independently from a cultural and from a societal point of view (Trigger 1968a : 61–90). This study has convinced me not only that both views of the same data are possible, but also that the two approaches complement each other and together raise important questions about the data under consideration. The pictorial representations on Gerzean pottery, for example, are interesting not only in terms of their stylistic origins and the light they may shed on Egyptian religious beliefs and practices at a particular stage in their development, but also because they shed light on the development of increasing specialization and mass production in the pottery industry at this period, which in turn can be correlated with other social and political developments. A further consideration of the relationship between the interpretations that result from the cultural and the societal approaches should encourage archaeologists to ask anthropologically significant questions about the relationship between culture and society. In a few years, these may be among the most significant questions with which archaeologists are grappling.

CONCLUSIONS

In Britain and America the basic concepts of prehistoric archaeology have shown surprising continuity in spite of progressive modification and development. The conceptual differentiation of culture and society is part of this general trend. This new interest grows out of the exploration of the functional and societal approaches. Thus the development of the basic ideas of prehistoric archaeology exemplifies the 'orderly, cumulative pattern' that Toulmin (1967 : 468) has stated is typical of the 'hard' sciences, but which he finds conspicuously lacking in certain of the social sciences.

It also appears that the theoretical differences between prehistoric archaeology as practised in Britain and America are less than is commonly stated (Clarke 1967) and tend largely to be superficial. British and American archaeologists clearly have different area interests and, until recently, discussions of common theoretical problems have been minimal (C. Hawkes 1954). In spite of this, the basic concepts of prehistory seem to have developed along more or less the same lines on both sides of the Atlantic.

The principal differences between the British and American traditions are ones of temperament and emphasis. In Britain, prehistoric archaeology has defined itself as a more autonomous discipline and has retained a stronger natural science orientation than it has in North America. Strong ties with the natural sciences are reflected in the publication in England of numerous archaeological books dealing with general palaeoecology (Cornwall 1964), plants (Dimbleby 1967), hydrology (Raikes 1967), soils (Cornwall 1958), raw materials and analysis of technology (Biek 1963; Hodges 1964; Rosenfeld 1965), archaeology and physics (Aitken 1961), bones (Cornwall 1956), stratigraphy (Pyddoke 1961), and general compilations of technical studies such as Brothwell & Higgs's (1963) *Science in Archaeology* or Pyddoke's (1963) *The Scientist and Archaeology*. American archaeologists, on the other hand, tend to be more self-conscious about the role of their discipline as a branch of anthropology, use a jargon borrowed from the social sciences and, in recent years at least, have focused much of their theoretical interest on investigating the methods by which an understanding of human behaviour, as derived from the social sciences, can be used to interpret the archaeological record (Chang 1967b; Deetz 1967; Trigger 1968a; S. and L. Binford 1968). These differences are in no way antithetical to one another, nor do they negate the fundamental communality of the basic concepts that are shared by the two traditions.

Archaeologists on both sides of the Atlantic share similar views of society and culture, in part because their concepts have been either shared with or borrowed from the cognate discipline of social (or cultural) anthropology. In both pre-historic archaeology and cultural anthropology, a unilineal evolutionary view of culture was followed by a diffusionary interpretation of culture process and then by the functional and societal positions that continue to influence cultural anthropology at the present time. During the early stages of this development, archaeological theory tended to be in advance of developments in cultural anthropology. Because of the nature of the archaeological data, the concept of parallel unilineal evolution was not well-received in archaeology and soon gave way to diffusionist and migration-based explanations of cultural change. An early interest in ecology also tended to introduce a semi-functional view into archaeology at an earlier date than it became an important concern in cultural anthropology. Both the systematic functional approach and the societal one appeared later in archaeology than in cultural anthropology, and both concepts clearly had their origins in the latter.

Considering the relatively weak ties that have held prehistoric archaeology and cultural anthropology together during the earlier part of the twentieth century (in spite of the desire of Americanist archaeology to affirm its role as part of anthropology), this systematic diffusion of concepts may seem surprising. It is understandable, however, when we recall that in spite of its special orientation towards natural history, arch-aeology has remained aware that the object of its study is man and his works and, therefore, that the conceptual tools for understanding its data stem from a knowledge of human behaviour. Even if archaeologists have borrowed many of their basic concepts from cultural anthropology, this borrowing until recently has tended to be indirect and unselfconscious and the concepts have been modified considerably to adapt them for dealing with archaeological data. In archaeology, functional and societal analysis is concerned primarily with inferring social structure and beliefs.

The intractable nature of archaeological data probably accounts for still another characteristic of prehistoric archaeology; its relative conservatism in replacing one conceptual approach with another. New approaches find themselves compelled to grow up alongside older ones and ultimately enrich the latter. The study of the history and development of individual culture traits did not cease to be important when the concept of the archaeological culture was introduced; it merely declined in importance relative to the new approach. Similarly, the efforts that have been made to reconstruct prehistoric cultures along functional lines have enhanced the importance of cultural data and rendered the study of diffusion more meaningful. Present trends seem to indicate that the new interest in a societal approach to the analysis of archaeological data, far from negating the value of established approaches, likewise will complement and enrich them.

Finally, it is worth remembering that all of these approaches reflect the growing richness of the archaeological data that prehistorians have at their disposal, without which few of the recent theoretical developments would have been possible. It is clear that the more conceptual tools the archaeologist has for the study of the past, the more demands he will make for data that are complete and of better quality. From the point of view of the enthusiastic fieldworker, this is surely what useful concepts are all about.

VII

The Concept of the Community

UNTIL RECENTLY, MOST ARCHAEOLOGISTS treated society as an attribute of culture. To describe an archaeological culture they assembled an inventory of traits that embraced the types of artefacts they had recovered, sometimes embellishing it with further conjectures about the nature of the subsistence pattern, social organization, and value system. Childe (1956a : 124–131) presented the outline of such an inventory under the main headings of economy, sociology, and ideology. Martin, Quimby, and Collier (1947) organized their resumés of the archaeological cultures of North America less systematically under human physical type, village plans, livelihood, pottery, tools, utensils and weapons, pipes, musical instruments, and burials.

All of these efforts are similar in that they treat society as 'social culture', rather than as a system of social relations. There is no reason not to describe the Amratian culture of Pre-dynastic Egypt as characterized by village life and probably lacking any form of state government. Yet because this 'norma-tive' approach treats such a conclusion as an end in itself, it does not constitute as productive an approach to the study of prehistory as does an attempt to reconstruct the social relations of an Amratian village or tribal unit. In the first case, society is being examined as an aspect of culture; in the second, culture is being viewed within the framework of a social system.

Some archaeologists have held that it is easy to find correla-tions between cultural configurations and social systems. Many have suggested, for example, that an archaeological component corresponds to a community, a culture to a tribe, and a series of related cultures to a culture area (MacWhite 1956 : 6–9). A brief reflection will show the inadequacy of these conclusions. No one would wish to classify an isolated cemetery, a small

115

fishing camp used for only a few weeks in the year, or a kill site where game is butchered, as a community.

It is apparent too, that no single social or political unit is invariably coterminous with a single pattern of material culture. Many examples can be found of people sharing similar material cultures yet having different social, political, or linguistic affiliations. Contrary situations also can be found where members of the same social grouping or tribe follow different ways of life. An example of this are the Fulani, some of whom are nomadic pastoralists, others sedentary cultivators, and all of whom live for the most part as an ethnic minority dispersed among other groups (Murdock 1959a : 413–420). In Early Dynastic Egypt, the local culture was coterminous with the Egyptian kingdom; yet the region embraced by Mesopotamian culture at the same period was divided up into a series of autonomous city states (Frankfort 1956). Even at a simple food producing level, there may be no one-to-one correlations between units of political, social, and material culture. Among the Five Nations Iroquois, local archaeological cultures can be distinguished which correspond to each (or at least to most) of the five historic tribes (MacNeish 1952). These tribes, however, formed a single political confederacy. Among the neighbouring Huron, who resembled the Iroquois in many ways, only one archaeological culture has been distinguished, although we know that this group constituted a confederacy divided into four tribes. In the Sudan, the Nuer and Dinka share a generally similar material culture, but constitute mutually hostile tribes.

Archaeological cultures clearly cannot be correlated in any mechanical fashion with societal groupings such as tribes, bands, or nations. The reason for this is not simply a technical one – such as insufficient data – but instead, because distributions of material culture do not necessarily conform with social and political configurations. Childe (1956a : 133) himself recognized this problem and stated that 'the sociological counterpart of an archaeological culture can only be designated by the noncommittal term "people".' *People*, however, is not a technical term, and we must question whether it has any useful meaning in the manner Childe employed it. In popular usage, the term implies a designated group sharing a sense of unity and common identity. This identity, however, rests on many different foundations. The Swiss speak four languages, but share a common sense of political identity; the Kurds, on the other hand, have a strong sense of ethnic identity, although they have never constituted a state, and different parts of their homeland presently are administered by Turkey, Iraq, the USSR, and Iran. Many examples can be found of groups who share similar (and in archaeological terms, probably identical) cultures, yet do not share a sense of identity because their first loyalties are focused on state institutions of more limited scope. The various Latin American nations are one case in point, the Scots and English another, and Anglo-Canadians and Americans a third. Moreover, a sense of identification often will vary according to the situation. Especially in more complex societies, an individual may have a wide variety of loyalties, varying from narrow ones to his clan or community, outward to the state and to mankind in general (Nadel 1951 : 184–188).

Thus, a uniform material culture does not constitute proof that the people associated with it necessarily had a strong sense of common identity, any more than differences in material culture prove the lack of such a sense of identity. If, however, the term *people* is used only to designate a group that shared a common material culture (as Childe evidently proposes to use it) then it is redundant and meaningless. Willey and Phillips (1958 : 48–49) are correct when they argue that an archaeological culture cannot be correlated automatically with any specific societal unit and that social units must be defined on their own terms. Childe (1956a : 121–124) also is right when he argues that any definition of an archaeological culture that is entirely typological and does not take sociological factors into account runs the danger of classifying different aspects of the life of the same group as different cultures. To resolve this dilemma, we must reconsider some of the basic concepts of prehistory.

While a culture, in the ethnological sense, is a way of life, it is also an assemblage of traits, each one of which also may be present in neighbouring cultures. For this reason, the borders of ethnological cultures usually are defined, at least in part, using societal criteria. Hence, when we speak of the culture of the Nuer, we refer to those traits possessed by a group of people claiming a particular name, whether or not those traits are possessed, individually or almost *in toto*, by neighbouring groups. In fact, there are probably few traits that are exclusively Nuer, except those related to the tribe's assertion of ethnic identity. This kind of association of cultures with particular groups of people is possible only because the ethnologist is able to examine all kinds of traits, including those of ethnic identity. It is difficult for the archaeologist to delineate ethnically significant boundaries as long as the only data at his disposal concern material culture. Archaeological cultures are, and no doubt will remain, units defined primarily in terms of material culture. It must be remembered, therefore, that groupings of components based on these criteria need not correspond to others which attempt to delineate various patterns of social relations. All interpretations begin with components, that is, with single periods of occupation in an archaeological site. It is in the primary analysis of components that alternative strategies can be employed to examine social and cultural units in greater detail.

A substantial number of inferences can be made concerning the social structure associated with a component. For example, it can be determined whether the component was a permanent settlement, a seasonal camp, or a special purpose site, such as a butchering place or a flint mine. This sort of information constitutes the basis for making inferences about the community structure associated with components or groups of components. By a community we mean those groups of people who normally live in face to face association for at least part of the year (Murdock 1949 : 79). In the case of permanent villages, the main component usually is equivalent to a community, while nearby encampments of the same culture often are part-time settlements associated with the main village. Among hunting and gathering cultures, however, it may be possible only to define communities statistically rather than to delineate them in terms of actual settlement patterns. The archaeologist may note, for example, that in a particular region he finds only one large winter settlement for every ten smaller summer ones. This might suggest that a band, having lived together during the winter, separated to form smaller and more scattered units during the summer. Where archaeological sites are distributed fairly evenly, it might not be possible to determine exactly which summer camps were inhabited by the people who lived

118

in a particular winter encampment. Nevertheless, it would be possible to say something about the average size and composition of the groups that had inhabited the region. In theory, the effort to define communities should reduce to a minimum the danger that the archaeologist would attribute seasonal expressions of the same culture to different groups. In practice, however, it frequently is difficult to determine the exact contemporaneity of sites and the time of year when each site was inhabited. This means that often our control of the data is far from perfect and interpretations involve a number of unproved assumptions. Nevertheless, once the archaeologist has defined a set of community patterns, he can proceed to assign those communities possessing similar material remains to the same archaeological culture.

In the study of more complex societies, other complications arise. In them, there are communities that are different from one another, yet are linked together in a network of functional interdependence. In a few such societies the ruling elite are of different origins from the people they rule and, in situations where both groups tend to preserve their own traditions, we may be justified in speaking of these groups as ethnically distinct (Murdock 1959a : 350). Where the rulers and peasantry share the same cultural background and are distinguished from each other only by their standard of living and degree of cultural refinement, these differences in life style usually are considered as being of a subcultural order. Hence, even if whole communities are part of one or the other of these subcultures, they are still part of a single culture.

An archaeological culture thus can be viewed as a group of communities sharing a similar material culture or displaying no greater variation in material culture than can be explained on the basis of occupational or class differences within a single cultural tradition. A culture is thus defined in terms of the typological similarities found among socially-defined minimal units (that is, communities). While there is no agreement as to the exact degree of similarity involved, there is, however, the further stipulation that a culture normally should reflect a self-perpetuating design for living.

What is of greater importance, however, is that communities also can be used to trace relationships other than those based

The Concept of the Community

on similarity in material culture. We have noted already that the political organization of the early city states of Mesopotamia was different from that found in Egypt. Even without written records, the excavation of many walled cities of similar size would suggest the possibility of city state organization in Mesopotamia; whereas the royal funerary establishments in Egypt, of which there is one for each reign, would suggest that the country was under powerful central control. The boundaries of many known kingdoms do not conform with the boundaries of the cultures that are associated with them. Indeed, many of the great empires of the past have embraced a large number of distinct cultures. In order to make inferences concerning prehistoric political units it is necessary to map the distributions of settlements, roads, and fortifications over large areas and, even then, the results are not always satisfactory.

Under rare circumstances, communities also can be grouped according to their linguistic affiliations, although this cannot be done with certainty using only archaeological data. Unfortunately, although certain general distributions of languages in prehistoric times have been worked out, it is often difficult, if not impossible, to draw linguistic boundaries with a high degree of precision. Frequently what is done is to associate a single language with a particular archaeological culture. There are, of course, dangers in doing this. It is unlikely, for example, that archaeological evidence alone would allow prehistorians of the future to determine which villages in northern Scotland presently speak Gaelic and which speak English. Similarly, while many archaeologists have identified the La Tène culture in western Europe with Celtic-speaking peoples, it has become clear, as a result of historical and linguistic research, that not all the Celtic peoples had a La Tène culture, while some people who were not Celts did (De Laet 1957 : 87). Whenever it is possible to reconstruct linguistic distributions independently of material culture, it is desirable to do so.

Archaeologists also are interested in tracing patterns of economic interaction. These studies may be concerned less with individual societies and cultures than with the flow of goods over long distances and the social mechanisms involved in this. Among the more obviously interesting kinds of sites are the Indus Valley trading establishments outside some Sumerian cities or the Assyrian trading posts that were built on the outskirts of Anatolian towns around the end of the third millennium B.C. (J. Hawkes and Woolley 1963 : 454, 609–610). Data of these kind not only help to track down sources of raw materials and manufactured goods and the routes over which they travelled, but also help solve such problems as whether trade was controlled by independent merchants or by the governments of various states. By adopting a flexible point of view, and using the community as a point of departure, the prehistorian is able to treat the social relationships involved as a functioning network, rather than having to view trade merely as external contacts between different archaeological cultures.

Treating the community as a basic unit, it becomes possible to link these units together using various criteria such as artefact types, political organization, economic relations, and language. The overall patterns which emerge when different criteria are applied are far from identical. The flexibility of this approach allows the prehistorian to examine various aspects of the past on their own terms rather than within a rigid framework of arbitrarily defined cultures. In this way, reconstructions approaching more nearly to the complexity of living cultures may be achieved.

The Concept of the Community

VIII

Race, Language and Culture

The Independence of the Variables

ANTHROPOLOGISTS TRADITIONALLY HAVE BEEN interested in the study of primitive 'tribes' or 'peoples'. Although the term tribe is defined in a variety of ways, it frequently is defined as a group possessing a territory of its own, and whose 'members feel that they share certain distinctive features of culture and language' (Goldschmidt 1959 : 151). The members of a tribe also are alleged often to conform to a particular physical type. Generally, it has been assumed that the tribes described in anthropological literature are objective divisions of humanity rather than units arbitrarily created by the people who have studied them.

The anthropological belief that tribes constitute cohesive social units stemmed in part from a belief that most primitive peoples regarded outsiders with fear and suspicion and tended to avoid them. The idea that each tribe had its own well-defined physical and cultural characteristics was based on the common-sense belief that people who interact freely with one another will tend to retain and develop traits in common, whereas those who are separated from each other will tend to develop along their own lines. The tendency to conceive of all change as the differentiation of originally similar tribal units, after the fashion of the biblical story of the tower of Babel, led prehistorians to attribute racial, cultural, and linguistic differences to the same ethnic separations. As groups spread they tended to develop regional peculiarities which, in turn, gave rise to new peoples and cultures. Pursuing this concept, it became logical to assume that tribes that presently are similar in culture or physical type, are so because their ancestors shared a common origin.

This particular view of culture history was based, however, on a serious fallacy; namely, the assumption that the racial, cultural, and linguistic differences among various peoples are all the result of the same process of differentiation (Sapir 1921 : 121–235). This assumption quickly led to the conclusion that any sort of similarity between two groups was evidence of a genetic relationship between them and, therefore, that the history of any group could be reconstructed from a patchwork of different types of data. For example, if several unrelated cultures were associated with racially similar types, it was assumed that these people had once constituted a single ethnic group and that cultural differentiation merely had gone on faster than racial differentiation. Hence, Africanists began to talk about cultures of 'Negro' or 'Hamitic' (Caucasoid) origin, as if at one time there had been a one-to-one correlation between race and culture in that area (for a discussion of this fallacy, see MacGaffey 1966). Likewise, if a number of different tribes spoke related languages, it was assumed that they had once been a single people with a common culture, and that any differences between them now were the result of changes that had taken place since the original group had broken up. Any linguistic, cultural, or racial similarities between peoples were interpreted as evidence that the groups involved had constituted a single ethnic group at some time in the past, and differences between them were seen as the result of subsequent modifications. Thus, whenever data of one sort were insufficient to establish an historical relationship between two groups, data of other sorts could be relied on.

From the start, however, grave problems confronted this method of interpretation. Had there not been so little data of any sort to go on, it probably would have been abandoned sooner. In particular, it seemed impossible to establish any sort of hierarchy for the relative rate of change in race, language, and culture. The genetic constitution of American Negroes may be largely African, but their language and culture are overwhelmingly of European origin. In like manner, American culture has shown surprising continuity in spite of the absorption of millions of immigrants who are not of the same Anglo-Saxon stock as the original settlers. The ability of human beings to learn new languages and new modes of behaviour, as

Race, Language and Culture

well as the capacity of social systems to assimilate newcomers, has meant that time and time again the racial, linguistic, and cultural history of groups has followed different paths. Consequently such similarities between groups are no proof that either the people or their culture shared a common origin. Because of cultural diffusion, people who are descended from a common ancestor may no longer share the same, or even a similar, culture; likewise, because of genetic drift, people who possess historically related cultures need share little genetic material in common. It is fairly obvious that gene flow and the diffusion of language and culture are not exceptions to the normal course of human development, but are at least as characteristic of it as is the development of differences through gradual separation.

Edward Sapir (1916) and Franz Boas (1940) summarized these objections when they pointed out that race, language, and culture had to be studied separately and their history treated as independent variables. The study of cultural areas in North America had suggested that traits tended to spread out from their point of origin and that as a result of diffusion similar cultures sometimes were shared by people with very different physical and linguistic characteristics. Hence, the latter characteristics cannot provide clues for the reconstruction of culture history, any more than cultural criteria can be used to reconstruct the history of the languages or physical type associated with any particular group. Examples to illustrate this can be drawn from European history. The Romance languages are all evolved forms of Latin, but only a small number of Romance speakers can possibly be biological decendants of the citizens of ancient Rome. Similarly, the fact that the majority of European nations speak related languages does not explain why they possess a similar culture. Much of the culture of modern Europe is not the heritage from a remote past, but rather is the product of shared cultural development which took place long after the various languages and nations of modern Europe had come into being. Europeans who speak non-Indo-European languages, such as Basque, Finnish, and Hungarian, have participated in this development no less than have other Europeans.

Because much is known about the history of Europe during the past 2000 years, no one would maintain that the most important cultural similarities in this area are vestiges of a common Indo-European culture many thousands of years old. Indeed, the great similarities in European culture, compared with the linguistic diversity, and the failure of linguistic and cultural (let alone political) boundaries to coincide, immediately would cast doubt on such an hypothesis, even if no historical data were available. Often such obvious incongruities between racial, linguistic, and cultural distributions prevent prehistorians from confusing these three sorts of data. Sometimes, however, fortuitous correspondences cloud the issue. For many years, the similar distribution of the Iroquoian languages and 'Iroquoian' culture in the region of the lower Great Lakes of North America was interpreted as proof that this culture had developed prior to the separation of the Iroquoian peoples into the various tribes that existed in early historic times (Parker 1916). The minor cultural differences among the various tribes were interpreted as the results of fragmentation. The 'Iroquoian' traits found among certain Algonkian-speaking tribes, such as the Mahican and Delaware, were viewed as 'acculturation' to Iroquoian ways, while 'Algonkian' traits found among the Iroquoians were attributed to trait diffusion in the opposite direction. The Iroquoians generally were regarded as late arrivals in the northeastern United States, who had come there as a single group with a common language and culture.

Today, an improved knowledge of Iroquoian archaeology and linguistics makes it probable that most of the tribal dialects had differentiated long before the development of the culture that characterized the Iroquoian peoples in historic times (Lounsbury 1961). Moreover, Iroquoian culture appears to have developed out of the earlier cultures of the Northeast, hitherto believed to have been associated exclusively with Algonkian-speaking peoples (MacNeish 1952). The similar cultures of the various tribes appear to have been the result, not of the differentiation of a single culture, but rather of shared development in late prehistoric times. For reasons such as this, prehistorians have realized that they must treat the history of race, language, and culture as separate problems.

Evidence that can be used to study the past is basically of two different sorts. The first is that recovered by archaeology;

the second is that of contemporary situations that can be used as a basis for making inferences about conditions and events in the past.

Cultural History

In the study of culture history, the most important evidence is provided by archaeology (McCall 1964 : 28–37). This evidence consists of products of human manufacture and the contexts in which they are found. From this material the prehistorian can try to reconstruct the economy, the social and political organization, and the art and beliefs of ancient cultures. He can also use it to study the development and spread of different types of artefacts and to trace the relationship between different cultures. The great advantage of archaeological evidence, especially since the development of carbon-14 and other geochronometric methods of dating, is the control it provides over chronology. It is possible to pinpoint both cultures and individual objects in time as well as place, and thus to evaluate more precisely the historical relationships among them.

The main weakness of archaeological evidence is the limited range of materials that survives. As we have noted, social relationships and culture (used in the sense of ideas) must be inferred from material culture. While it is relatively easy to deduce subsistence patterns from material artefacts, it is considerably more difficult to reconstruct social organization and ideology (C. Hawkes 1954 : 161–162). Even subsistence patterns are not always self-evident, since artefacts vary in their ability to survive according to age, climate, and material. In very dry climates or in permafrost almost everything survives; in a tropical forest one is fortunate if even stone tools manage to do so.

Anthropologists have attempted also to use the distribution of ethnographic traits as a basis for reconstructing cultural relationships in prehistoric times. The term 'culture history' often is reserved for this sort of study. While some scholars have limited themselves to reconstructing the history of individual items or segments of culture, such as panpipes, outrigger canoes, dice games, or megaliths, others have attempted to work out the history of whole cultures. Both of these efforts involve assumptions about the nature of culture which are

126

based on elaborate, but arbitrary, schemes of cultural development. Many of the assumptions concern the probability of similar traits having developed independently in different parts of the world, or of their being historically related. Another disadvantage of distributional studies, compared with archaeological ones, is the difficulty of determining at what period traits diffused from one area to another or often even of finding out in what direction they moved. Their advantage lies in the fact that they allow anthropologists to study all aspects of culture, not merely those that are reflected in the archaeological record. Murdock (1959a : 42) argues that the historical reliability of conclusions based on this sort of approach is enhanced if the prehistorian attempts to reconstruct the history of several major categories of traits independently and then cross-checks to see if the various reconstructions support or contradict each other. On the whole, culture historical studies seem to be most reliable when they are used in conjunction with archaeological evidence.

Another source of information about the past is the stories living peoples tell about their own history. This is often referred to as oral tradition (Vansina 1965 : 1–18; McCall 1964 : 37–61). Such traditions frequently reflect contemporary social and political conditions as much as they do historical reality, and even in cultures where there is a strong desire to preserve their integrity, such stories unconsciously may be reworked from generation to generation. The oral traditions of Polynesia, which were famous for the fidelity with which they were supposed to be transmitted, are now known to be out of line with archaeological and other sorts of evidence (Suggs 1960 : 47–56). Hence it is no wonder that many anthropologists doubt the historical reliability of all oral traditions. Murdock (1959a : 43) has claimed (without documentation) that African oral traditions concerning the origins of a tribe that are over a century old are correct less than 25 percent of the time.

The scientific study of oral traditions is obviously an exacting task and requires a careful evaluation of the reliability of sources, the identification of stereotyped motifs that may distort historical evidence, the checking of the stories told by one group against comparable information supplied by others, and, finally, the checking of these stories against independent sources of information such as archaeological evidence. Used in this way, oral traditions may supply valuable information about the not too distant past. Used uncritically, however, they can be a source of much confusion and misunderstanding in prehistoric studies.

Physical Anthropology

Studies of racial history are also of two types (McCall 1964 : 101–106). Skeletons belonging to different cultures can be unearthed and used to determine changes in physical type. Where there is enough data, the physical characteristics of various populations can be reconstructed and gradual changes that result from natural selection or the slow diffusion of genes may be distinguished from those resulting from the influx of new populations. When data are available over a wide area, it may also be possible to determine from whence new traits or new populations arrived. The main shortcoming of this approach, like that of archaeology, is that, except under very special conditions, relatively few characteristics are preserved. Non-skeletal features, which are the ones most frequently used to distinguish living races, have long since disappeared.

Present racial distributions, on the other hand, provide only limited clues concerning racial history. One can assume, for example, that any pre-Columbian group in the New World is likely to have been of Mongoloid stock, since no other stock is known among the peoples indigenous to this area. On the other hand, any historical reconstruction based on the assumption that African and Oceanic Negroes are descended from a common ancestor runs up against the possibility of parallel development in similar environments. Only a detailed study of prehistoric skeletons throughout the tropical regions of the Old World ultimately may be able to prove which of these theories is correct.

The reconstruction of more precise historical events from physical types alone is also difficult. The Tutsi of Rwanda have a Nilotic physical type, unlike that of the Hutu whom they rule. Both groups, however, now speak Bantu. Although the differences in physical type between the present-day Tutsi and Hutu are sufficient to show that the former are intruders into Rwanda, and to relate them with the Nilotes to the east, it

128

would be impossible to determine, from this evidence alone, when or along what route the Tutsi migrated into this area. Only archaeological evidence, aided perhaps by their own traditions, can provide this information.

It is even more dangerous to base theories of population movement on the comparison of ancient skeletal evidence with the physical characteristics of various living peoples. It is foolish to argue, for example, that a group of people living in the Nile Valley around 2000 B.C. is related to the modern Shilluk, since this argument assumes that the gene pool of the latter has remained the same over a 4000-year period. In view of the considerable amount of gene flow and natural selection that may have gone on in Africa during this period, this is something to be proved rather than assumed. To do this archaeological evidence concerning physical types is required.

Linguistics

Defined literally, prehistory is a text-free discipline. Since the prehistorian lacks written evidence about ancient languages, all of his linguistic speculations concerning prehistoric times must be based on information derived from present-day languages or at least on linguistic data recorded later than the period he is studying (McCall 1964 : 62–71). Fortunately, the historical linguist has at his command techniques for working out historical relationships among languages which are far more exact than comparable procedures available to the culture historian. Whenever several related languages are known, the phonemics, lexicon, and grammar of the ancestral language can be reconstructed with some degree of accuracy. Through the systematic comparison of fundamental vocabulary, genetic relationships between whole languages can be distinguished from superficial borrowings (Greenberg 1957 : 39) and through lexicostatistical procedures the relative degree of historical relationship between different languages can be worked out with considerable accuracy. The special form of lexicostatistics known as glottochronology shows promise of being able to determine approximate dates for the separation of different languages over a period of several thousand years (Gudschinsky 1956).

Race, Language and Culture

Determining the geographical distribution of languages in prehistoric times is much more difficult. A linguist may be able to reconstruct a protolanguage and even be able to say when this language was spoken, yet have difficulty in determining where it was spoken or by what culture or group of cultures. In order to handle this situation, linguists, mainly through the application of various culture-distribution theories, have worked out certain rules to help determine where a particular language family originated. Such points of origin are sought either near the centre of the distribution of the language family's major branches or else where one finds the greatest variation among languages currently belonging to the family (Sapir 1916 : 76–78). Since, for example, three branches of Nubian presently are spoken in Kordofan and Darfur, and only one in the Nile Valley, it is likely that the former regions were the original homeland of the Nubian people. This particular conclusion is supported by additional archaeological and historical evidence (Trigger 1966). There are exceptions to these rules, however, and because of historical events – such as the rapid expansion of certain languages in recent times – not all languages are amenable to this sort of analysis.

Attempts to identify where certain language groups originated have been made by reconstructing the environment that is suggested by cognate words for plants and animals that have survived in the vocabularies of the modern languages belonging to the group. On this basis it has been suggested that Indo-European was originally spoken in a region where salmon were found and where there were beech trees, probably, it is suggested, in the vicinity of the rivers Vistula, Oder, and Elbe (Thieme 1964 : 594–597). This particular conclusion does not seem to be supported, however, by archaeological evidence (Gimbutas 1963). The same technique has been used to reconstruct various aspects of the culture associated with proto-Indo-European. In the future this may permit a closer correlation of the archaeological and linguistic evidence. Similar work is under way on proto-Bantu (McCall 1964 : 69). The principal danger confronting studies of this sort is the possibility that technical terms can diffuse far and wide and give a false impression of being part of the protolanguage.

Especially in the study of African prehistory, there has been a tendency to place too much trust in language distributions as conclusive evidence of ethnic movements (Lewis 1966 : 38; MacGaffey 1966 : 13–17). It must be remembered that languages can spread without major population movements, as Latin did among the subject peoples of the western Roman Empire and that people, when moving, do not always carry their ancestral language with them. Caution is needed not to interpret the diffusion of languages as resulting only from the migrations of peoples.

It is possible to learn something about the racial, linguistic, and cultural changes that took place in prehistoric times. Each of these fields must be investigated independently, using the data that are appropriate to it. Only when this has been done, is it possible to combine these different categories of data in order to investigate what has happened to specific groups of people in prehistory.

Race, Language and Culture

PART THREE

Inference and Interpretation

IX

Archaeology and Ecology

Historical Survey

PREHISTORIC ARCHAEOLOGY BEGAN TO develop in the
first half of the last century with the realization that a coherent
study of the past could be based on archaeological data alone.
Since that time, archaeologists have engaged in a continuing
search for theories and techniques that will permit them to
wrest from their data as complete an understanding of human
behaviour as possible. Yet, in spite of these ambitions, they
have been apologetic about the nature of their data, which,
they generally have agreed, are more limited in scope and
more difficult to interpret than are those employed by historians and ethnologists. It is not surprising that much of the
theorizing in archaeology has been concerned with stratagems
which, it was hoped, would maximize the information output
of archaeological data and permit archaeology to compete
on a more equal footing with the other social sciences. These
stratagems sometimes have led archaeology astray and to some
extent continue to do so.

The earliest of them reflected the important role that was
played by the concept of unilineal evolution in the last century.
At that time, it was widely maintained that all societies evolved
in a fixed sequence; the only variable and apparently unpredictable feature being the rate of development. Less advanced
societies that survived to the present were viewed as examples
of stages which the more advanced societies had outgrown. All
present-day societies were arranged in a single continuum from
simplest to most complex. This was assumed to represent all
but possibly the most primitive stages through which the most
advanced cultures had developed. The strictly archaeological

aspect of interpreting archaeological data was thus limited to determining the level of sociocultural development particular artefact assemblages had reached; the rest was no more than an exercise in applied ethnography (Clark 1957 : 170–2; Daniel 1968a, 1968b : 57–63).

As interest in unilineal evolution declined, the concept of cultural diffusion quickly grew in importance. Although the early diffusionists frequently were rigorous in their methodology and paid much more attention to the formal properties of artefacts than their predecessors had done, they were no more interested in studying artefacts as parts of a cultural system than the latter had been. Instead, they concentrated on tracing the origin and spread of specific types of artefacts (Montelius 1899; Childe 1925). Yet long before matters were carried to an untenable extreme in the hyperdiffusionary theorizings of ethnologists such as G. Elliot Smith and W. J. Perry, most archaeologists were at least vaguely aware that the concept had limited explanatory potential. Above all, it was realized that in order to be able to explain why diffusion had occurred, the archaeologist needed to understand the nature of the recipient culture. Attempts to acquire such knowledge led British archaeologists to develop two approaches, both of which were concerned with adaptive features of individual cultures and therefore were, at least implicitly, ecological. This encouraged the development of a functional and systemic view of culture in place of the early diffusionist 'bits-and-pieces' interpretation.

The first and more rudimentary approach was a geographical one, which became popular in Britain through the cartographic work of O. G. S. Crawford (1921), and the studies by H. J. Fleure and W. E. Whitehouse (1916) of prehistoric distributions of population in Wales. While often criticized for being overly deterministic, Cyril Fox's work (1923, 1932) demonstrated beyond doubt the value of a geographical approach to prehistory.

The second, and more important, result of a growing interest in adaptation was the development of what Grahame Clark (1953) has called the 'economic approach' to the study of prehistory. This approach, which was inspired in part by developments in social anthropology (Clark 1974), led to a

135   *Archaeology and Ecology*

complete restructuring of the goals and general orientation of British archaeology and has provided the foundations for modern archaeological interpretation. While concepts borrowed from ecology played an important role in this development, their main effect was to increase the interest archaeologists had in the empirical study and comparison of individual archaeological cultures. The result was the formulation of an implicitly functional approach to the study of prehistoric cultures, within which interest was to remain focused largely on the economic sector. Site reports such as *Excavations at Star Carr* (Clark 1954) and synthetic studies such as *Prehistoric Europe: the Economic Basis* (Clark 1952) illustrated the success of this approach.

Growing interest in adaptation encouraged British archaeologists to collect data that permitted a far more detailed reconstruction and interpretation of the economic basis of individual prehistoric cultures than had been attempted hitherto. From the 1920s on, increasing attention was paid to plant and animal remains in archaeological sites with a view to reconstructing patterns of subsistence. Artefacts took on new significance as elements within systems of production and distribution. Archaeologists had to forge closer links with palaeoecology and to develop, or adopt, an imposing array of techniques for eliciting new information from their data (Biek 1963; Brothwell and Higgs 1963; Cornwall 1958; Dimbleby 1967; Hodges 1964; Rosenfeld 1965; Semenov 1964). More specialized techniques for recovering data also had to be developed and this encouraged ever greater attention to detail in excavation of sites.

As a result of these developments, archaeologists gained confidence in their ability to use archaeological data to reconstruct and interpret the economic patterns of individual prehistoric cultures. On the other hand, they grew generally less optimistic about how much could be inferred about the social, intellectual, and spiritual life of prehistoric cultures (Childe 1951 : 55). Christopher Hawkes (1954 : 161-2) was expressing a widely-held view when he argued that the techniques which produce artefacts were easy to infer, subsistence-economics fairly easy, social and political institutions considerably harder, and religious institutions and spiritual life the hardest of all.

Nevertheless, a theoretical justification for this approach

was evolved, which served to minimize the significance of the seeming weakness of archaeological data for reconstructing social customs and beliefs. It was argued that economic institutions played a leading role in any culture and determined, at least in a general way, the social structure and value systems that were associated with it. The materialist view that was implicit in this position corresponded in a general way with much of the thinking of the period and, in particular, with Marxist theory, which Childe (1936, 1942, 1946a) proclaimed was the basis of several of his own highly influential interpretations of archaeological data. Progress had been made, however, in two directions. First, instead of the whole culture being reconstructed on the basis of vague ethnographic analogies, only its non-economic aspects were. The economy itself now was studied directly from archaeological data. Secondly, archaeologists generally regarded analogies of this sort as being far more tentative and speculative than their predecessors had done. On the whole, the idea was rejected that broad general theories could be used to predict in detail the nature of specific cultures.

The American Systemic Approach

It was to be expected that as the interpretation of prehistoric economic patterns became increasingly routine, enterprizing archaeologists would seek to devise methods to study the apparently less tractable aspects of prehistoric cultures. It is perhaps no accident that the first explicit demand to move in this direction was made in the United States, where archaeological studies lagged behind those in Britain and where the close academic ties that had bound archaeology and ethnology together during the period when unilineal evolutionary theory was in the ascendant never had been dissolved. A concern to justify and strengthen this association appears to account, at least in part, for the unprecedented outpouring of programmatic statements there during the 1960s (S. and L. Binford 1968; Chang 1967b, 1968; Deetz 1967).

The intial step in this direction was the publication of Walter W. Taylor's (1948) *A Study of Archeology*. This book was a much-deserved reaction against the prolonged survival in

American archaeology of an interest in identifying culture units, working out local chronologies, and tracing external cultural connections, much in the spirit of the early diffusionists. Taylor attacked the neglect of non-material aspects of culture and the failure of archaeologists to consider artefacts in a functional context. Yet, instead of advocating that Americans adopt the British approach, he argued that they should view their arte-facts as products of total cultural systems and attempt to reconstruct these systems, at least in general outline. The functionalism that Taylor was advocating, differed from that of the British by being much more explicit and seeking to embrace as much of culture as possible. Taylor was attempting, in effect, to introduce into archaeology a view of culture broadly similar to that which Malinowski had advocated for studying contem-porary peoples.

Taylor argued that archaeologists should strive to create conditions in which archaeological and ethnographic informa-tion could be used for the same purpose: to generalize about the nature and working of culture. The very different nature of the two kinds of data was not seen as an obstacle to archaeology and ethnology sharing common goals and constituting homo-logous branches of a single discipline. Taylor's point of view was adopted by Willey and Phillips (1958), who paraphrased Maitland's famous dictum with the statement that 'American archaeology is anthropology or it is nothing' (p. 2). Later, L. R. Binford (1962) challenged the assumption that most of the information to be derived from archaeological data concerns technological and economic matters. He argued that artefacts must be viewed as products of total cultural systems, which, in turn, are made up of functionally interrelated subsystems. Especially when viewed in its archaeological context, every artefact may provide information, not only about the economy, but also about the social structure, aesthetic concepts, and religious beliefs of its makers (and/or users). Binford suggested that the unequal amount of information that archaeological data shed on various aspects of culture may result not so much from the nature of the data, as from the failure of archaeo-logists to develop adequate interpretational skills. This was undeniably an antidote against naive complacency!

On a programmatic level, Taylor's approach had far-reaching impact. There is widespread agreement that artefacts

138

must be studied as products, and therefore as reflections, of cultural systems. There is also growing interest in developing techniques to elicit new kinds of information from archaeological data; particularly concerning social (and to a lesser degree political) structures. Much more attention now is being paid to the microdistribution of artefacts within individual sites in the hope that these distributions will shed light on the social behaviour of the people who made or used these artefacts (Hill 1966, 1968; Longacre 1968). Related to this is an increasing concern with settlement patterns, which are viewed as the fossilized stage on which social action has taken place (Chang 1958, 1962a, 1968; Trigger 1965 : 2). Multivariate analysis of stylistic variation, along lines pioneered by James Deetz (1965), has helped to shed valuable light on prehistoric residence patterns, although archaeologists have tended to draw unwarranted inferences about other features of social organization from such data (Aberle 1968). Archaeologists also have been making forays into the ethnographic literature to search out detailed correlations between aspects of material and non-material culture that can be used to interpret archaeological data (Chang 1958, 1962a; Cook and Heizer 1968). Many of these studies require manipulating vast quantities of data and have been practicable only with the assistance of computers.

Although attempts have been made to view burials as fossilized rituals (Fox 1959; Sears 1961), there were few, if any, comparable advances in the study of belief systems or aesthetics in the 1960s. Efforts have been made to discover regularities between art styles and certain aspects of social organization (Fischer 1961). Yet the most successful studies remain those which are text-aided or grounded in the direct historic approach. In several highly successful attempts to deal with more general problems of interpreting art and burial customs, P. J. Ucko (1968, 1969; Ucko and Rosenfeld 1967) has reaffirmed that the best use that can be made of ethnographic analogy in these areas is to broaden the archaeologist's awareness of unsuspected alternatives in the possible significance of his data. Yet, even if recent efforts to interpret the non-economic aspects of prehistoric cultures so far have had their greatest success in dealing with socio-political organiza-

Archaeology and Ecology

tion, they mark the beginning of an attempt to extend the empirical reconstruction and explanation of prehistoric cultures into new areas and to upgrade field methods to provide new kinds of data.

These practical developments have helped to stimulate interest in a thorough reappraisal of the theory and assumptions of prehistoric archaeology. The ultimate purpose of these discussions is to define the future aims of prehistoric archaeology and to establish an effective relationship between this discipline and the other social sciences. In the course of these discussions, almost every concept that has ever been considered by archaeologists has come under scrutiny (Bayard 1969; L. Binford 1962, 1965, 1967c; S. and L.Binford 1968; Chang 1967b, 1968; Clarke 1968; Deetz 1965; Trigger 1968a). Some of these concepts have been made more explicit, but in many cases clarification has resulted in hitherto unforeseen points of disagreement being recognized. It is indicative of the continuing importance of the British economic approach that much of the debate about cultural theory (as distinguished from general methodology) concerns problems that can be grouped under the general heading of ecology. Here two opposing views can be distinguished: one tending towards a narrower and more deterministic conceptualization of ecology than has prevailed among archaeologists hitherto; the other tending towards a broader and more empirical approach. Many individual positions fall somewhere between these two extremes and a discussion of these tendencies as ideal types may do injustice to the subtlety of these positions. Nevertheless, such a discussion may shed significant light on the general issues that are involved. It will also demonstrate the extent to which current controversies are embedded in the past history of archaeological theory.

Deterministic Ecology

Deterministic ecology has been influenced heavily by the cultural materialist approach in American anthropology, the growth of which is closely linked to that of cultural ecology and neo-evolutionary theory generally (Harris 1968). Yet, in spite of its largely American origins, the deterministic approach in archaeology shares many of the key concepts of the

140

British economic approach. Total cultures are studied as adaptive systems, as Grahame Clark advocated they should be. Both approaches share a materialist bias, but in place of the tentatively expressed British assumption that loosely-defined economic institutions play a leading role in the development of other features of culture (Childe 1946b : 250), deterministic archaeologists have tended to adopt Leslie White's (1949) more rigorous premise that total cultures are the product of their technology interacting with the natural environment. In one study, for example, we are informed that 'the settlement pattern . . . is an essential corollary of subsistence' and that 'Variations between cultures are responses to differing adaptive requirements of specific environments; accordingly, varying ecological potentialities are linked to different exploitative economies and the latter, in turn, to differing integrative requirements met by differing forms of social structure' (Struever 1968a : 134–5; 133); in another study, on the advice of David Aberle, Struever (1968b : 311) has expressed a less deterministic approach to ecology.

While White (1945a : 346) has warned that his general theories cannot be used as a basis for making inferences about the specific features of individual cultures, not all archaeologists have chosen to take this admonition seriously. They assume that if White's deterministic hypotheses are correct, any archaeologist who is able to reconstruct the technology and environment for an individual prehistoric culture should be able to predict what the rest of that culture, or at least its key features, was like (Meggers 1960). Shortcomings in such reconstructions are considered as being the result of inadequacies in general anthropological theory, not in archaeological data or the archaeologist's ability to interpret these data. Archaeological studies which concentrate on subsistence patterns and assign to them a leading role in the evolution of other aspects of culture have examined both simple (Struever 1968b) and complex (Sanders 1968; Sanders and Price 1968) societies.

Evolutionary theory in anthropology always has been preoccupied with problems of cultural typology and has operated on the assumption that the degree of variation in the total morphological pattern of individual cultures is strictly limited (Rouse 1964). Moreover, the search for causal relations has

Archaeology and Ecology

been conceived of as an effort to explain the similarities, rather than the 'unique, exotic and non-recurrent particulars' (Steward 1955 : 209), observed in these patterns. This is equally true of the unilineal evolutionism of Leslie White (1959) or the multilinear evolution of Julian Steward (1955), even though the latter attempts to account for patterns of variation resulting from adaptations to various different kinds of environments. The cultural theory that underlies both approaches is, in fact, very similar (Sahlins and Service 1960). Cultures are viewed as made up of 'core' features, which are basic to their general structure, and other features which are not. The core features are mainly technological and social-structural and are posited to develop in response to the adaptive needs of a culture. They occur, therefore, in a limited number of total patterns, which represent responses to specific classes of environments by peoples at various levels of technological development. Thus, by determining which total cultural pattern corresponds most closely to his data, the archaeologist is assumed to acquire knowledge of the key features of a culture. In this manner, cultural evolution becomes a 'practical research tool' for archaeologists (Meggers 1960).

It is regrettable that just as new techniques are being devised to elicit independent information about social structure from archaeological data, arguments should be advanced that resemble so closely those advocated by earlier schools of archaeological interpretation to justify not basing their interpretations on a detailed exegesis of such data. Technology and environment have replaced index fossils and the economy as a datum line, but some archaeologists continue to believe that cultural patterns are limited enough in variety that the major outlines of any culture can be inferred from knowledge of only one part of it.

Another important feature that the deterministic approach has in common with neo-evolutionary theory is its anti-diffusionist bias. An interest in diffusion is interpreted as being antithetical, or irrelevant, to the study of cultures as adaptive systems. It is argued that diffusion occurs less frequently than uncritical archaeologists have claimed and that it is usually trivial in its consequences, at least as far as adaptation is concerned. It is also maintained that if conditions are right for a trait to be adopted in a recipient culture, a homologous trait, or one that has similar socio-economic significance, ultimately will evolve even if that culture remains totally isolated (L. Binford 1963; Sanders and Price 1968 : 58–73; Renfrew 1969). Such a position is the mirror-image of the early diffusionists' lack of concern with the manner in which traits became integrated into recipient cultures.

On the whole, the deterministic approach tends to be more narrowly focused and more dogmatic than its economic predecessor. None of its major concepts is new and, taken individually, each of them has been criticized in various ways. The deterministic approach has been unduly protected by the theoretical prestige that has accrued to it through its close ties with cultural materialism and neo-evolutionism. To point out its shortcomings does not necessarily imply a negative evaluation of these more general hypotheses. What the archaeologist must be concerned with is the degree to which these concepts are of practical value for interpreting his data.

Cultural materialism and its allied approaches, whatever their ultimate value, are, as yet, neither sufficiently sophisticated nor comprehensive to be able to explain the cultural variability noted in the ethnographic record, even if interest is confined to 'core' items. Most ecological explanations of ethnographic data are *ad hoc*, in the sense that they adduce plausible reasons to account for what is observed, but are unable to demonstrate that, given the same set of conditions, alternative solutions would be either impossible or highly unlikely. Widely differing explanations are offered concerning how particular features of culture are adaptive, and anthropologists are far from agreed that all behaviour can be interpreted best in this manner (Harris 1966).

Because of the complexity of cultural phenomena and the inadequacy of our present understanding of culture process, all deterministic, and indeed all functional, approaches remain essentially non-predictive, except at very general or mundane levels. An analogy with the biological sciences is perhaps instructive. Although the understanding of biological processes far exceeds that of socio-cultural ones, the biologist is unable to predict the specific changes that any particular species will undergo through time. This is largely because he is

143   *Archaeology and Ecology*

unable to control, to a sufficiently accurate degree, for a large number of external variables, including geological, climatic, and solar conditions, as well as for the other plants and animals that are part of the ecosystem. Thus, the complexity of the parameters that must be controlled for, even more so than the problems of understanding process, rules out the possibility of detailed and far-reaching predictions, either forwards or backwards in time. The current inability of social scientists to control for the even greater number of variables that affect cultural processes rules out the possibility of cultural theory being used by archaeologists as an 'effective research tool' for reconstructing individual prehistoric cultures.

A sharp distinction must be drawn between the manner in which non-archaeological evolutionists seek to reconstruct the past using only their understanding of cultural theory and of present conditions and the archaeologists' efforts to understand the past as it is reflected in the archaeological record. The scenarios of cultural evolution that non-archaeological anthropologists have produced to date are largely descriptive generalizations, often highly impressionistic ones, rather than adequate explanations of the processes that have shaped the evolution of culture. For the archaeologist, the latter must be synonymous with the actual record of human development as revealed by culture historical research. The general schemes of cultural evolutionists can neither aid the archaeologist to interpret individual prehistoric cultures, nor, being themselves the product of cultural theory, can they contribute information that will permit archaeologists to understand cultural processes better.

There is a tendency, as Paul Tolstoy (1969 : 558) has pointed out, for determinists to consider worthy of attention only those traits with which their theories appear equipped to deal. These studies generally are restricted to dealing with structural features that are cross-culturally recurrent; the implication being that fundamental causal relationships (that is, those which concern adaptation to the environment) can be discovered only through the examination of such features. Although no criteria ever have been established that can discriminate objectively between the core and non-core features of a culture, it is generally agreed that the former are those which play an active roll in adapting the culture to its environment. Other features

144

such as art styles or tokens of rank, are treated as 'outward symbols', functionally related to the core, but of only peripheral structural significance. While concentration upon structural features can be extremely useful, at best it offers a partial view of culture that must be complemented by an examination of less obviously recurrent or adaptive features. Archaeologists must never lose sight of one of anthropology's basic assumptions: that culture as a whole (and not merely those aspects which are causally related with the environment) is orderly. They must strive therefore to explain the total range of variation in their data and not be content merely to deal with gross structural similarities.

Another major shortcoming of deterministic ecology is its tendency to study individual cultures as isolated systems; a procedure reminiscent of the organic fallacy in social anthropology. This bias clearly is related to the desire to examine environmentally adaptive features of culture, but when applied dogmatically it is unrealistic for understanding both structure and process. Few cultures, if any, have existed in total isolation from all others. Many have been in such close contact with their neighbours that they lack the clear-cut boundaries which anthropologists find so convenient (Trigger 1967 : 151). Networks of social, political, and economic relations tend to proliferate across cultural boundaries and link cultural systems together.

Viewed in structural terms, the impact that different cultures have had upon one another is far from insignificant. No one would deny, for example, that the spread of industrial technology, and of an associated international economic system, has had an enormous impact outside the area of western Europe where the Industrial Revolution was initiated. Because of variations in local culture, as well as in natural resources and the circumstances under which industrial technology was introduced, the impact of this technology has been different in each of these areas, and from what it was originally in western Europe. Some determinists postulate that eventually all industrial societies will evolve a similar set of social, economic, and political institutions that are suited ideally to an industrial technology. Yet to dismiss the experience of the Third World as being of little evolutionary interest, as White's unilineal

Archaeology and Ecology

approach would lead us to do, clearly is inadequate both from an historical and a processual point of view. While it is legitimate, and highly desirable, to study the history of particular peoples in terms of the continuing evolution of their social systems, this does not provide a theoretical justification for ignoring either diffusion or the impact that interacting societies have had upon one another's socio-political institutions. Cultures clearly must be treated as important components in each other's environment.

Finally, we must reject the last-ditch defence that a deterministic ecological approach is better suited to the interpretation of technologically-simpler societies than it is to more complex ones. Such an argument is based on the assumption that structurally less complex societies are more directly dependent on their environment and, therefore, strictly limited in terms of the adaptive responses that are open to them. Such an argument is based on an unduly simplistic view of small-scale societies (Lee and DeVore 1968) and is reinforced by the relatively small amount of archaeological data that is available concerning any single small-scale culture. Complex societies, such as those of ancient Egypt or of the Maya, simply leave behind too wide a range of archaeological evidence not to give rise to doubts about such formulations. This has helped to expose overenthusiastic attempts to distort such societies and fit them into unsuitable preconceived patterns. There is neither archaeological nor ethnological evidence to support the assumption that small-scale cultures are necessarily any more lacking in adaptive variation than are complex ones.

Deterministic ecology thus appears to combine many of the weaknesses of the older evolutionary and economic approaches and fails to take advantage of recent significant advances in the interpretation of archaeological data. Its attempt to reconstruct prehistoric cultures on the basis of an assumedly limited variation in total morphological pattern seems to be theoretically unjustified and unproductive of new insights, such as are derived from attempts to explain in detail the archaeological evidence for particular cultures.

Non-deterministic Ecology

What I have called non-deterministic ecology consists of a body of assumptions shared by various archaeologists who nevertheless have never thought of themselves as members of a particular school of archaeological interpretation. Because of this, there is less programmatic literature associated with this approach than there is with deterministic ecology, although the number of substantive studies is probably greater. Most of the assumptions of the non-deterministic approach are in accord with recent developments in cultural ecology generally and they reflect growing confidence among archaeologists in their capacity to interpret archaeological data. For these reasons, the non-deterministic approach appears to be a more progressive, and ultimately a more productive, development than deterministic ecology.

The non-deterministic approach is based on the assumption that cultural ecology is concerned with the total manner in which human groups adapt to and transform their environments. Cultures are conceived of as being at least partially open systems, some of whose institutions may be tied in with those of other cultures. Because of this, simplistic efforts to treat cultures as selfcontained units may impede the interpretation of archaeological data. Cultural systems are seen as having to adapt to a total environment made up both of natural elements and of other cultures.

Non-deterministic ecology assumes that there is a considerable degree of individual variation among both ethnological and archaeological cultures. While cultural phenomena are assumed to be orderly and hence subject to scientific enquiry, the non-deterministic approach insists that any explanation of culture must prove its worth by being able to cope with patterns of variation observed in real cultures, rather than with the variations hypothesized to exist among a limited number of ideal types, such as the neo-evolutionists postulate. Order must be sought, not in neat cultural typologies, but rather through understanding those processes by which cultural similarities and differences are generated. Only in this manner can sufficient allowances be made for the wide variety of contingent factors that influence the development of any one culture. The non-deterministic approach also argues that, because of the complexity of these external factors and the archaeologist's inability to control for them adequately, it is not possible to reconstruct the whole of a cultural system from knowledge of only part of it. Instead, it insists that every facet of a prehistoric culture that can be reconstructed must be so done, through the interpretation of data relevant to that part. For the same reason, it is doubted that the core features of any one culture can be distinguished on an *a priori* basis from non-economic, non-adaptive features.

Non-deterministic ecology remains interested in subsistence patterns and economics, but assumes that developments affecting any one aspect of culture ultimately will produce further adjustments throughout the system and affect the system's relationship with its natural environment. Hence, non-deterministic archaeologists are equally interested in studying trade, communications, political organization, warfare, population movements, religious ideas, disease patterns, and other features of, or influenced by, culture, as far as this can be done from the archaeological record, in order to construct as complete a picture as possible of factors which influence the adaptation of a society to its total environment, both natural and cultural (Trigger 1970b). Moreover, while interest remains high in studying whole cultures, there is also a growing interest in examining in detail the functional relationship between restricted segments of prehistoric cultures, such as irrigation systems and political organization. Such studies are important from an ecological point of view because they contribute to the better understanding of the adaptive features of a culture.

The non-deterministic approach has been one of several factors promoting a growing interest in the study of archaeological settlement patterns. It is assumed that the quantity, type, and distribution of the material remains of human activities (including settlements, houses, fields, and artefacts) constitute reliable evidence concerning the manner in which former inhabitants adjusted to their environment and that all of the factors that influenced this adjustment are reflected, either directly or indirectly, in the settlement pattern. Broad attempts to explain settlement patterns therefore should result

148

in a more comprehensive understanding of this adaptation than should a study that concentrates on subsistence patterns or the economy and which tries to explain the settlement patterns only, at best, in terms of these factors (Struever 1968a : 134–5). It is recognized, of course, that a settlement pattern is the product of a variety of factors, some of which reinforce certain trends, others of which are opposed to one another. The pattern therefore is often a compromise among a number of conflicting tendencies. A simple example is the contradiction in some agricultural societies between the desire for dispersed homesteads in order to be near fields and for nucleated settlements for protection against enemies. It is not always possible to untangle the forces that have been at work, given the sort of archaeological data that normally are available. Nevertheless, an attempt to explain an archaeological settlement pattern constitutes a dynamic approach to the study of the cultural ecology of prehistoric societies.

The first substantial effort to study settlement patterns in this manner was Gordon Willey's report on the Virú Valley in Peru (1953). Willey demonstrated that not only the development of subsistence patterns, but also political and economic competition between valleys and changes in the relationship between the sacred and secular areas of cultures had played important roles in shaping the development of settlement patterns in the Virú Valley. Moreover, the development of subsistence patterns only became intelligible once these other factors had been taken into account.

In *Land Behind Baghdad*, R.M.Adams (1965) carried the approach further by using archaeological and historical evidence to demonstrate that political and economic factors had played a more important role than had technological ones in shaping the development of irrigation systems in a part of Iraq over a 6,000-year period. Similarly, studies of Nubian culture history have shown that the size and distribution of population in this region, from at least 3000 B.C. to the present, have been determined not only by subsistence patterns but also by trade, warfare, political organization, religious beliefs, and disease patterns, and especially by Nubia's relationship with Egypt (Trigger 1965; 1970b). The vast array of factors that has been shown to influence settlement patterns in these

Archaeology and Ecology

regions clearly demonstrates the theoretical limitations of deterministic ecology. Moreover, in none of these studies is it claimed that the full range of factors has been deduced or their relationship to one another completely worked out. In each study at least some of the factors are known from historical rather than from archaeological data.

Within a non-deterministic framework, studies of subsistence patterns take on new significance. Michael D. Coe (1969) has pointed out that hitherto most theorizing about ancient ecosystems has been limited to the 'supposed permissive or limiting effects of major biomes, such as desert, steppe, or tropical forest' upon cultural development. He cites, as examples of such theories, Wittfogel's (1957) thesis that despotic states arise to provide the controls needed to administer large-scale irrigation systems or Meggers' (1954) related theory that tropical forest environments preclude the independent rise of complex societies and eventually destroy such of them as are introduced from outside. Coe and Flannery (1964) argue that such general theories do not take account of the variations within major biomes and for this reason frequently are not in accord with the facts. This is essentially the same kind of objection that already has been levelled in this paper against the neo-evolutionist approach to the study of culture. In their work on lowland Mesoamerica, Coe and Flannery suggest that the explanation of cultural development requires a detailed knowledge of the micro-environments to which individual people actually adapt. It is through an understanding of such micro-environments and of the kinds of adjustments that the members of any one culture have made to those available to them that a picture of subsistence patterns and of their carrying capacity may be built up. Alternatively in a discussion of his work at Oaxaca, Flannery (1968) has pointed out that some groups do not adapt to micro-environments as much as to a small number of plants and animals that cut across several such environments. He has suggested that cybernetic-type models may help to provide useful explanations of stability and change in such adaptations (for a discussion of this suggestion see Doran 1970).

Coe (1969) has followed the recent lead of geographers and economists in arguing that agricultural systems must be viewed not as independent variables in the study of culture but rather as parts of a much broader cultural system and there-fore as responsive to changes initiated in various other parts of the system. He stresses that social, cultural, ceremonial, and religious factors may influence subsistence patterns, par-ticularly insofar as they effect changes in population. He also stresses the potential value of analytic concepts borrowed from geography, such as central-place theory, nearest neighbour analysis, and von Thünen's 'isolated state' theory, for the analysis of archaeological data and the generation of new explanatory models. The tendency to view population, not as an automatic response to food production, but rather as related to the total cultural pattern and hence influenced by many different kinds of factors is clearly an integral part of a non-deterministic approach. Such ideas serve to connect arch-aeology with modern ecology in general.

CONCLUSIONS

Archaeologists must learn to live with the realization that their desire to study whole cultural systems cannot be realized. Much of the weakness of modern archaeology results from a tendency among archaeologists to treat their discipline as being merely the 'past tense of ethnology' or a kind of 'palaeoanthropology', rather than defining its goals in terms of the potentialities of its data. Archaeologists must learn to ask the kinds of questions with which their data are equipped to deal (Clarke 1968 : 12–24).

The relationship between archaeology and ecology is bound to be affected by such questions. As long as ecology was con-ceived of in a deterministic fashion, it appeared to be an ap-proach totally adapted to take advantage of the strong points of archaeological data and to circumvent their weak points. Now, however, it is apparent that because archaeology is unable to reconstruct whole cultural systems, an ecological approach at best can be applied partially and that the lessons drawn from it will tend to be limited to the relationships between certain adaptive features of culture. From a theoretical point of view, the main contributions that prehistoric archaeology is likely to make in the near future will concern the manner in which specific economic, social, and demographic variables interact with one another in specified environmental settings over long periods of time. Subject to these limitations, prehistoric archaeology has a unique contribution to make to an understanding of the manner in which culture has evolved prior to the beginnings of recorded history.

X

The Archaeology of Government

Introduction

IN RECENT YEARS ARCHAEOLOGISTS have shown increasing interest in processual studies that attempt to explain the development of complex societies. In them, importance is placed on the explanation of changes in political organization. They also have shown a less explicit but long-standing interest in the political behaviour of early civilizations that seems to reflect the historians' traditional interest in political events. In spite of this, little attention has been paid to the interpretation of political organization as an archaeological problem. Most archaeologists probably would agree that political organization, like other aspects of social behaviour, falls into Christopher Hawkes's (1954) middle range of amenability to archaeological study; generally more difficult to interpret than technological processes or subsistence economy, but less so than religious beliefs. Indeed, the supposed difficulties of studying all types of social processes long have resulted in archaeology being characterized as chiefly concerned with studying the material adaptation of societies to their environment; although few archaeologists would now argue that social organization and beliefs can be explained as simple epiphenomena produced by the economic substructure. In fact, the literature shows that political organization is now of considerable interest to archaeologists. Prehistorians not uncommonly assume that hypotheses about political organization can be validated archaeologically; what is needed is for these assumptions to be made explicit and adequately tested. The development of reliable techniques for using archaeological data to test assumptions about political development is important, since the complex causality of most social institutions makes it possible to propose alternative explanations for particular processes without being able to establish which of these explanations is superior to another.

The Political Subsystem

The political may be seen as a subsystem of the total socio-cultural system, which ideally is the object of archaeological study. In general terms, the political system is concerned with broad processes that regulate the functioning of societies. These processes relate to: (1) foreign relations, (2) defence from external attack, (3) maintaining internal order, validating and maintaining patterns of authority, and regulating the competition for power, and (4) organizing complex activities relating to the welfare of the society as a whole (Balandier 1972; Lloyd 1965 : 72). These activities sometimes are described as attributes of the state (Renfrew 1972 : 363), but in one form or another they apply to the simplest as well as to the most complex societies. In common with most social anthropologists, I disagree that political activities are a feature only of complex societies. Simple and complex societies vary in the degree to which political activities are professionalized and institutionally-differentiated from the general kin-based patterns of social interaction that characterize smaller-scale societies. This institutionalization of political activities Sears (1968 : 134) refers to when he cites 'specialized sub-organization' as being a characteristic of the state. The complexity of social institutions is assumed to vary with the demographic scale (but not necessarily the population density) of the social unit and with the complexity of other institutions. Though all the elements of the social system inter-relate, political phenomena are distinguishable from aspects of social organization such as residence, family, descent, and inheritance on the one hand, and from law and other aspects of belief and values on the other.

Inferring Political Organization

Purely archaeological data do not help us to study significant problems of interpersonal competition for power, which is an important element in the ethnological study of political be-

154

haviour. Even dynastic marriage patterns, which may be important for understanding the political interdependence of states, may not be amenable to study for the majority of prehistoric states. In spite of this, elements in the archaeological record may permit the delineation of many of the basic elements of political organization, such as the hierarchy of decision-making and the military system.

The strength of archaeological data for the interpretation of socio-political behaviour currently lies in their ability to provide information concerning community size and distribution of population, division of labour, relative distribution of goods and services, and the symbolic representation of status differences. Throughout the rest of this paper, I will attempt to survey how these data may improve an understanding of political organization. I am deliberately restricting this survey to the type of problems encountered in dealing with societies for which documentary evidence is not available. In doing so, I accept that many important archaeological studies of ancient political systems have been based on a combination of archaeological and historical data, and I agree that it would be foolish to reject written sources of information when available. In the long run, information gathered from the study of such societies may make it possible to interpret societies for which such information is not available. Nevertheless, the intrinsic interest of societies for which written records exist has diverted attention from the study of the correlations between political organization and material culture needed to interpret archaeological cultures that lack written documentation.

As a general rule, because of the complexity of social phenomena, the results gained from any one line of investigation may be deceiving. This suggests the need to study a problem along as many lines as possible and to cross-check the results of these studies for their coherence. Five basic types of approaches may be distinguished, as follows:

1) *Demographic*. Recent studies of the effect of population size on other aspects of human behaviour offer the hope that significant inferences can be based solely on knowledge of the size and distribution of population. The interest of anthropologists in such problems derives in part from K. Oberg's (1955) paper in which he argued that numerical increase and

concentration of population were the principal factors influencing the development of social structure among indigenous peoples of Central and South America. Later, when establishing the *World Ethnographic Sample*, G.P. Murdock (1957) made gross size of population the only variable for distinguishing his political types: Autonomous Local Community (1,500 or less); Minimal State (1,500–10,000); Little State (10,000–100,000); State (more than 100,000).

Some regularities relate to community or group size. Naroll (1956 : 690) has collected data which suggest that where maximum gatherings do not exceed a few hundred people authoritative officials are not needed, but beyond 500 they are necessary. At first, the authority seems to take the form of a council of chiefs recognizing a paramount headman as their spokesman. Where local groups exceed 1,000 people (my own work would suggest 1,500) officials in addition must be able to exercise police functions. It may be significant that the maximum size for Murdock's autonomous local community is also about this level, since this would be the point at which if a stable community were to increase in size and hold together it would have to transform itself from a village into a small city state.

Multi-community groupings require less political integration since, especially if the technology remains relatively simple, local groups can manage most of their own affairs. Tribal governments are concerned largely with suppressing internal blood feuds and regulating relations with other groups. Because of this, larger numbers of people may come together as members of a single political entity without developing a state than can remain together in a similar condition in a single community. Kroeber (1955 : 309) has observed that in many parts of North America, Indian bands tended to break apart if they acquired more than 500 members. The same appears to hold true for New Guinea at the present time (Forge 1972). This upper limit seems to apply in cases where, for various reasons, clans or small local groupings cling to their autonomy, and rankings of headmen fail to develop. Where councils of headmen do develop, the upper limit is many times higher.

Baker and Sanders (1972 : 163) suggest that simple tribes have a maximum population of 5,000 to 6,000; chiefdoms normally number 10,000 to 12,000 and ones four times as large can exist for a short time before splitting, or developing into a state. Even if this observation is valid, serious problems are encountered in using it to interpret the archaeological record. For example, archaeologically the seventeenth-century Huron Indians of eastern Canada appear as a culturally homogeneous cluster of settlements with a population of about 20,000 people, hence they would be interpreted as a chiefdom. Historically, we know that the Huron were a confederacy made up of four tribes, each approaching Baker and Sanders's maximum of 5,000 to 6,000. Chiefs were ranked up to the level of the confederacy council but power was validated by the ability of a clan leader to distribute goods and in no way by coercive pressure (Trigger 1969a). Clan autonomy and individual rights consistently were prized above all other political ideals and no one familiar with their institutions has suggested that the Huron or Iroquois confederacies constitute examples of chiefdoms. We have already noted that centralization can emerge among political units of 6,000 people or less, as evidenced by small city states. Population density does not appear to predict political organization, since groups like the Chimbu number 400 per square mile yet lack ranking or social stratification (Flannery 1972 : 406). Nor, as the contrast between the Yoruba and Ibo illustrates, does population density alone serve to promote the development of urbanism and thus shape political systems (Bascom 1955 : 452).

While theoretical sophistication has not yet reached the point where demographic data can serve as more than a very general predictor of the nature of political systems, the intrinsic value of the approach suggests that further research along these lines may be highly rewarding.

2) *Cultural.* The idea that political units normally ought to equate with cultural ones is derived from Kossinna's and Childe's general proposition that an archaeological culture is the expression of a single people. This notion was strengthened further by the European political dogma that the state is the logical expression of a common nationality. Recently this idea has been applied more or less self-consciously to the interpretation of archaeological data from the southeastern United States and Peru. While Sears (1968) admits the possibility of multi-ethnic states, he assumes that most Mississippian

The Archaeology of Government

polities in the southeastern United States grew by expanding and replacing local populations. Hence he argues that identifying a prehistoric state in this area requires defining an ethnic group by archaeological criteria, determining its extent, and finding evidence of its political organization by locating the ceremonial centres or hierarchy of such centres which served to govern and co-ordinate it. In Peru, the unification of several coastal valleys into single stylistic units is taken, along with other evidence, as indicative of the development of centralized political control (Earle 1972).

In spite of this, historical evidence indicates clearly that in some instances patterns of material culture greatly exceed the boundaries of any one government. This may be observed in the city state systems of ancient Mesopotamia, Greece, or Mesoamerica. Conversely, a single state may incorporate groups possessing diverse cultural patterns. This is normally so with empires, but also may occur when peoples speaking diverse languages or with different economies live in close proximity. In the case of mature states, spreading by replacement is probably rare, since it is in the interests of rulers to increase their wealth by increasing the number of their subjects regardless of the latter's cultural background. Another feature of imperial states that should be amenable to archaeological study is the forced resettlement of conquered populations for political reasons. This is particularly the case when, as in Peru, these are largely rural populations who may be expected to retain their native culture in a new setting.

In societies where at least some goods, such as pottery, are mass-produced, the wide-scale distribution of these items provides evidence of trading zones and associated lines of communication (O'Connor 1974). Yet, as W. Y. Adams (1970) has pointed out, these trading zones may not correspond in any specific way with ethnic groups or political frontiers, since trade flows across such boundaries as often as it does not. Among tribal societies, where pottery is manufactured by women for household use, a more widespread homogeneity of pottery styles may result not only from political alliances and intermarriage but also from warfare and the capture of women by both sides. Hence many different lines of evidence may have to be explored before the significance of variations in pottery styles can be understood.

In complex societies the material culture associated with high status groups may provide the best clue to the political structure of an area, since sharing a common style may serve as a badge of political identity. Particularly in areas of diversity in village culture, an elite culture may serve as evidence of political unity.

On the other hand, the high, and indeed the low, status cultures of whole city state systems may share a common style in spite of political diversity. An intrusive elite may adopt the material culture of an area they have conquered, so that only their language or other archaeologically elusive features provide certain evidence of their presence. This is particularly likely to be the case when the older culture is recognized as being superior to that of the newcomers. Examples are provided by the Kassites or the Amorites in Mesopotamia and the Mycenaean rulers in Crete. It is clear that, like other criteria, cultural ones are rarely useful alone; however, they may be more informative when used in combination with other criteria.

3) *Societal.* In the long run, the increasing wealth and its increasingly unequal distribution, as observed in the archaeological record in many parts of the world, must have led to conflict and to the development of political systems that could protect these arrangements (Lloyd 1965 : 78). In complex societies status correlates with the ability of certain individuals or groups to appropriate a disproportionate share of society's wealth for their own use, but there is no inevitable correlation between status and property. In band societies, status is derived mainly from initiatives that contribute to the common welfare of the group and is imperilled by attempts to retain an unequal share of material possessions. Hence in these societies status consists mainly of intangibles that are not apparent in the archaeological record. In more complex societies, the relative wealth of clan groups or of age and sex divisions within such groups may be apparent from differential distributions of material possessions, but this does not reveal how such differentials were socially regulated and supernaturally justified. Even slavery may be associated with stateless societies in which prestige must be validated by gift giving. This is exemplified by the Indian tribes of the west coast of Canada among whom prisoners of war were set to work for the economic benefit of

The Archaeology of Government

their captors and sometimes were slain as part of displays involving the conspicuous consumption of wealth.

Elaborate goods in limited numbers of children's graves may indicate a society in which high status was assigned at birth to members of particular clans or families (Flannery 1972 : 403), but this reveals nothing about the political basis of such power. Moreover, as P.J.Ucko (1969) has admonished us, grave goods do not correlate inevitably with wealth (or status) in life; therefore, alternative explanations of such graves, such as that they result from ritual sacrifice, ought at least to be considered. Such an alternative once was entertained with respect to the Early Dynastic 'death pits' excavated at Ur of the Chaldees. Only the subsequent discovery of one text apparently alluding to retainer sacrifice in connection with Mesopotamian royal burials has tipped scholarly opinion decisively in favour of them being royal graves (Kramer 1963 : 129–30).

Inferences about political organization must be based on a broad pattern of access to goods and services as preserved in the archaeological record. Only at the point where it can be demonstrated that the privileges of the elite are based on wresting significant surpluses from the society at large for their own use can the existence of a state confidently be posited. Such conclusions cannot be based simply on demonstrating that there was a centralized redistributive system in the society. It requires proof of marked asymmetry in the system, with the elite appropriating much more than they put into it.

The development of this type of redistributive system is an evolutionary process and for transitional societies it may not be possible to determine whether or not a state was present; however, some classes of evidence that definitely suggest the existence of a state are the following: (1) building programmes of a labour-intensive nature that are specifically designed to affirm the personal glory of high-status individuals or to display the power of the state. Such projects include the construction of graves, palaces, and temples. Some of these constructions, such as large tumuli over royal graves, may involve relatively little technical skill, but the manpower required makes the resulting structure a symbol of royal authority. It has been argued, however, that monumental construction can be carried out without the coercive authority of the state (Kaplan 1963; Erasmus 1965). In this respect, Colin Renfrew's distinction

160

between group-orientated and individualizing chiefdoms (might the latter better be called states?) may be conceptually useful. In the first, monumental works are of a community nature; in the latter they display the power and eminence of rulers to their subjects (Renfrew 1973b); (2) the emergence of full-time specialists to serve the needs of the elite and the state apparatus which they control. In general, these specialists fall into four classes: artisans, bureaucrats, soldiers, and retainers. Workers of this sort are enabled to specialize to a much greater degree than full-time specialists whose services are available to the society as a whole and who first appear at an earlier stage of social development. The appearance of 'master specialists' is correlated with the development of new sources of patronage, namely, rulers who can cover the high overhead needed to support them. Their presence leads to the creation of an elite culture or what Robert Redfield has called a 'Great Tradition', as distinct from the 'Little Tradition' of the peasantry. Archaeologically, the presence of a Great Tradition can be measured by the refinement of technology and the appearance of sophisticated and coherent art styles, as exhibited in the palaces, temples, tombs, and goods that are manufactured for the elite. In pre-industrial societies such goods are shared to a very limited degree, if at all, by the lower classes, except in the form of cheap and clumsy imitations. The distribution of workers or of variant local styles may reveal much about the degree of centralization of patronage and power in a particular political system; (3) large-scale human sacrifice in connection with high status burials. Such retainer sacrifice, which is essentially different from the killing of prisoners of war in simpler societies, was common to many ancient states in both the Old and New World (Childe 1944 : 96). It must be remembered, however, that the state is a precondition for the development of civilization (if defined as associated with a Great Tradition) and for this reason many simpler states may go undetected using these cultural criteria (Trigger 1968a : 53–4).

4) *Geographical*. All complex societies produce a wide range of special purpose structures: palaces, temples, storehouses, military camps, meeting places, and administrative buildings. Some of these structures clearly relate to political activities

The Archaeology of Government

and the study of them and their distribution may reveal something about the political organization. Care is needed, however, to determine correctly the functions of such buildings, which are not always clear from their location, lay-out, and contents. Some of the problems involved in determining the functions of buildings are exemplified by the recent debate whether the 'Official Palace' at Tell el Amarna was a palace, temple, or combination of both (Uphill 1970; Assmann 1972). At least part of the latter controversy seems to stem from the difficulty of applying modern (or medieval) concepts about the function of buildings to ancient ones. Likewise, in dealing with tribal societies, it is of less importance to correlate the largest house in a village with a village headman than it is to determine whether the house reflects his greater affluence or was made large to serve as a communal meeting place for the whole village.

Archaeologists have begun to use locational theory to work out hierarchies of settlement types and to attempt to explain their geographical distribution. Normally this analysis involves determining different levels of service functions. Even at a simple tribal level centrally-located, fortified towns may provide protection for neighbouring small villages. Such an arrangement represents a reasonable compromise between a need for protection and the desire of horticulturalists to live as near as possible to their fields. David Clarke (1972) has applied locational analysis to Iron Age settlements and hillforts in England, interpreting different sizes as centres of different rank orders. Even in cases where economic factors may be the primary determinants of settlement size, their size may correspond in a general way with their position in an administrative hierarchy; if so, this can be confirmed by the further correlation of specific types of high status residences or official buildings with sites of a particular rank. Where centres of political administration do not correspond with centres of population and economic activity, as in some feudal societies, this can be determined easily. Multiple or itinerant capitals, for example, may represent the attempt of a central government to overcome problems of communication and internal disunity (Balandier 1972 : 137–8).

Political factors play an important role in influencing the size and location of settlements. At the tribal level these seem mainly to be correlated with military considerations. Where warfare is endemic among closely neighbouring groups, as in New Guinea, protection may be achieved by kinsmen living in small dispersed hamlets, not all of which can be attacked at one time. Elsewhere, dispersed farming or herding groups may share a common fort to which everyone can retire in times of danger. For the most part, however, communities depend on increased size for protection or locate themselves in easily defended locations, as far removed as possible from sources of danger (Doxiadis 1968 : 141, 143).

Elsewhere I have argued that craft specialization will tend to produce a hexagonal distribution of cities of approximately equal importance, each having perhaps 5,000 to 50,000 inhabitants (Trigger 1972). Cities of this size also appear to be normal for a city state system; however, when such cities become the capitals of larger states they are subsidized as administrative and cult centres and grow much larger and more opulent than they would have done otherwise. This expansion of cities as they gain hegemony within a city state system easily can be documented for ancient Mesopotamia (Ur, Babylon), Classical Greece (Athens), and highland Mesoamerica (Tenochtitlan), and a similar phenomenon may explain the relatively large size of Tikal among the classic Maya centres. Supercities, with populations of 100,000 or more, such as Rome and Ch'ang-an, achieved and maintained their high size as centres of vast empires. A similar explanation probably holds for all pre-industrial cities of this magnitude. Within these large-scale states it is often possible to distinguish not only a capital, but also secondary and tertiary administrative centres corresponding to regional and smaller divisions. In Egypt, where little archaeological information is available concerning habitation sites, a hierarchy of tomb types seems roughly to parallel the administrative hierarchy. The tendency of provincial officials to locate their tombs in their administrative centres rather than in the royal necropolis has been found to serve as a useful measure of the relative degree of centralization or decentralization at different periods. Even without written records, no archaeologist could doubt the political unification of Egypt at the time when the largest pyramids were constructed (O'Connor 1974).

The Archaeology of Government

In some instances, political unification may be attested by the extent of state projects such as irrigation or transportation systems. While the degree to which small-scale irrigation systems can operate on a consensual basis is a matter of controversy, it seems fairly clear that the integrated multi-valley systems of coastal Peru or the large water-control systems of the Old World presuppose the existence of a central authority to plan and maintain such projects. These projects may be combined with important transportation systems, such as the Grand Canal joining the Huang Ho and Yangtze rivers in China. In many large states, special road networks were constructed for administrative and military purposes. These road systems tend to be co-extensive with the state and in the case of the Roman and Inca empires, where they have been relatively well studied, they would serve to reveal the extent of these empires even without written records. Particularly with the growth of aerial reconnaissance, this type of evidence has proved increasingly amenable to study (Deuel 1973).

Where rival city states exist in close proximity to one another it is not unusual for each urban centre to be fortified. On the other hand, administrative centres often are fortified within large states so they may serve as control centres for the central government and places where the elite can live in relative security. This was the case with traditional Chinese cities (*ch'eng*) (Fei 1953 : 95). By contrast, the lack of fortifications around Roman cities in the early centuries of the Christian era was a measure not only of security against external attack, but also of the control that the Roman administration was able to exercise over the surrounding countryside.

Frontiers between states may be demarcated in a variety of ways that can be studied archaeologically. Sometimes formal boundary markers may be recovered; in other cases states may be separated as a matter of policy by no-man's-lands. Work done by Parsons (1971) and Dumond (1972) suggests that during the Classic period in highland Mexico Teotihuacán and Cholula were separated by a broad, sparsely-settled zone which may have functioned as a no-man's-land. Elsewhere elaborate border defences may separate one state from another or protect settled areas against the incursion of barbarian tribesmen living beyond the borders of the state. Examples are

164

the elaborate defences that the Egyptians built along their southern frontier in the Middle Kingdom, the Great Wall of China, and the Roman *limes*, which vary from a single fortified line along the northern frontiers to broad defensive belts in Syria and North Africa (Deuel 1973 : 93–120). Even without written records, a study of forts and border defences would enable archaeologists to trace the frontiers and history of expansion of the Roman Empire. That such fortifications are not only a feature of empires is shown by Offa's Dyke, the linear earthwork between Wales and Anglo-Saxon Mercia. Analogous fortifications appear to have demarcated the borders of coastal states in Peru (Deuel 1973 : 226–6).

5) *Iconographic.* The art of some cultures, such as Shang China and the Indus Valley civilization, appears to be singularly poor in information about political subjects. In other cultures, artistic representations of rulers and their activities abound. These representations often are highly formalized and based on a limited repertoire of themes. The relative size and positioning of figures, the elaborateness of costumes, and particular iconic symbols (crowns, parasols, etc.) may denote the rank of those being depicted (Marcus 1974). Without writing, such representations may be difficult to interpret, as witnessed by the long uncertainty as to whether Maya rulers were priests or secular rulers. It is possible, however, that even without written explanations, a detailed contextual analysis will reveal the fundamental significance of differences in the attributes associated with these figures.

Certain features that recur in this 'iconography of power' (*Machtkunst*) in widely separated early civilizations are of special interest, since they appear to be parallel responses to similar circumstances among historically-unrelated groups. Among the most obvious themes are the following: (1) the relative size of figures and elaborateness of costumes tend to correlate positively with their political importance; (2) defeated enemies are shown simply dressed or naked in the presence of their elaborately-costumed conquerors (examples from Egypt, Mesopotamia, Maya, Mochica culture); (3) a king is often portrayed dominating a supine enemy (Egypt, Maya, Aztec). Resemblances of this sort suggest that the iconography of early civilizations may be a source of insight not only into the political structure of these societies but into their political psychology as well.

CONCLUSION

A broad range of data concerning political systems is embedded in the archaeological record. The present survey only touches the surface of this subject but suggests that careful attention to this area will further an understanding of archaeological cultures for which written records are lacking and for testing more general theories of cultural evolution. For the present, few conclusions can be based on only one line of inference; instead they must be based on the convergence of different lines of investigation.

XI

The Determinants of
Settlement Patterns

THIS SURVEY PAPER IS a preliminary exploration of the range of ways in which the concept of settlement patterns can be useful for interpreting archaeological data. My chief interests are in the nature of settlement patterns and in the relationships they bear to the rest of culture. I shall analyze: (1) the relationships that exist between settlement patterns and other aspects of culture, and (2) the ways in which archaeologists can use the knowledge of such relationships to further an understanding of the cultures they are investigating. The first step requires a cross-cultural investigation of: (a) the range of factors that correlate significantly with settlement patterns, and (b) the manner in which these factors articulate with one another to produce the settlement pattern of a particular society. My main interest will be the determinants of settlement patterns, by which I mean those classes of factors that interact with each other to produce the spatial configurations of a social group. Since individual determinants may tend toward results that oppose as well as reinforce one another, a settlement pattern may be a compromise among a number of conflicting determinants. There are still other factors that are functionally related to the settlement pattern but whose relationship is a dependent rather than a determining one. These, however, lie beyond the scope of this study.

It is first necessary to clarify what is meant by a settlement pattern. To do this I must review some of the work that has been done to date. The concept of settlement pattern was first put to substantial use in the field of archaeology by Gordon R. Willey in his book *Prehistoric Settlement Patterns in the Virú Valley* (1953). There, Willey delineated changes in the form and distribution of sites in a small Peruvian valley during the course of several millennia, and related these changes to socio-economic trends and to historical events. In his Introduction he described settlement patterns as a 'strategic starting point for the functional interpretation of archaeological cultures' since they reflect 'the natural environment, the level of technology on which the builders operated, and various institutions of social interaction and control which the culture maintained' (p1). Since then, a considerable number of studies have been concerned with settlement patterns. Some are basically factual studies aimed at ascertaining the types of settlement patterns associated with a given culture. Others have attempted to use settlement patterns to reconstruct the social (Chang 1958; 1962a) or religious (Sears 1961) institutions of ancient cultures. Some have concentrated on the layout and house types associated with individual sites (Willey 1956b); others, on the distribution patterns of large numbers of sites (Trigger 1963a). The cultures studied range from small hunting and gathering ones (Chang 1962a) to complex civilizations (Coe 1961), and the interpretive approaches range from simple, straightforward analogy to systematic cross-cultural comparisons using ethnographic material.

One of the chief merits of Willey's definition of settlement patterns lay in its breadth and its clearly functional view of settlement pattern phenomena. The value of settlement patterns for reconstructing prehistoric cultures was seen as a result of the variety of institutions that are 'reflected' in the settlement pattern. Despite such a healthy emphasis on variety and on a range of possible uses of data, two approaches dominated settlement pattern studies into the late 1960s.

The first was primarily ecological and often was based on the assumption that the settlement pattern was a product of the simple interaction of two variables – environment and technology. This sort of ecological determinism actively had been promoted as a determinant not only of settlement patterns but also of culture in general by Leslie White and his students, and, in archaeology, particularly by Betty Meggers. The ecological approach was primarily an investigation of how the settlement pattern reflected the adaptation of a society and its technology to its environment.

In the second kind of approach, settlement pattern data were used as a basis for making inferences about the social, political, and religious organization of prehistoric cultures. Chang
168

(1958; 1962a) and Sears (1961) have used the term 'community pattern' to refer to 'the strictly social aspects of settlement patterning'. E. Z. Vogt (1956 : 174–175) has even suggested that these two approaches, along with studies of process, might be considered as separate branches of the study of settlement patterns. These two kinds of study were distinguished not only by approach but also to a large degree by their choice of data. The first was concerned with the size and distribution of whole sites, whereas the second concentrated on patterning within individual settlements. Mayer-Oakes (1959 : 167) distinguished between *community types* and *zonal patterns;* Sears (1961 : 226) between *site* and *areal* patterns, referring to the former as *microcosmic* and the latter as *macrocosmic*. Chang used the terms 'microstructure' and 'macrostructure' to describe the socio-cultural systems of individual settlements and those made up of a number of settlements, respectively.

I believe, however, that archaeologists and other anthropologists can conceive of settlement patterns more profitably in terms of three levels. The first of these is the individual building or structure; the second, the manner in which these structures are arranged within single communities; and the third, the manner in which communities are distributed over the landscape. Each of these levels appears to be shaped by factors that differ in kind or degree from the factors that shape other levels; hence the combined study of all three is likely to shed more light on archaeological cultures than is the study of a single level.

Although work to date has done much to advance the study of settlement patterns, the heavy concentration on only two approaches has not been without its disadvantages. So far, archaeologists have been more interested in using the evidence as a basis for reconstructing individual cultures than in studying the nature of settlement patterns for its own sake. Hence there is little in the way of a systematic understanding to guide the archaeologist. In the long run, however, settlement pattern data can be used with a full knowledge of their prospects and limitations only when some attention has been paid to the nature of this phenomenon in living societies. My aim in the first part of this paper is to assemble a list of the various factors that scholars have suggested play a part in determining the structure of individual buildings, settlements, and overall distributions. This list is based on the work of geographers, sociologists, and historians. Material from both simple and complex societies will be considered, since circumstances peculiar to each may help to point up problems common to settlement pattern studies as a whole. Since this part of my paper is essentially a survey of other people's ideas, my illustrations are drawn from many different parts of the world.

Determinants

1) *Individual buildings*. There has been relatively little in the way of a systematic investigation of our most basic unit, the individual structure. Perhaps the most common use that has been made of house types has been in tracing historical connections among different groups. Therefore, much that I say here must be in the form of queries rather than answers. There is great variety in the structures of complex societies – various types of houses, as well as temples, forts, tombs, and other types of buildings. In the simplest societies, there may be only one, quite uniform, house type and no special-purpose buildings. Yet even this single house type may represent an accommodation to a considerable variety of factors.

One of these factors is the subsistence regime of the society. Migratory peoples tend to have houses that are either transportable or easy to build; even semisedentary swidden agriculturalists are less inclined to invest in buildings than are most completely sedentary populations. For migratory societies, there seems to be an even more specific correlation between house types and the availability of building materials. In areas where such materials easily can be come by, a new shelter can be erected at each camping place, but in deserts or steppe country where such materials are scarce, buildings tend to be of a sort that is moved from place to place. Examples are the portable tepee of the Plains Indians, the light goat-hair tent of the Arab Bedouin, and the *yurt* of Mongolian herdsmen. In the *yurt*, insulation against the cold climate is provided by two layers of felt stretched, one on the inside, the other on the outside, of a collapsible wooden trellis (Fitch and Branch 1960 : 141–142).

Thus a house represents an attempt to meet the challenge of an environment with the building materials that same environment offers. In a short but important study of primitive architecture, Fitch and Branch (1960) have noted that the structural design of many primitive buildings 'reflects a precise and detailed knowledge of local climatic conditions . . . and . . . a remarkable understanding of the performance characteristics of [local] building materials' (p. 134). They suggest that the principal climatic factors to which houses adapt are the diurnal and yearly variations in ambient and radiant temperatures, air movement, and humidity. They find that houses in different regions of the world often show adaptations that are of 'surprising delicacy and precision' (p. 136).

The dome-shaped igloo of the Central Eskimo, for example, is built quickly and easily of local material that is readily available. The dome offers minimum resistance and maximum obstruction to winter gales. This shape also exposes as little of its surface to the cold as possible, and can be heated effectively by a point source of heat, such as an oil lamp.

In hot deserts, there are marked differences in temperatures between day and night, as well as between seasons. In such regions, buildings with heavy walls of stone and clay absorb heat during the day and reradiate it at night in a manner that helps to flatten out the uncomfortable diurnal fluctuations of the coldest months. Such buildings are common among the Pueblo Indians of the American Southwest, in North Africa, and in the Middle East. Roofs are either of vaulted mud brick or of mud slabs laid on beams. In moister regions, such as Nigeria, a mud dome frequently is covered with thatch so that it sheds water.

In wet, tropical regions, temperatures vary rather little, but shade and ventilation are essential to comfort. Walls are reduced therefore to a minimum to allow for ventilation, while a large, steeply sloping roof projects beyond the living space as protection against sun and rain. A raised floor also serves to fend off dampness and wild animals. Houses of this sort can be constructed easily out of available saplings and fibres.

In some of the preceding examples, not only the general structural principles but also the shapes of the houses are adaptations to the environment. The igloo and the sloping roofs of houses in rainy regions are cases in point. The Naskapi house is a conical wigwam braced by a ring of stones and covered with bark or skins. G. I. Quimby (1960 : 383–384) has observed that no other shape would be as efficient in an environment where frozen ground and lack of soil make it impossible to sink poles into the earth. Moreover, certain types of more complex structures, such as houses built around an open court, are less practical in cold climates than in warm ones. Not only is the usefulness of the courtyard, which normally is the centre of much family activity, reduced in a cold climate, but also heating such a house is considerably more difficult than heating a compact one. Climatic factors also may influence the orientation of houses. Doors or windows may face toward the sun, away from an unpleasant prevailing wind, or toward a lake or river. Such practical considerations certainly enter into the Chinese art of *fung-shui*, or geomancy, where they are embedded in an elaborate system of symbolism and magic (Durkheim and Mauss 1963 : 68, 73).

Yet a building is more than an adaptation to climate. It also reflects the skills of its builder and his technology. This technical know-how affects the range of materials that are available, and through the materials the shape and design of buildings. Skill in stone and brickwork permits the erection of larger and more elaborate structures. In different societies, building techniques may develop along divergent paths that, in part, reflect the different materials used. The brick and stone architecture of Europe and Western Asia gave rise to buildings the weight of which rested primarily on the walls. In Eastern Asia, however, a tradition of wood architecture was developed in which walls tended to be 'hung' on a pole-and-beam construction that supported the roof (Willetts 1958 : 689–723). Specific techniques also make new designs possible. The dome, for example, made it possible to roof over unencumbered spaces of considerable size.

The size and layout of buildings also may reflect the structure of the family. A house occupied by a nuclear family may contain one or more rooms, but the function of these rooms will relate to the needs of a single family. If the house belongs to a lineage, nuclear family units are likely to be found repeated within the house, although food stores may be common to the whole unit. Chang (1958) has suggested that even in large houses, such as those of the Witoto of South America which house a whole village, the household can be distinguished by (1) interpreting the use of equipment, (2) distinguishing the partitions that separate households, and (3) identifying separate kitchens. In a polygynous household, on the other hand, each wife may have her own living area and kitchen, but the rooms belonging to the head of the household will be without a kitchen, since he will be fed by his various wives in turn. Alternatively, a polygynous family may have a common cookhouse (Murdock 1934 : 559). From archaeological evidence alone it might be difficult to distinguish a household consisting of a master and his resident servants from that of a lineage, especially if social differences within a society are not strongly marked in material possessions. Moreover, although various forms of multi-family houses may indicate lineages or polygynous families, similar institutions also are found associated with nuclear family houses and so can go undetected.

Particular forms of houses also may be related to forms of family organization. The longhouse as a unit of residence seems to be associated closely with lineage organizations. In this case, the main archaeological problem is to distinguish residential longhouses from buildings such as men's clubs. In Melanesia, some of the latter have not only the plan of a longhouse but also a row of fireplaces down the centre, associated not with nuclear families but with particular status groups within the club (Codrington 1957 : 101–105). Any site in which a few 'longhouses' occur alongside a large number of nuclear family houses should be suspect, and the buildings subjected to careful investigation before functions are assigned to them.

The structures in a community may reflect differences in wealth and rank, as well as various social institutions. The economic egalitarianism of many primitive societies is reflected in uniformity in the design and size of shelters, but with increasing social complexity the design and functions of buildings become increasingly differentiated. Among the Huron, the most important chiefs in a village occupied the largest longhouses, which served as gathering places for meetings and rituals (Trigger 1963b : 156). In societies where authority or class divisions are more pronounced, the houses of the elite become larger and more elaborate. In such places as the Marquesas, for example, the elaborateness of the platform on which a house was built reflected the importance of its owner in the social hierarchy (Suggs 1960 : 124). In addition to such differentiations in house types, special-purpose structures are more common in a class-differentiated society. Some of these structures are also residential. Visitors or bachelors may sleep inside the clubhouses that are common in Oceania (Codrington 1957 : 69–115); while in Sparta and more recently in some parts of Hungary (Hollander 1960), adult males normally lived apart from their wives and families. The age grade system of the Masai found expression in special camps where the warriors and unmarried girls of a village lived together until they reached the age when they were permitted to establish homes of their own (Forde 1934 : 302–333).

Elsewhere, various special-purpose structures that are not lived in may serve the needs of the community as a whole or of some of its members. The Arab guest house, which is used to feed and accommodate travellers, functions primarily as a meeting place for the men of a tribe or village (Salim 1962 : 72), as did the sweat house among the Pomo. The Plains Indians constructed large triple tepees where some of the ceremonies of their men's societies were performed (Forde 1934 : 57). Huts or houses also may be built to isolate members of society. Among the Indians of the Northwest Coast of America, girls frequently were secluded for a time at puberty, either in a small hut or behind a curtain. In complex societies, there is often a considerable variety of public buildings devoted to secular group activities, such as schools, libraries, stadia, public baths, and museums. Once their function has been determined, these buildings permit us to assess the nature of community life and the values of ancient civilizations.

The specialization of production also is reflected in the individual structure, in the form either of workshops added on to houses or of separate buildings that serve as workshops and storerooms. Likewise, the transportation and sale of goods stimulates the growth of marketplaces, stores, and caravanserais. By determining the use that was made of individual buildings, the archaeologist can recover much information about patterns of production and trade in ancient societies.

The religious beliefs of a society may influence house types and also may result in the construction of shrines, temples, or tombs. The royal funerary temples of the Khmer civilization were built as a model of the universe. The central structure with its five towers on a large pyramid represented Mount Meru, the centre of the universe; the surrounding walls were the rock wall that bounded the universe; and the moat beyond was the primal ocean (Coe 1961 : 71). Mircea Eliade (1960) and others see houses as the representation of a people's conception of the universe. Such 'habitation symbolism' is said to be very clear among the subarctic peoples of North America and Siberia. Among them the centre post is symbolically identified with the 'pillar of the world'; among the pastoralists of Asia, and the 'archaic Chinese', the mythico-ritual function of the pillar has been 'passed on' to the overhead smoke hole.

Special religious buildings include temples and plazas where rituals can be performed. The *kivas*, or ceremonial lodges, found among the Pueblo tribes of the American Southwest are interesting for two reasons: first, the *kiva* may be the retention of an earlier form of round house, long abandoned as a dwelling; and second, the *kivas* were owned by religious fraternities that were associated with the various clans of the community. Sears (1961) already has demonstrated the value of studying temple and tomb complexes as settings for ritual. In this way, much can be learned about the religious practices of prehistoric societies. The whole relationship between structures and ritual remains to be studied in a comparative fashion both on a worldwide basis and within particular culture areas. Archaeologists must beware equating the study of religious buildings with the study of religion itself. The importance of cult buildings varies a good deal from society to society. Gods may have no temples at all, and ceremonies may be performed in the open or in public places that normally have other uses. To understand religious practices, the archaeologist also must look for household shrines and cult images and symbols, whatever the architectural complex may be.

Political institutions also affect house styles. In areas where crime is common and police controls ineffective houses tend to be built with an eye to security. The inward-facing house is one example of this sort of building. A few fierce dogs also may provide protection for a house or tent, but this sort of defence would not likely be obvious in the archaeological record. The lack of proper defences on a higher (community or national) level may result in houses themselves being adapted for such purposes. The towering, thick-walled dwellings found in southern Arabia often were strong enough to ward off attacks by Bedouin. A more complex political organization also will generate buildings to serve its own needs, such as administrative offices, jails, and barracks.

Nor can the influence of secular tastes and fashions be ignored. These are reflected in the design and layout of houses, and may account for the spreading of particular types of buildings into areas for which they were not designed and may not be well-suited. The layout of a house also may reflect such tastes as a desire for individual or group privacy. The former will be reflected in the clear division of a house into rooms and the separation of the rooms by doors. Secular tastes also may produce special summer or country houses that may differ considerably from normal ones. Huron women are described as going with their children to live in the fields during the summer, not merely to be nearer their work but also to be away from the crowded conditions of village life (Trigger 1960 : 18).

2) *Community layouts.* The next level is the layout of the structures constituting a single community. By community I mean 'the maximal group of persons who normally reside in face-to-face association' (Murdock 1949 : 79). In general, a community corresponds to a single settlement and therefore can be identified with the archaeologist's *component* (Willey and Phillips 1958 : 21, 22). Yet, in areas of dispersed settlement such an equation may not hold, nor will it hold for migratory hunting and gathering peoples who shift their community through several settlements in the course of a year, or among whom the community may be forced to disperse in small family groups during seasons of scarcity. In these cases, the community, as socially defined, would be associated with more than one settlement or site. The archaeological definition of the aggregate of settlements associated with such a community would require ascertaining at what time of year different settlements were occupied and what kinds of settlements were utilized at each season. It also would require the detection of whatever central meeting places exist in the pattern and estimations of the size of a community that could be associated with a particular mode of subsistence. Then, on the basis of complementary distributions, the pattern itself could be worked

176

out, at least as a statistical possibility. Despite some violence to the sociological concept of community, I also have extended the term to cover the whole of large stable units of settlement, such as cities, which, if they cannot be defined as communities, at least represent stable interaction patterns.

The maximum size and stability of a community quite obviously are limited by the environment and the effectiveness of the subsistence technology. The latter includes the means of acquiring or producing food, as well as storing, processing, and transporting it. The three last factors often are crucially important: effective means of storing food allows the population to expand beyond the numbers that could survive the period of least production; processing allows foods to be used that otherwise would be inedible (e.g. acorns and bitter manioc); and transportation determines the size of the area over which food can be collected and concentrated. These ecological factors play an important role in determining the major types of community pattern as they have been defined by Chang (1962a : 30). They determine, for example, whether or not a community can complete its annual subsistence cycle at a single site, and whether a single site can be inhabited permanently, as would be the case with irrigation agriculture, or only semipermanently, as with most swidden agriculture. When sedentary life is not possible, a community may have to occupy a network of scattered settlements in the course of a year. In some cases the annual subsistence region in such a network will remain unchanged from year to year, and the main seasonal settlements will be revisited annually. In other cases the group will exhaust the ecological potential of one region and be forced to move on to fresh territory.

Within any region, people will tend to establish their settlements in places that are close to drinking water, sources of food, and, as far as possible, in places that are safe and pleasant. The hunters and gatherers of the temperate forests sought to locate their camps not only close to food supplies but more specifically on sand banks by the edges of lakes or rivers, where they would be dry, and where the breeze would keep away bothersome insects. Agricultural groups seek locations where the soil and weather are favourable to their crops and methods of cultivation.

The Determinants of Settlement Patterns

Whereas community size and location are influenced to a large extent by ecological factors, the layout of communities appears to be strongly influenced by family and kinship organization – especially in primitive societies. These relationships are not necessarily totally independent factors, since kinship relations are determined at least partly by ecological factors that operate through the relations of production.

In a study of circumpolar groups, Chang (1962a) has distinguished between communities of a 'Siberian' type and those of an 'Eskimo' type. The Siberian type is composed of individuals 'unilineally determined by descent and/or unilocally recruited by marriage. It is a basic unit of economic cooperation and is strongly integrated as a cohesive body' (p.33). This type of society often occupies a multi-dwelling village that has individual or multifamily houses laid out in a planned fashion. When there is more than one lineage present, each occupies its own section of the village, and when the community splits up for its seasonal movements it splits along lines of kinship, with the same groups returning to the same winter base year after year. The Eskimo type of community is characterized by the looseness of its organization, by fluctuations in group membership, and by bilateral kinship. Such groups tend to be incoherent conglomerations of families, each family settling where it likes and moving elsewhere when new districts offer greater advantages. Even the winter settlements are characterized by this irregularity. Chang's distinction between 'Siberian' and 'Eskimo' community types is similar in many ways to Steward's (1955) distinction between patrilineal and composite bands. The first type of community is associated with a more stable and more sedentary subsistence pattern than is the second; its subsistence being based more often on fishing than on hunting. Chang suggests that the kind of solidarity associated with the Siberian type 'tends to call for a symbolic projection of the community structure in the lay-out of the settlement site' (p.37).

This same theme forms the basis of Chang's (1958) study of neolithic village patterns, which suggests a high degree of correlation between community plans and village social organization, and postulates land ownership as an important determinant of neolithic community types. Chang's survey of neolithic societies demonstrates a strong correlation between planned villages and communities composed of a single lineage, and between segmented planned villages and communities composed of more than one lineage. Although there are perhaps more neolithic societies with a scattered homestead pattern than Chang's sample suggests, his conclusions remain valid so long as they are presumed to read: the absence of x settlement pattern does not necessarily imply the absence of y community type, but the presence of x strongly suggests that y is present also. The idea that kinship organization is reflected in village plans or in the distribution of communities is not new in anthropology: the relationship between social and geographical space was one of the main themes explored by Evans-Pritchard in *The Nuer* (1940). Nor is this phenomenon confined entirely to primitive societies. In medieval Arab cities, different quarters sometimes were established for different tribes. Likewise, the Aztec city of Tenochtitlan was divided into sections, each with its own temples and schools and belonging to a separate *calpulli*, probably an endogamous deme (Soustelle 1962 : 7–8).

In complex societies, not only social classes but also religious and ethnic groups may live in well-demarcated areas of the community, which often are separated from one another by a wall. In these communities, special sections may be set aside for foreigners or for ethnic groups such as Jews. In these areas, such groups can live under the protection and regulation of city officials (Sjoberg 1960 : 100). Ethnic areas also may be found within modern communities, where they develop as a result of associational patterns rather than formal rules. Although divisions of the community resulting from disparate levels of wealth may be defined fairly easily from the quality and size of dwellings, more informal ethnic divisions may be difficult to trace in the layout of a site. A district populated by prosperous foreign traders could perhaps be distinguished from the local elite quarter by a preponderance of store rooms, by alien house plans, or by evidence of foreign cults. The section of the Spanish settlement of Nueva Cadiz in Venezuela that was inhabited by Negro and Indian slaves was identified by Indian pottery representing various tribal groups and by the lack of such permanent habitations as were found in the European quarter (Rouse and Cruxent 1963 : 134–138). The best hope of identifying ethnic groups at an archaeological site seems to lie in investigating distributions of artefacts to discover whether particular symbols or written materials are associated with houses in one part of the site but not another. Even where these efforts prove fruitful, it is difficult to demonstrate that an ethnic difference – as opposed, for example, to a religious or tribal difference – is involved. The presence of Huron captives in historic Seneca villages in New York State is attested in the archaeological record by the presence of many Huron-style potsherds among those of native design. Without historical documentation, however, it is likely that these would have been described as trade sherds and their real social significance misunderstood (MacNeish 1952 : 46).

In more complex societies, subsistence factors, in the narrow sense, are not so important as determinants of the size and location of communities. Trade may provide a source of wealth and stimulate the growth of large cities in remote regions, and the wealth amassed from such trade in turn may serve either to finance the development of novel agricultural systems in areas where they would otherwise be impractical, or to effect the importation of food from distant regions. Settlements also may spring up in wastelands where rare and valuable minerals are discovered. In ancient times, copper smelters were built at Aqaba on the shores of the Red Sea, a region rich in copper but lacking in agricultural potential.

Specialization on a local or village level can develop in relatively simple societies. When a number of villages are linked together in a trading network, they can better transcend local limitations in natural resources. A trading network also fosters greater specialization and better quality products than does an autonomous village economy. Thus a careful investigation of trade and of the nature of production is a prerequisite for explaining the size and the social and cultural complexity of communities. The archaeologist must determine what goods were present and produced in his sites. Data concerning production relationships can be obtained by studying the layout of stores and workshops within a community. The study should note whether places of work and residence are together or separate; whether the workshops of one trade are located in the same part of the community or at scattered points; the degree to which the production and sale of goods are handled as a single operation or as separate functions; the importance of public markets, as opposed to stores; and so forth. Data of this sort, considered together with what can be learned about the social organization of the community from other sources, will permit more detailed and accurate reconstructions of prehistoric social organization.

Graveyards provide interesting clues to social and political organization. Status differences often can be traced in graves even better than in house types or village patterns. This is especially so at a neolithic or advanced collecting level, where there may be considerable differences in status but little difference in standards of living. Social relations and kinship also may be reflected in the relationship between communities and their cemeteries. Chang (1963 : 65) has noted that in the Yangshao phase in North China each village had its own cemetery, but as the population increased and villages split, villages that had shared a common ancestry often continued to share a common graveyard, so that the ratio of cemeteries to villages declined. In historic times, the tribes of the Huron confederacy held a ceremony every decade or so in which members of the various tribes who had died in the interim were reinterred in a common ossuary as an expression of political solidarity. A careful cross-cultural study of the relationship between burial practices and social structure might reveal correlations of considerable interest and value.

Little formal work has been done by archaeologists on the relationship between special-purpose structures and the community as a whole. Gideon Sjoberg (1960) has noted that in most preindustrial cities the major temples and palaces and the homes of the elite are concentrated in the centre of the community. In support of this observation, one can call to mind the location of the agora and the acropolis in Athens, the Roman forum, the temple centre of a Sumerian city, and the palaces and temples of a Chinese city like Peking. In the New World, similarly, the centre of Tenochtitlan was occupied by the main temples, palaces, and markets of the city, and Cuzco, the Inca capital, appears to have consisted of palaces, temples, and a ritual square surrounded by villages of royal retainers (Rowe 1944). In cities like Tenochtitlan that were organized on a segmental principle, each of the divisions of the city also had its own secondary centre. However, in some cities the elite centre appears to have been at one side or in one corner of the city. In some of the cities of Chou China the elite centre was a walled-off corner of the city (Chang 1963 : 180–195), and in the cities of the Indus Valley civilization the citadel was to one side (Wheeler 1960 : 18), as was the elite centre in the ancient Egyptian town of Kahun (W. Smith 1958 : 96–98).

The kind of buildings associated with such civic centres also provides some indication of the values and orientation of a particular society. In simpler societies, houses often are grouped around a central plaza that may serve as a market, a work area, and a meeting place, and may contain or be bordered by such public buildings as temples or council houses. In the dispersed pattern of the American farming community, such special-purpose buildings as schools, churches, and general stores are foci of public activity. Yet, the reconstruction of community activities on the basis of the layout of public buildings within the community must be undertaken with caution. It may be difficult, from archaeological evidence alone, to determine the full range of uses that was made of a plaza. Norms may require that various structures important in community life be located outside the settlement, as for example the clubhouses of the secret societies in Melanesia. Temples or cult centres likewise may be located in sacred spots outside the residential area. The Egyptian pyramid complexes, with their small colonies of attendant priests, were built as the foci of royal mortuary cults. The priests lived near the pyramid and maintained themselves through agriculture and craft occupations (Kees 1961 : 157–160). Monastic communities, with carefully organized routines and often with rigidly laid-out buildings, are still another example of whole communities that are religiously based. Pilgrimage centres like Mecca would be humble desert villages were it not for the tourist industry that sustains the local population.

The development of complex political organization gives rise to similarly specialized communities. Isolated forts and garrison towns are built to guard frontiers or to police the countryside. Royal courts commonly are established within cities, but some constitute independent communities. The king of Buganda, for example, lived in an oval enclosure over a mile long that also housed his guards, retainers, and slaves. The roads leading to this compound were lined with the houses of important chiefs and officials (Murdock 1934 : 525). Warfare and defence play important roles in determining the site and layout of communities in many parts of the world. Where warfare is endemic, as it was among the Iroquois, villages commonly were built on hilltops or at the bends of rivers. Where walls or stockades are used for defence, houses often are crowded together to conserve space. When the Roman empire was defended adequately by its armies, cities tended to grow into sprawling agglomerations, but when the defence system collapsed in the third century A.D. the inhabitants of cities such as Barcelona were forced to abandon their suburbs and crowd together behind hastily built walls (Weiss 1961). Large numbers of pastoralists often camp together for protection, and smaller groups of Bedouin will camp with their tents arranged in a circular fashion (Forde 1934 : 317). Similarly, the Masai *kraal* consists of a thorn fence and a ring of houses surrounding a central area where the domestic animals are secured for the night. The central area of a city often is similarly walled off, both to separate it from the city as a whole and so that it can be a place of last retreat. In Mexico, temple platforms served the latter purpose, and the capture of the main sanctuary symbolized the capture of a city (Soustelle 1962 : 211). The presence or absence of fortifications cannot be considered as direct evidence of the prevalence of warfare, since the effectiveness of such means of defence depends in part on whether offensive or defensive warfare is in the ascendant.

It also is argued that community patterns, like house plans, reflect cosmological conceptions. According to Eliade (1960), communities often are laid out as an *imago mundi*. In Hindu culture, the central feature of any town is regarded as a symbol of the pillar of the universe. When a village is constructed in Bali, a space is left vacant in the centre to be used for a cult house, the roof of which symbolizes the sky. Likewise, Roman cities were laid out according to a divine plan, their division into four quarters being the earthly manifestation of a heavenly prototype (Müller 1962). In all such examples, either the community is laid out in some general fashion according to a prescribed pattern, or there is a tendency to read such a pattern into an existing plan. Lévi-Strauss (1953 : 534) has argued that the elaborate layout of a Bororo village – where houses are arranged around a circle according to moieties, clans, and ranked subdivisions of clans – is a realization not of unconscious social organization but rather of a model of society consciously existing in the Bororo's minds. Unfortunately, many of these symbolic plans would be difficult, if not impossible, for the archaeologist to detect, let alone to explain, without non-archaeological sources of information.

3) *Zonal patterns.* The overall density and distribution of the population of a region is determined to a large degree by the nature and availability of the natural resources that are being exploited. As long as other land is available, settlers tend to avoid districts that are naturally poor or where diseases or other dangers are common. Factors such as availability of game have a strong bearing on the size of hunting territories and on the distribution of permanent and transient bases. The attractions of fishing and collecting shellfish and the difficulties of overland travel through bush or jungle may result in concentrations of population along bodies of water (Kroeber 1953 : 143–146). In Ontario, for example, the late Iroquoian occupation, which was based on agriculture, was confined to the warm and fertile regions in the southern part of the province, and to areas that were close to rivers and had light soil. Such populations were notably absent in central southwestern Ontario, which is relatively high and cold and also an area of hard clay soils, few rivers, and flat, forested lands. At best, such areas were used as hunting territories by neighbouring tribes (Trigger 1963a). Similar correlations have been noted between the neolithic Danubian culture and löss soils in Europe (Narr 1956 : 139–140); the Sangoan culture and the tropical forest zone in Africa (Cole 1954 : 26); and the eastern Gravettian culture and the mammoth in ice-age Europe (Hawkes and Woolley 1963 : 83–86). In complex societies, fertile regions become centres of population and hence of political and cultural importance. In Japan the main fertile areas have been the Kanto, Nobi, and Kinai plains on the east side of Honshu Island. The chief cities and cultural centres have been located on these plains, and Japanese history largely has been a struggle for control of these areas, and through them, of the country (Sansom 1958 : 5–6).

Because archaeologists and geographers have had fairly good success in reconstructing both prehistoric subsistence patterns and prehistoric environments, the study of the relationship between these two sets of factors has become popular. Since the relationships of production strongly influence many other aspects of culture, even more stress has been placed on the ecological approach to the reconstruction of prehistoric societies (see, e.g. Kehoe 1964). This is a perfectly legitimate approach so long as it is used in a responsible manner, but it should not inhibit anthropologists from following other avenues of research that also may shed light on prehistoric cultures. For example, if we know that a prehistoric society depended on shifting agriculture, it is reasonable to suggest that it may have had a lineage-based social structure, and if long-houses are excavated the statement becomes even more probable. But determining whether the society was matrilocal, like the Iroquois, or patrilocal, like the Tupinamba, is much more difficult. Knowledge about the division of labour may shed some light on the problem (White 1959 : 150–152), and useful correlations may be found between art styles or religious practices and lineality (Deetz 1965).

As contiguous regions become more interdependent, zonal patterns are modified to an increasing degree by economic factors, as opposed to merely subsistence factors. In particular, trade plays an important role in establishing new communities and in increasing population density. Many of the most densely populated industrial regions of the modern world produce neither enough food to support their own population nor the raw materials needed to support their industries; both are obtained through trade and production. Trade, however, can be important even between simple societies. Among the Alaskan Eskimo, trading partnerships between sea-orientated and inland hunters helped to level off periods of poor hunting for both groups and promoted greater community stability (Dunning 1960 : 26). In northeastern North America, agri-culturalists and hunters occupying contiguous but different ecological zones exchanged their respective products to such an extent that even before the European fur trade began, the Huron villages in southern Ontario were clustered in a small area favourable for this kind of trade. Long-distance trade has been seen as a major factor in the rise of medieval European cities, such as Venice (Pirenne 1925), and the coastal cities of the ancient Levant, such as Tyre (Revere 1957). In the Hellenistic period, a series of cities including Petra, Palmyra, and Hatra, all of which depended on trade, grew up around the margins of the Arabian Desert. Many of the important cities in ancient southern Arabia were built in the desert east of the fertile mountain region but along a major trade route to the north (Bowen 1958). Even earlier, special colonies were established for trade in foreign regions; such as the Assyrian *karums* in Anatolia (Ozguc 1963) and the self-sufficient colonies established by the Greeks around the Black Sea and in the western Mediterranean.

The overall distribution of settlements also is affected by political organization. Internal security may require garrisons or administrative towns in the various sections of the country. Hsiao-tung Fei (1953 : 90–100) describes the *ch'engs* or administrative towns in imperial China as instruments of power in the hands of the ruling classes. The emperor's representatives and the state bureaucracy lived in these towns and administered the countryside from them. Landowners, living off the rents from their estates, also frequently lived there for protection. In a centrally-organized state, such towns would form provincial nuclei within a milieu of villages and scattered homesteads, and the national capital would be characterized by its greater size and luxury. Although the relative wealth of city states may differ considerably, it is doubtful that in such a system a single city state would predominate to the same degree as the capital city in most national states (Lambert 1964). In civilizations where cities are less important, the distribution of shrines or ceremonial centres likewise may reflect political organization. Although little is known about Maya political organization, the distribution of a large number of minor ceremonial centres around the large centres reflects unmistakably the subordination of the former to the latter. On the other hand, even without written records, such immense undertakings as the Egyptian pyramids of the Fourth Dynasty would be interpreted as evidence of a powerful central government controlling a vast domain. This impression is strengthened by noting that the tombs of the nobles in this period are not to be found elsewhere in Egypt but cluster around the pyramid of the reigning king in a fashion as centralized as that of the government they served (Baer 1960 : 301).

Warfare is another factor shaping the overall distribution of settlements. Hunting bands may have a strong sense of territory, and in everyday life avoid one another. Since most of these groups have little in the way of immovable property they may simply move out of the way or scatter when danger threatens. Pastoralists, on the other hand, often band together in larger groups to defend their herds. Agricultural peoples can respond in a number of different ways. Scattered communities may join together to build a common fort to which they can flee at time of danger. In Bronze Age Palestine, these forts often were the headquarters of local chiefs (Albright 1960 : 205). Where there are a number of small villages, the people may choose to fortify one of the larger ones, which, like the fort, can be used as a place of refuge in times of danger. In most city states the capital serves this purpose.

One feature of warfare may be the development of buffer zones between belligerent factions. Where the population density is low, warring neolithic groups often are separated from each other by lakes or broad stretches of forest. During the Middle Ages, the rich plains of Burgundy, which had been thickly populated, were abandoned because of the repeated incursions of the Vikings (Bloch 1961 : 41–42). In large states the defensive system may become an important specialized feature of the overall settlement pattern. The Roman *limes* and the Great Wall of China were Maginot Lines of their day, designed to keep out the marauding tribes to the north. Both required elaborate constructions and the establishment of garrison communities. Similar frontier defence systems had been built by the Egyptians as early as the Middle Kingdom (Kees 1961 : 317). The need for quick movement of troops and messengers may result in extensive road systems.

Religious factors also can affect the overall settlement pattern. Among the Maya, ceremonial centers served as community and state foci for the population that lived around them. In the Middle East, Judaeo-Christian religious communities, driven by persecution or a desire to escape the world, established settlements in lonely and forbidding regions, which they developed, often with great difficulty, to produce their needs. European monastic orders pioneered settlement in many parts of northern Europe; the Benedictines were active in clearing the forests of the Dauphine and the Ile de France, and were followed in other regions by the Cistercians (Darby 1956 : 194). In North America, utopian religious communities had curious and erratic careers, and Mormonism played an important role in the colonization of Utah.

Taste and symbolic factors appear to play a fairly limited role in determining zonal patterns. They are involved to some degree in determining the location of villas or pleasure resorts serving the main centres of population, in the establishment of summer and winter capitals in some tropical countries, and in the preference for suburban living among the more affluent inhabitants of Western cities. It has been suggested that the twelve great cities making up each of the three Etruscan leagues in Italy were not an accidental number but a ritually auspicious one, perhaps emulating the league of twelve cities in Ionia (Pallottino 1956 : 131–135). The designation of the twelve cities appears to have taken place after the fact, and played no role in their foundation or location. In general, social, economic, and political factors seem to find more expression on the zonal level than do ideational ones.

So far, we have been considering settlement patterns as a reflection of a variety of more or less stable conditions. To the factors we already have noted as determinants, we must add the more dynamic factors of migration and population change. These may alter the settlement pattern of a region more or less completely. Homans (1962 : 127–181) has argued that two contrasting types of settlement in medieval England, the compact village of the central region and the dispersed settlement of Kent and East Anglia, were the result not of geographical or technological variations but of different traditions of land use that were brought from the continent. Neither was sufficiently unsuited to the new environment that it was forced to change. The rise or fall of population in response to economic factors or disease also may affect the settlement pattern in various ways. Land crowding may be an important factor stimulating migration to urban centres. As a result of wars and bubonic plague, large areas of farmland in central Europe reverted to thick forest between 1350 and 1450 (Darby 1956 : 198).

Integration

It is clear that settlement patterns represent responses to a number of different kinds of factors that influence them in different ways and degrees on different levels. For example, ecology, warfare, and religion influence individual structures, community plans, and zonal patterns, whereas symbolic factors tend to affect only the first two of these levels. Certain factors leave a very clear imprint on one or more of these levels: war may result in fortified houses, walled settlements, or large defensive works, and trade may produce specialized buildings and communities. At the same time, these factors also may be reflected indirectly, in terms of the prosperity or lack of prosperity associated with them.

If we conceive of the settlement pattern as an outcome of the adjustments a society makes to a series of determinants that vary both in importance and in the kinds of demands they make on the society, we must consider not merely the range of factors affecting settlement patterns but also the manner in which different factors interact with one another to produce a particular pattern. Factors vary in importance according to both the local situation and the temporal relationship they have to one another.

We have noted that primitive agricultural communities threatened by attack may respond in a number of different ways. In other situations the range of choice may be considerably more restricted. A shift in the settlement pattern of the Shukriya Bedouin is especially interesting because it was brought about primarily by political changes rather than by economic or environmental ones. The Shukriya, an Arabic-speaking people, live in the Butana Desert, east of Khartoum in the Sudan. In the last century their camps and their herds were menaced constantly by raiding parties. In self-defence, they began to move about in groups that were two to three hundred tents strong. Because the sparse, scattered desert pastures could support the correspondingly large herds for no more than 15 to 20 days, the groups were forced to move frequently from one place to another. With the establishment of British rule, the threat of raids was lifted, and the large tribal

The Determinants of Settlement Patterns

groups broke up into smaller family units, each able to occupy a single stretch of the pasture year-round without exhausting it. As a result, these smaller groups tended to become sedentary and some even took to agriculture in a small way (Crowfoot 1920 : 86–87). In terms of subsistence patterns, two alternatives always had been open to the Shukriya: large groups could exhaust individual pastures one by one and move on, or smaller groups could occupy a larger number of pastures simultaneously, each group remaining on the same pasture throughout the year. But was this choice really open to the Shukriya? The answer would seem to be no, inasmuch as the fear of raids necessitated a defence best achieved by staying together. Moreover, even if neighbouring tribes had agreed to remain at peace, it is unlikely that conflict could have been avoided prior to British rule. Slow increases in population would have begun to tax the grazing areas, and new outbreaks of fighting would have resulted. The same British rule that brought peace also provided the Shukriya with new opportunities in a national economy. Conflict and a subsequent need to band together for defence seems characteristic of pastoral economies in areas where pasturage is limited. A culture wherein the variety of settlement patterns that is ecologically possible is limited by a restricted range of possibilities in another of the culture's aspects can be said to exhibit a *principle of functional limitation*.

A variation on this pattern is one in which a form of settlement may be highly desirable in some respects although unfavourable in most others. For example, an area well-placed for trade may be ill-equipped to support a large population. Nueva Cadiz already has provided one example of such a situation. The town was founded on an island off the coast of Venezuela that was close to pearling areas and protected from the Indians on the mainland. On the other hand, both food and water had to be imported. As a result, the colony survived only so long as the pearl fisheries were profitable. Similarly, the city of Samarra was founded in A.D. 836 by the Caliph Mu'tasim, on a site removed from the major trade routes of the Middle East but considered to be a safer residence for the Caliph than the turbulent city of Kufa. Despite the removal of many merchants and artisans to the new site, the city endured for less than fifty years before it was abandoned and its inhabitants drifted back to the 'natural' centres of population in Mesopotamia. Likewise, the city of Akhetaton, which was founded in honour of the new god of the Egyptian Pharaoh Akhenaton, was inhabited for only 17 years. The trading cities in Arabia and desert mining outposts like Aqaba flourished in regions poorly suited for agriculture. Each of these communities was abandoned when the function it was designed to serve ceased to be important. In other cases, the determination of a settlement pattern may involve a choice between opposing considerations: modern cities, for example, are vulnerable to attack from the air and therefore a liability to their military defenders, but they are essential for efficient industrial production. In such cases, the course of development reflects the relative importance attached to different functions: advantages gained through trade may make a large investment in land development worthwhile, or the agricultural worth of an area may justify elaborate defences. We may call this the *hierarchical resolution of conflicting tendencies*.

When a problem may have several alternative solutions, the course of action that is followed may be determined by the manner in which a previous problem was resolved. A city, for example, is functionally distinguished from a town or village by a high concentration of the facilities needed for the specialized functions characteristic of complex societies, such as temples, administrative buildings, the residences of the elite, workshops for artisans, and defence facilities. It is evident, however, that some early civilizations, such as those of ancient Egypt and Peru, and of the Maya, existed without large cities. In such societies the main temples might be located in one place, forts in another, and the royal court in still another. Craftsmen, both full- and part-time, could live in the scattered villages and exchange their produce at market places or through a state-operated redistribution network. Such a settlement pattern, though clearly workable at a certain level, is nevertheless cumbersome, and one would expect that with increased cultural complexity there would be a tendency for different functions to converge toward a common centre. The pattern of convergence may differ considerably from one society to another. A fort may become the residence of a chief and his retainers; as immovable property accumulates, the well-to-do may move into the fort, so that a town begins to develop; and artisans may settle in the town in order to sell their wares to the townsfolk and to farmers who come to trade and to worship at local shrines. In other cultures, a cult centre also may serve as a fort or marketplace and in this way become the nucleus of a city. In Shang China the city apparently consisted of a walled elite centre surrounded by villages that probably were self-sufficient in terms of subsistence and local handicrafts, but because many of these villages were also centres of particular occupational specialties, the whole tended to be bound together as a political and economic unit (Chang 1963). In the Chou period, probably largely in response to warfare, these specialist villages tended to cluster close to the elite enclosures and finally both were incorporated to form a large walled city. Even without the stimulus of war, a court may attract public servants, attendants, and the merchants and menials who serve them, as well as temples and state buildings. If such nuclei attract trade, or serve as forts or administrative centres, they eventually may become viable cities, whether or not the court remains.

There is considerable variation in the rate and degree of this concentration in different areas. In Mesopotamia, large urban communities arose at an early period within a context of warring states. In Egypt, where a strong territorial state was established early, there was no need for fortified towns, and less of a tendency for administrative centres to attract large populations (Frankfort 1956). In Mexico, cities seem to have developed early. This tendency perhaps was stimulated by the growth of inter-regional trade. In the lowland Maya region, this tendency seems to have been much weaker. Thus, a flourishing centre whether established first for political, economic, religious, or defensive reasons, or for a combination of these, gradually may take on additional functions until it becomes an important and diversified centre of population serving the needs of a complex society. The basic patterns of growth within a given culture will be shaped by local circumstances and by general configurations of development. This sort of development can be seen as illustrating a third principle, that of the *convergence of functions*.

CONCLUSIONS

I have defined three 'levels' that are the object of settlement-pattern studies: the individual structure, the layout of communities, and the manner in which communities belonging to a society or culture distribute themselves over the landscape. The patterns displayed at each of these levels can be viewed as being functionally related in some way to all aspects of a culture and therefore able to shed light on a variety of problems. Yet each level displays tendencies especially appropriate to the study of particular aspects of society: individual structures furnish information about family organization, craft specialization, and perhaps the relative importance of different aspects of the social structure, and the layout of shrines may elucidate religious rituals; community plans have yielded useful information about lineage organization and a community's adaptation to its physical and cultural environments; and areal patterns reflect many aspects of the social and political organization of complex societies, as well as of trade and warfare. Problem-orientated approaches exploiting the potential of each of these levels simultaneously would seem to be highly desirable.

The Determinants of Settlement Patterns

XII

Inequality and Communication
in Early Civilizations

DAVID CLARKE (1968 : 88–101) WAS AMONG the first to point out the potential value for archaeologists of treating culture as an information system. Since then a growing number of British and American archaeologists have argued the importance of communications as part of a broad systemic analysis of prehistoric cultures (Flannery 1972; Johnson 1973; Renfrew 1975; see also Segraves 1974). In this paper I wish to compare and contrast some general features of communication in societies at differing levels of socio-cultural complexity. My aim is to shed fresh light on functional relationships that previously have tended to be overlooked. I will also make tentative efforts at quantification, although these will concern technologically-simpler rather than more complex societies. The need for quantification is great if anthropologists are to deal with the major theoretical problems of their discipline in more than a conjectural fashion.

Band Societies and Autonomous Villages

Since the work of Emile Durkheim (1893), no social scientist has been able to ignore the importance of the division of labour as a key to understanding society. The proverb about a jack-of-all-trades being a master of none embodies a comparative perspective that is possible only in a technologically-evolved society. In small-scale societies, whether they are of hunters and gatherers or are small, politically-autonomous horticultural communities, everyone knows and performs all the essential tasks appropriate to his or her sex. This does not rule out the possession of special, esoteric knowledge by individuals, although such knowledge is limited in complexity and its transmission frequently is hazardous. In such societies, the

194

small scale also makes it possible for those individuals who must interact with one another to do so on a familiar basis. It is possible for each member of such a society to know in a general way what the total network of individual relationships within his or her society is like at any one time. Resources tend to be shared as far as individuals are in need, with prestige rather than material riches accruing to unusually skilful or industrious producers. Each male and sometimes each female member of such a society is viewed as an independent agent, who is as free as any other to determine his or her own conduct. The only effective sanctions that can be brought to bear against an individual are those supported by strong public opinion (Sahlins 1968; Service 1966, 1971 : 46–132).

Even the smallest bands, however, have members who in certain respects act as leaders. Such a role may be acquired in an informal manner or the office may be the prerogative of a particular family or lineage, as it was among the Montagnais of southern Quebec in the seventeenth century (Bailey 1969 : 91). While this sort of leader may play an important role in directing the economic affairs of his people and in mediating their internal disagreements, his primary role is as a spokesman when his band has dealings with other groups. Yet in speaking for his band the headman must reflect faithfully the opinions of his followers, since no agreement he makes can have more force than each individual is willing to give it.

On the basis of data from New Guinea, Anthony Forge (1972 : 374) has argued that in societies with no more than 30 adult male members (or a total population of about 150), basic egalitarian principles are generally respected and internal rivalry tends to be low-keyed because there is an insufficiency of challengers to leaders of strong personality. In societies of up to 75 or 80 adult males (or a total population of 350 to 400) individualized competition occurs, but this too safeguards the egalitarian structure of society. Only when the number of males rises above 80 do their face-to-face relationships reach the limit that each player can handle successfully. Above that limit, for lack of sufficient information the game becomes disorganized and unbalanced, causing tension to increase. If the ecological situation allows for dispersal, such a group may split apart, establishing two separate bands or communities.

Kroeber (1955 : 309) set the limit at which Indian tribes in many parts of North America tended to break apart at 500 members. Alternatively, the society may increase in size, but in order to do so it must adopt new principles of organization. It is at this point that internal segmentation is resorted to, thereby permitting a classification of relationships. This facilitates a reduction in the amount of information that any one actor has to carry about in his head.

Tribal Societies

The type of society thereby created, like the sedentary groups discussed above, is still at the tribal level. It is exemplified by larger, sedentary, and frequently horticultural groups such as the Huron. In these societies, as in the smaller-scale ones, each man and woman possesses the full range of skills necessary for his or her nuclear family's subsistence. Craft specialization is limited and constitutes a minor part of any individual's routine. Within communities, redistribution is highly-valued and reinforced by public opinion. Those who are stingy risk being accused of witchcraft, which in turn may entail severe penalties. At the same time, self-reliance and individual autonomy are prized highly (Trigger 1976a : 27–90).

Among the Huron, the minimal unit of settlement was equivalent in size to the individual band-type societies discussed above. It was a village consisting of about 300 people. Its core of lifelong inhabitants apparently were members of a single clan that was made up of a number of matrilineal extended families. Like many other American Indian groups, each clan unit had two headmen; one for peace and one for war. At least the former office was the property of a specific lineage of each clan.

The advantage of a small village was that it kept cultivators close to their fields, and exhausted the surrounding soil and sources of firewood more slowly than did larger ones. Yet, as a defence against warfare and blood feud, many villages had 1,500 or more inhabitants. Such a village was composed of four or five clan groups, each of which appears to have occupied its own portion of the community. Each clan group retained as much political independence within a large village as it had when it constituted a separate community. Suspected inter-
196

ference in the internal affairs of a clan group by members of other clans was deeply resented and not infrequently resulted in the break-up of large villages.

The collective affairs of a large village were regulated by a council attended by the peace chiefs of the various clan groups and less regularly by lineage heads and old men. One of the clan heads was recognized as spokesman for the entire village. This office also tended to be hereditary. The council concerned itself with co-ordinating the ritual activities of the community, supervising village-wide redistribution of resources (when necessary), and resolving disputes between (but never within) the clans making up the village. The recognition of one clan chief as village spokesman constituted a categorization and implicit ranking among headmen not found in smaller-scale societies.

Among the Huron, several villages constituted a tribe, each of which averaged 5,000 members. Each tribe had its affairs co-ordinated by a council, which at least in theory appears to have been made up of the peace chiefs of all of the clan groups within the tribe. One of these chiefs, again usually on a hereditary basis, was recognized as being the official spokesman for the tribe. The tribal councils were concerned primarily with co-ordinating trading with other groups and foreign policy generally, and with preventing blood feuds when disputes involved more than one village. Finally, at least in historic times, four or five neighbouring Iroquoian tribes often constituted a confederacy embracing up to 20,000 people. Each of the tribes belonging to the confederacy might be separated from the rest by its own hunting territory (as among the Iroquois) or they might all live in close proximity (as among the Huron). The confederacy council was composed of the same peace chiefs who sat on the tribal councils. One chief may have been the traditional convenor of the council, but various specific functions were assigned on an hereditary basis to individual council chiefs, so that it is unclear to what degree any of them could be considered a spokesman for the confederacy. The French quickly recognized the tribal spokesmen among the Huron and had important dealings with them. By contrast, the convenor of the confederacy council remained a shadowy figure, even to the Jesuits after they had lived among

Inequality and Communication

the Huron for many years. The primary concern of the confederacy was to prevent blood feud and other forms of conflict among its members. Efforts also were made to co-ordinate warfare, although relations with non-Huron groups were handled mainly at the tribal level.

The Huron regarded it as a matter of principle that an individual could not be regarded as bound against his will by any decision made by the confederacy council or by tribal, village, or clan spokesmen. Public opinion might influence an individual's conduct but coercion could only be practised openly by a man or woman's nearest kinsmen, usually in the form of threatened expulsion from an extended household. Any other coercion would anger the victim's lineage and clansmen and constitute a threat to the stability of community life. Because of this, spokesmen had to refer every decision that was made back to their constituents for individual approval and implementation. It was therefore essential for a spokesman to be well-informed about his constituents' opinions. Discussions aimed at achieving a consensus. A decision normally was reached when remaining supporters of a minority opinion would neither support nor oppose a particular policy. A minority faction would remain silent and inactive until changing events produced a shift in public opinion and their policies might once again attract support. European observers regarded such latent factions as a source of strength rather than weakness for the Iroquoians, since they allowed for great flexibility in dealing with changing circumstances, especially in intertribal relations.

The one coercive power that chiefs possessed was to pronounce an individual guilty of witchcraft. According to Huron law anyone might slay a known witch while the victim's relatives were forbidden to resort to blood revenge to avenge such a killing. It was, however, only the chiefs who could determine publicly whether an accused person was in fact a witch. This power could be exercised only for the benefit of the society as a whole or of the chiefs as a collective interest group, since to be effective all of the chiefs, including the spokesman for the accused person's own clan, had to co-operate in condemning him. In spite of this limitation, threat of a formal accusation for witchcraft appears to have been a potent instrument of social control (Trigger 1963b).

198

The Huron demonstrate that individual villages of up to 1,500 people and societies of up to 20,000 people and with as many as four levels of government could be made to work by relying only on public opinion and on the individual's voluntary implementation of each decision. Most of an individual's regular activities were related to his clan, a unit that was structurally very similar to the bands and autonomous villages discussed above. It was also in terms of the clan that all of an individual's basic rights and responsibilities were defined. Larger communities consisted of a number of clan modules politically integrated by a council on which the clans were represented primarily by their peace chiefs. These headmen attempted to co-ordinate policy but could not commit their individual constituents to a particular line of action. The principal innovation of such a council was to recognize one clan chief as spokesman for the whole village. Factionalism can be documented as endemic in the larger Huron settlements and it would appear that a population of approximately 1,500 represents the upper limits of stability for this type of political organization (Heidenreich 1971 : 129–134).

In a study comparing settlement size and social organization in 30 pre-urban societies, Naroll (1956 : 690) has observed that 'when settlements contain more than about five hundred people they must have authoritative officials [a Huron council-type arrangement?], and if they contain over a thousand, some kind of specialized organization or corps of officials to perform police functions'. Foster (1960 : 178) has suggested 1500 as the upper limit at which a settlement 'can function as a single community'. This suggests that if a settlement is to have a population larger than 1,500 on a long-term basis, some form of coercion may be required as part of the regulatory mechanism of its government. From a communication point of view, no mystique or even the necessity to invoke class considerations is required to explain this sort of development. As a community grows in population above 1,500, it becomes cumbersome and often dangerously time-consuming to refer all of the routine decisions necessary to govern the community back to the population at large. In place of generalized consultation, some form of executive representation is required for government at even a minimal level of effectiveness. Coercion can be viewed as one means by which community decision-makers are assured that their routine decisions will be executed.

The Huron example also demonstrates, however, that in the form of tribes and confederacies multi-community political units of 20,000 people or more may function without recourse to coercion or the delegation of decision-making powers. In terms of population, the confederacy appears to fall within the same size range as the chiefdom, to which Baker and Sanders (1972 : 163) attribute an average of 10,000 to 12,000 members. The higher levels of Huron government seem to have worked because the issues with which they dealt were limited and because the same clan representatives functioned at each level. Moving from village to tribe to confederacy, these clan representatives met in larger groups, but less frequently and to handle fewer issues. The continuity of these clan personnel through the higher levels of government minimized the misunderstandings and conflicts that might have arisen from misinformation. It also ensured that every Huron clansman had ready access to information about what was being discussed at every level.

It is unclear whether it is realistic to ask if there is a demographic point at which an entire society (as opposed to a community) must delegate decision-making authority and equip its leaders with coercive powers. Baker and Sanders (1972 : 163) suggest that chiefdoms may grow to about 50,000 inhabitants but in the long run large ones will tend either to fall apart or to develop into coercive states. Apart from demographic factors, it seems clear that at a certain point entire socio-cultural systems grow sufficiently complex that delegated decision-making becomes necessary for their regulation, which in turn requires some form of coercion.

State Societies

There is another saying, which is only partially true, that knowledge is power. This was certainly not so for the skilled craftsmen of ancient Egypt, who were scorned as mere manual labourers by the bureaucratic scribes who integrated the national processes of production and distribution (Childe 1958a : 93–97). While some craftsmen may have enjoyed prestige, power traditionally accrued to those in control of the processes of production and distribution. In the ancient civilizations, government developed as a fully-specialized subsystem within the social order, and ruling constituted for the first time a wholly-specialized profession. The rulers of these early civilizations were assisted by various categories of full-time personnel: scribes (bureaucrats), soldiers, personal retainers, and elite craftsmen. The societies were administered by a multi-tiered hierarchy in which officials at each level owed their services to a superior official or officials and were answerable to them for the conduct of lesser people who were in their charge.

It has been proposed that the State may be equated with an administrative hierarchy that consists of three or more levels, as reflected in a hierarchical arrangement of settlements of varying size and complexity (Johnson 1973 : 2, 15). If the employment of coercion to supplement public opinion as a means of effecting policy is still accepted as an important criterion of the state (as I believe it must be), this operational definition may not serve to identify the smallest and simplest states. Nevertheless, the hierarchical characteristics that it stresses are associated with all state-organized societies from Renfrew's (1975 : 12–21) Early State Modules to the largest empires of antiquity or modern times.

Kent Flannery (1972) has noted that cultural evolution correlates with an expanding capacity to process, store, and analyse information and specifically has characterized political and religious institutions as data-processing systems. Johnson (1973 : 3) has identified the functions of such institutions as being to collect data, make decisions, and disseminate information. Flannery (1972) views these institutions as achieving power by *promotion*, that is by rising in a developing hierarchy of control to assume a higher-level and often transformed role. Their power is further enhanced by *linearization*, or cutting past lower-order controls, often after the latter have failed to function in an increasingly complex situation.

Yet, however much administrative hierarchies are concerned with processing information, they are by no means neutral entities attending impartially to the interests of the whole society. On the contrary, rulers regard such hierarchies as the means by which their personal (albeit culturally-conditioned) ambitions may be realized. The truism that provides the point of departure for most of Service's (1975) recent arguments about the nature of early civilizations is his observation that no state can be held together by force alone. For a regime to survive, a majority of its subjects must remain convinced that there is no reasonable chance of seeing it replaced by a regime that might better serve their interests.

Yet even if no government can ignore public opinion totally, the elimination of the ruler's accountability for routine decisions introduces an element of privacy and secrecy into the governing process. This change correlates with major alterations in the fabric of society. Prestige no longer is maintained by massive redistribution on the part of leaders. Instead, vast surpluses are placed at the disposal of rulers, which they may employ in a wide variety of ways. Powerful individuals are not compelled to redistribute by fear of being accused of witchcraft if they do not. On the contrary, they can reverse the former practise by directing accusations of witchcraft against the traditional recipients of their bounty, should individuals' claims prove burdensome (Macfarlane 1970). This lays the basis for the development of extensive usufruct and private property. Not being in a position to know for certain what a public figure possesses or does makes it harder for a subject to accuse him of wrongdoing.

Concomitant with rulers obscuring many of the everyday details of government business is their energetic promotion of a mystique of office. Few rulers even today do not try to claim some element of supernatural sanction for their power. Michael Coe (1972) notes that early kings sought to have themselves credited with divine status and their lineages recognized as being of divine origin and therefore generically different from those of their subjects. These claims helped to justify not only their failure to redistribute goods equitably but also the conspicuous consumption in which the elite of the early civilizations indulged so heartily. Yet familiarity breeds contempt. Rulers of small-scale societies, in particular of city states, always had a much harder time establishing claims of omnipotence than had the rulers of large empires. Conversely, the more large states were agrarian, the less scepticism there seems to have been. Some of the most far-reaching claims of divinity were advanced by the Inca rulers of Peru and by the Egyptian Pharaohs (Spath 1973; Trigger, in press).

The assumed need for complex societies to make and implement decisions quickly, requires the majority of individuals to surrender a direct role in the decision-making process. This allows political systems to develop that are hierarchical and centralized; hence can process information and respond to challenges more efficiently. Within such a system the officials who channel and process the sorts of information that the state regards as vital to its functioning are in a position to decide how quickly and by whom this information can be used. Rulers may withhold information from their subordinates and from dissenting and competing groups or feed false information to these groups if they believe it to be in their own interest to do so (Adams 1975 : 453). The system also permits subordinate officials to withhold information from their superiors.

The ability to control a system of this type, even imperfectly, allows rulers to use the surplus resources of society to pursue goals that to some degree are of their own choosing (Eisenstadt 1963). These may be to conquer neighbouring kingdoms, to increase the extent and value of royal domains, to alter the religious system, or to engage in the personal excesses of a Nero or Akhenaton. The successful pursuit of these goals depends upon the effectiveness with which the ruler is able to mobilize the surpluses of society for his own ends. To do this well he must control not only the primary producers but also his officials. In a state that is controlled effectively by its king or his chief officers, these officials function primarily as tax collectors and civil servants for their royal master.

The more a king can dominate neighbouring regions, the more resources he can control and the more effectively he may promote and reward his own followers. As A. L. Oppenheim (1964 : 117) has observed 'real prosperity came to a Mesopotamian city only when it had in its midst the palace of a victorious king'. Because the fortunes of a militarily-successful monarch and his own people are so mutually interdependent, the internal authority exercised by such a ruler is likely to be great. By contrast, a weak and tributary ruler is less likely to enjoy the respect of his own people and the affairs of his kingdom may be turbulent and disordered. This no doubt explains why, in their relations with other states, powerful

Inequality and Communication

rulers of ancient states or those who believed they had a chance to become powerful were willing to hazard their fortunes by adopting strategies emphasizing a maximization of returns rather than a maximization of security, such as normally characterizes the behaviour of the poorer elements of society and possibly of petty rulers as well (Shimkin 1973 : 275). Yet Robert M. Adams (1975 : 453–454) has observed that these rulers had to make important decisions about internal as well as external policies in the face of vast uncertainties about the actual situations that were confronting them and the possible consequences of particular lines of action. Today political leaders must cope with awesome imponderables but it seems likely that, in spite of the greater size and complexity of modern states, advances in communication and data processing, as well as improved scientific knowledge about the consequences of policy decisions, have reduced this uncertainty by comparison with what confronted the rulers of the early civilizations.

Data Processing Systems

Rulers find it advantageous to be regarded as omniscient as well as omnipotent. Yet in the early civilizations data collecting and record keeping were expensive, labour-intensive undertakings frequently requiring highly-trained staff. Maintaining lines of communication grew increasingly burdensome as the size of political units increased. The far-flung Persian, Roman, and Inca empires had extensive road systems that were built and maintained to facilitate the movement of their armies and of the government courier service. Innis (1951 : 40) has described the government of the Persian Empire as 'an elaborate administration based on a system of roads and the use of horses to maintain communication by post with the capital'. He also accepted the suggestion that the greater stability of Near Eastern empires in the second millennium B.C., as compared with those of earlier times, can be attributed to the acceleration of official journeys as a result of the introduction of the chariot (p. 95). Yet the speed at which messages could be transmitted along even the best roads was that at which a relay of couriers could run or ride. A week or more might elapse before the report of an invasion or revolt in an outlying province reached the imperial capital; meanwhile, the road system might accelerate the advance of the enemy. The only more rapid form of communication, using signal fires, was vulnerable to bad weather and limited in terms of the messages that could be conveyed. The principal advantage of a royal courier service could scarcely have been its absolute speed (which was far from ideal) but that it was faster than what was available to those who were not authorized to use it.

Not long ago anthropologists equated civilization with literacy. Many archaeologists working in the Near East still believe that writing is highly likely to develop as a data-storage technique when a given level of complexity is reached (Johnson 1973 : 3). This seems to be supported, for example, by the apparently extensive use of writing for bureaucratic purposes in ancient Egypt: to record ownership of land, payment of taxes, the assignment of materials to individual workmen, and the presence or absence of men on specific work shifts. Yet, evidence from Africa and the New World reveals that complex societies can exist without fully-developed writing systems and that those early civilizations that lacked writing were of comparable complexity to those that had it. Whether we are considering collections of city states, such as those of the Maya or the ancient Mesopotamians, that were literate or of the highland Mexicans, that were not, or much larger polities, such as Dynastic Egypt which was literate or the Inca Empire which was not, there is no obvious functional reason why some of these should have developed writing systems and not the rest. The Inca managed to do their bookkeeping with knotted ropes (*quipu*) and by conceiving of work teams as decimal units. The eighteenth-century Dahomeans did the same by means of pebble counting and appointing female officials to note and remember what their male counterparts did. This suggests that writing *per se* was not as vital for data-storage in the early civilizations as has been imagined. Karl Polanyi coined the term 'operational device' to cover the wide range of techniques other than writing that were used for accounting, census-taking, and record-keeping in pre-industrial societies (Dalton 1975 : 99–100).

The rationale for the development of writing may have to be sought in the detailed structure of specific cultures. It is here that the seminal writings of Harold Innis (1951) may yet prove to be of special value. In particular, writing appears to have assisted the development of private property, of specific types of long distance banking, and of promulgated as opposed to traditional law. The survival over very long periods of time of cumbersome logosyllabic scripts and the fact that the Roman Empire was able and (what is more significant) willing to keep its accounts in Roman numerals suggest that governments made relatively small demands upon ancient writing systems as a means of data-storage and manipulation.

William Rathje (1975) has utilized certain propositions derived from General Systems Theory to construct a developmental scheme that purports to account for the manner in which developing early civilizations coped with the problem of processing an increasing amount of information. By implication, what he says can be applied specifically to the evolution of political institutions. Rathje proposes that in the early stages increasing complexity was coped with by a markedly disproportional increase in information processing and deciding components (in plain words, by having more bureaucrats). Later, an attempt was made to forestall the growth of bureaucracy beyond economically-acceptable limits by resorting to greater standardization. The development of standard, system-wide codes decreased the amount of accounting that was necessary. Still later, efficiencies were effected by promoting more autonomy at lower levels; the whole society being integrated as a series of interdependent, interacting components.

Rathje's scheme looks like a rationalization of American laissez-faire idealism. While examples of each of these processes probably can be shown to have been employed by the governmental institutions of any early civilization at any phase in its development, the scheme as a whole does not impress me as being plausible. The principal means by which ancient bureaucracies at any stage of their development had their task rendered manageable was by limiting linearization to essentials. In this respect, any comparison between a modern state and those of former times is inappropriate. The detailed penetration of the modern state into the lives of its citizens, made possible by electronic computers, was impossible for pre-industrial states. On the contrary, officials at the highest levels of such societies limited their interventions into the affairs of the common people or of distant provinces to matters related directly to securing the goods and services necessary to achieve their own specific goals. Local rulers and officials generally were accorded something approaching plenipotentiary powers over their province, district, or village, so long as they could convince their superiors that they were in control of the situation and could supply them with what they wanted or what traditionally was owing to them. Such relationships produced what seems to us to have been curious behaviour. Chinese provincial officials frequently claimed that their districts had smaller populations than they really had so that they would not have to admit to the central government that they were unable to collect the full rate of taxes from powerful landowners. So long as such behaviour produced adequate revenue, the central government tolerated it, rather than admit a lack of control which would imply a weakening of the Mandate of Heaven (Ho 1959 : 3–97).

Politics and Communication

The deliberate avoidance of the establishment of lower-level controls is dramatically evident in city state hegemonies as manifested in Early Dynastic Mesopotamia, or in highland Mesoamerica in the sixteenth century A.D. In these areas, the governments of conquered city states frequently were left to function more or less freely, so long as they paid tribute to their hegemon. The same principle was applied differently but no less strikingly in the Achaemenid Persian Empire, whose provinces or satrapies, though artificial creations, rapidly evolved into sub-kingdoms within the empire (Olmstead 1948 : 59). At their empire's greatest extent, the Romans promoted local government. They continued to regard the city state, the archetypal government of early Rome and of its neighbours, as the fundamental unit of political organization. Because of this, they undertook at great effort and cost to transform tribal areas that they conquered (such as southern England) into a mosaic of what appeared to them (if not to the conquered peoples) to be city states. Hyperlinearization (meddling) has been stated to be one of the pathologies to which ancient civilizations are susceptible (Flannery 1972). Yet the evidence suggests that, in general, rulers were keenly aware of the limitations of their systems of communication and record-keeping and deliberately avoided overtaxing the capacities of their bureaucratic systems, by needlessly eliminating low order controls.

The most striking linearization did not result from a conscious desire to control the everyday functioning of lower-order structures but from uncontrollable social forces. The Inca Empire and Pharaonic Egypt are particularly interesting in this respect. In spite of the celebrated decimal-regimentation of the Peruvians and the mania for record-keeping of the Egyptians (which dealt mainly with state business), the vast majority of the population of both of these states were farmers dwelling in hamlets or small villages. Surpluses had to be produced as taxes for the central government and a variety of labour services provided, which occasionally took a fraction of the men away from their villages. Relations with the government probably were mediated through clan or village heads, who served among other things as the lowest-level officials in the administrative hierarchy.

By contrast, the number of people whose lives were transformed radically by the elite traditions of these civilizations was relatively small. They included rulers, priests, and their bureaucratic assistants, as well as some full-time soldiers, attendants, and craftsmen. These people were the sole inhabitants of the relatively small administrative centres of Egypt and highland Peru. In spite of the cultural sophistication of these societies, urbanization was notably restrained; only the royal capital and a few regional centres having populations of more than a few thousand people. While the elite cultures of these societies greatly had transformed the lives of rulers and their entourages, most people continued to live in villages, where everyday life was governed by local institutions that had altered little from pre-state times (Frankfort 1956 : 90–120; Lanning 1967 : 157–172).

By contrast, southern Mesopotamian civilization developed as a mosaic of small city states. By the Early Dynastic Period most of the sedentary population of that region appears to have been living in the urban centres that were the nuclei of these states. Warfare in late prehistoric times had induced the inhabitants of the villages and towns located within a 5 to 15 kilometre radius to abandon these communities and cluster in what became walled urban centres. These provided greater

208

security for an individual's person and household goods and could cope more effectively with prolonged military or natural crises. Yet, while urbanization increased the prosperity, and offensive and defensive strength, of a small elite, it imposed greater demands for taxes and military and corvée service upon most individuals (Adams 1972).

Most of the inhabitants of the Mesopotamian cities, unlike those of Inca or Egyptian administrative centres, engaged in subsistence production. The urbanization of these agricultural producers transformed them socially, politically, and culturally to a far greater degree than their peasant counterparts in Egypt or Peru had been transformed. As urban dwellers, they observed the upper classes at first hand and hence had the knowledge and inclination to share in the material benefits of urban life. Power was shared by the representatives of a number of different institutions within each city state; unlike the monolithic organization of the Egyptian and Inca ones. Priests, councils, and military leaders often competed for power openly. Although in the long run it was the military leaders who won out, this rivalry probably worked to the permanent advantage of the ordinary people. The archaeological evidence suggests that the average Mesopotamian had far greater access to the fruits of technological innovation than did the average Peruvian or Egyptian (Frankfort 1956 : 49–89). Because the Mesopotamian city tended to be small, its members could observe each other and it embraced representatives of all occupations and all classes. This made it a pressure cooker that transformed the totality of Mesopotamian life. By contrast, the Egyptian and Peruvian peasant lived most of his life in nearly total isolation from such forces. It was the very alienness of the upper classes to his everyday experience that made credible royal claims of divine status such as no ruler of a city state was able to establish. A self-interested policy may have dictated the decline of such independent urban or proto-urban centres as were encompassed by the Egyptian and the Inca realms (Lanning 1967 : 163).

The physical problems that impeded communication in the early civilizations heightened mistrust between officials at different levels in the administrative hierarchy and in large states complicated relations between the central government and officials in outlying regions. Repeatedly and in widely-separated instances we find rulers utilizing a limited range of devices to cope with these problems. The deportation of elites from newly-conquered territories to the centres of empires provided hostages to ensure the good behaviour of those who were left behind. Sometimes, powerful rulers deported whole populations whose loyalty was suspect. The settling of trusted subjects in regions thus vacated, or as in the case of the Roman Empire the establishment of colonies of army veterans in newly-conquered territories was also common. This provided a force that could be counted on to watch for trouble and to resist uprisings until the officials of the regional or, if necessary, the central government could employ their own forces to quell such insurrections. Tension might persist for generations between the newcomers and the resentful original inhabitants of a region, making these policies of more than short-term usefulness to the central government. A more subtle but widely applicable stratagem was a version of divide and rule that involved encouraging local particularisms among subject peoples in order to discourage them from uniting to oppose the central government. Innis (1951 : 135) saw an early manifestation of such a policy in the Persians' encouragement of ethnic religious cults within their empire.

To defend the borders of their empires, especially when these were resource-poor areas, weak and strong rulers alike resorted to bribery, clientage, and subtle diplomacy in an effort to play off neighbouring groups against one another. An astutely-managed policy repaid the cost of supplying and withholding arms and other resources from various groups in turn. Those who were dominant at any one time, often against their own will constituted a defensive ring protecting the metropolitan state against incursions by pastoral or nomadic tribesmen. Although the maintenance of such a policy required political finesse, it did not necessitate constant supervision by the central government but was managed by local officials in the provinces.

In the absence of means for continuous surveillance, central governments resorted to various devices to control provincial officials. One such method was to create checks and balances by dividing the administrative responsibilities of a province among a number of independent officers. Each province of the

Persian Empire was governed by a satrap, a military commander, and an intendant whose authority was independent of one another, and who were each directly responsible to the king. The satrap's secretary also was empowered to report directly to the king (Olmstead 1948 : 59). Another device, utilized at certain periods by the ancient Egyptians, was to rotate senior officials from district to district to prevent them from acquiring a local basis of political support. A successful career was one that moved upwards through a hierarchy of offices that culminated in a major appointment at court (Frankfort 1956 : 101). Both of these strategies had their disadvantages. Divided authority often produced rivalry, mistrust, and obvious hostility, which adversely affected the quality and effectiveness of the administration; rotation meant that senior officials were unable to acquire the detailed knowledge of a particular region that was necessary for its optimal administration. Rotation also may have encouraged the rapacity of officials in their dealings with the people of any one region (Bernier 1916 : 227). In both situations the central government was willing to sacrifice major advantages in order to safeguard its own authority. Another form of control was the use of inspectors or spies who kept watch on provincial officials of the central government. The 'King's Eyes' and 'King's Ears' visited each province of the Persian Empire annually and reported directly to the king what they had learned (Olmstead 1948 : 59). In this way, the Persian kings sought to forestall revolts or secessions by ambitious provincial officials. Yet ensuring the loyalty of these spies entailed its own problems.

Some of the most serious problems posed by difficulties of communication in the early empires occurred at the highest decision-making levels of government. These problems were first analysed in detail by the Arab medieval historian Ibn Khaldun (1967). His analysis does not apply so much to the rulers of small states or lower-level officials in large states, since these inevitably remained in touch with the people they governed. In larger states, however, there was a tendency for kings to become encapsulated within the highly artificial elite life-style that was centred on the royal court. As a result, they no longer made decisions that were based on personal knowledge of the real world. Instead, their decisions were based on information that was mediated through a variety of court officials. In some societies, the seclusion of the monarch, which was related to the concept of divine kingship, encouraged such practises. In others fear of usurpation or the desire of court officials to dominate rulers resulted in heirs to the throne being kept isolated and inexperienced. In the later Ottoman Empire, the former system by which princes were trained in the field gave way to one in which potential royal heirs were isolated in the harem and their education limited to what the permanent inhabitants of that institution could provide. Sometimes such a situation began when a monarch, tiring of administrative duties, retired from public affairs to enjoy the pleasures of his wealth and power. A variety of officials could carry on government in his name but they could not replace him as a focus of loyalty. The unconstitutional nature of such government was conducive to political intrigues that undermined the stability of the regime. At the same time, the unchecked indulgence of the sovereign diverted the resources of the empire into unproductive and ultimately counter-productive channels. The increasing separation of the ruler from reality encouraged politically ambitious leaders, often on the periphery of the state, to found independent states or to make their own bid for imperial mastery.

The rate at which such a cycle is run seems to be slower in both small states and large empires than among states of middle range. In small ones the ruler does not so easily become isolated from reality and in the large ones it takes longer for the effects of his isolation to corrupt the political fabric. It is dangerous, however, to generalize about the length of dynastic cycles, since the latter is affected by many different institutional factors. For example, the failure of the Romans to work out a pattern of legitimate succession resulted in the frequent seizure of the throne by military officers who had acquired a wide range of administrative experience. This seems to have more than compensated the system for the disadvantages of an unstable succession.

Transformations

What may we conclude from this brief survey of the relationship between inequality and communication? At the highest level of abstraction, I would agree with Forge (1972 : 375) when he hypothesizes that human beings can handle only a finite number of intense interpersonal relationships and that as the number of relationships increases classification must be employed to keep them within manageable limits. I would also conclude that information, in the form both of traditional knowledge about how to do things (culture) and of fresh data entering the cultural system (news), can be shared equally by all the males or females of a society only within the simplest band structures. As group size increases, specialization occurs with respect to both types of information. The information-processing necessary to co-ordinate large groups generates an hierarchical administrative structure that acquires more levels and greater internal complexity at each level as political units increase in size and become economically more complex. Within such a hierarchy, power correlates directly with an individual's ability to collect, process, and control the distribution of information that is judged vital to manage society. This does not mean that lower-level officials cannot withhold such information from their superiors or feed them with false information. When this happens, however, it is usually an indication of the weakness of higher-level officials or of the control hierarchy generally.

When a system has reached the point where the referral of routine decisions for general approval must be eliminated in order for the affairs of the group to be managed successfully, the basis is laid for the breakdown of equitable redistribution and hence for the acquisition and retention of resources by those who are politically powerful. From this point on, rulers utilize administrative hierarchies to attempt to achieve goals that they themselves perceive as necessary or desirable. They avoid wasting the resources of their kingdoms to support un-necessary and ultimately counter-productive administrative operations. This is done by not exercising higher-level controls over aspects of the system that are or can be made self-regu-lating. Even so, most early civilizations stretched their regu-latory mechanisms to the utmost. The authority of even effec-tive rulers was a skilful blend of shadow and substance. The limitations that were imposed on the administration of early civilizations by their cumbersome systems of communication

Inequality and Communication

and record-keeping are an accurate reflection of the fragility of the socio-political order as a whole.

In discussing bands and villages, I suggested that there might be critical thresholds of population size, which if exceeded necessitated the elaboration of specific kinds of decision-making arrangements. If confirmed, such thresholds could be of considerable assistance to archaeologists in interpreting settlement data. Within societies at any one level, however, and particularly when dealing with complex societies, the nature of systems for procuring and processing information becomes extremely complex. Simplistic models cannot deal adequately with real situations, which require detailed analyses similar to those which social anthropologists provide for their data. Robert M. Adams (1974 : 248) has argued that archaeologists ought to pay more attention to the historic role of conscious decision-making. This includes recognizing 'that goal-motivated behaviour has been a decisive factor in many social transformations'. The concept of goal-motivated behaviour also questions the assumption, long-challenged but now all too prevalent among archaeologists, that all processes of change occur in the form of graceful, uninterrupted, and irreversible trajectories. As Adams (ibid.) again points out, changes in the early civilizations often took place in 'dizzyingly abrupt shifts'. This happened as rulers sought, with varying degrees of success, to maximize their position by dominating weaker neighbours or crushing internal rivals. Such 'historical' events are among the most difficult phenomena for archaeologists to discern and explain.

Yet, especially where some written records survive, the analysis of political transformations of this sort, although arduous, is not wholly beyond the archaeologist's ken. A better understanding of such situations partly may be facilitated by the development of analytical procedures that will permit a better understanding of communication systems. Archaeologists have made rapid progress in adapting the rigorous techniques that geographers have developed for locational analysis to the needs of settlement archaeology. Communication is clearly a relevant aspect of the hierarchies revealed thereby (Renfrew 1975). The mathematical approaches that Torsten Hägerstrand (1967) has developed to model the diffusion of innovations and the application of stochastic models to study social processes (Bartholomew 1967) suggest that other more rigorous quantitative approaches can be applied to studying the processes of communication in early civilizations. This, in turn, may provide archaeologists with a sounder basis on which to investigate the development of administrative hierarchies, social inequality, and class-based societies.

XIII

The Inter-Societal Transfer
of Institutions

The Status of Diffusion

IN RECENT YEARS THE CONCEPT of diffusion has fallen into gross disfavour, and indeed disrepute, as British and American archaeologists have turned to studying the development of societies or cultures as functionally-integrated systems. Many formerly fashionable diffusionary explanations of archaeological data are now viewed as erroneous or as attempts to avoid a more demanding explanation of cultural change framed in terms of internal developments (Childe 1956a : 154).

Julian Steward (1955 : 182) heralded this change when he proposed in a comparative study of early civilizations that every borrowing might be construed as an 'independent recurrence of cause and effect'. Thereafter Marvin Harris (1968 : 377–378) in his widely-read *The Rise of Anthropological Theory* dismissed diffusion as a 'nonprinciple'; a view shared by American archaeologists as diverse in their orientations as L.R. Binford (1968b : 8–10) and K.C.Chang (1962b : 190–191).

This attitude among archaeologists reflects a general lack of interest in diffusionary theory in the social sciences in recent decades. T. Hägerstrand's (1967) geographical analyses of the micro-processes of the spread of innovations represent a major contribution to the study of human behaviour, but so far his findings have been applied to the investigation of archaeological data only by Ian Hodder (1977 : 259–262). Of immediate, but largely unrecognized significance to archaeologists are H.E.Driver and W.C.Massey's (1957) statistical comparisons of native American cultures, which demonstrate clearly that functional correlations can account only in part for actual trait distributions. On the basis of these findings, Driver

216

(1974) concludes that when cultures are ripe for change, solutions already adopted in neighbouring societies often are of crucial importance in determining what happens. Driver maintains that the most unassailable evidence demonstrates conclusively that independent invention is rare by comparison with diffusion, while the capriciousness of diffusion is matched by that of internal development. Although the smaller-scale societies ought not to be regarded as being as uninventive as many archaeologists used to assume, Driver's work should stand as a warning against the equally facile counter-claim that such societies 'are inventing all the time' (Renfrew 1969).

Colin Renfrew (1973a : 109–112) provides a temperate and well-considered formulation of the new point of view. He does not deny that 'ideas, and innovations and inventions' diffuse but argues that 'what matters is not to know whether some ingenious idea reached the society in question from outside, but rather to understand how it came to be accepted by that society, and what features of the economic and social organization there made the innovation so significant'. To do this the archaeologist must study the processes at work within the recipient society. The mere assertion of diffusion provides no understanding of the processes of cultural change, which require elaboration and documentation. Diffusion is therefore a portfolio expression which is best abandoned in favour of terms denoting specific modes of cultural contact (Renfrew 1975 : 21).

Childe (1929 : vi), now regarded as 'the arch-diffusionist' in European archaeology, made a similar point in *The Danube in Prehistory*. There he stated that the term *influences* 'has only a minimal connotation. It may mean actual movements and mixings of peoples, intertribal barter, imitation, or some other form of contact. Often it is merely a confession of ignorance, and in no case must it be taken as an explanation. Where any indications are available to guide us, we attempt to give 'influence' a precise meaning in concrete cases'.

Diffusion was a methodologically valid concept so long as archaeologists and ethnologists were preoccupied with the related questions of how inventive man was and whether psychic unity or diffusion explained more of the cultural parallelisms found throughout the world. These psychological propositions may or may not be relevant to the study of man and archaeological evidence may or may not be of particular importance for their solution. In any case, they have become unfashionable and without them the term diffusion becomes redundant. But, as Renfrew has noted, this does not mean that the concrete processes once grouped together under the heading of diffusion do not occur. It seems generally to be admitted by archaeologists that they do (Martin and Plog 1973 : 337–341).

The role of cultural borrowing is, however, likely to be seriously underestimated if we think of it as limited to 'ideas, innovations and inventions' – the elementary building blocks of culture. This implies that systemic aspects of culture do not diffuse, or do so only very rarely. While this *in situ* view of development, if correct, would greatly simplify the study of cultural systems, it is manifestly untenable. In the following case studies, I will demonstrate that cultural borrowing is not limited to traits or trait complexes but extends to institutions and entire cultural subsystems. It will also be made clear that such diffusion in no way obviates a functional and systemic view of cultural development. Rather, it must be seen as an important aspect of it.

Case Studies

The first institution I will examine is the Christian church about the middle of the first millennium A.D. Whether in its Roman, Orthodox, or Coptic variants, the church was a clearly-delineated and complex institution, serviced by a disciplined, multi-level hierarchy of priests, possessing considerable property, claiming to monopolize religious rituals, and enunciating a comprehensive and unified body of dogma. While the church, as a hierarchical and propertied institution, could not exist in the absence of the state, it claimed to be universal and often a particular church extended beyond the borders of any one state.

Significant parallels emerge from a comparison of the conversion to Christianity of Anglo-Saxon England and Nubia. In spite of their very different geographical settings, the two areas shared a number of significant features. Each had formerly been part of a flourishing empire: Britain having been a Roman province and Nubia roughly co-extensive with the

218

Meroitic state. In lowland England what remained of Roman civilization, including literacy, urban life, and Christianity, had been erased after the fourth century by incursions of Anglo-Saxon settlers, who formerly had lived beyond the borders of the empire. By the sixth century, twelve small states had emerged, each ruled by a king belonging to a family that traced its descent from a Germanic deity (Fisher 1974 : 108–110). Strong rulers forced their weaker neighbours to pay tribute, so that by A.D. 850 all but four of these states were reduced to the status of dependent provinces. The strongest king of the day was recognized as Bretwalda or high king of Britain (Blair 1956 : 196–202; Whitelock 1974 : 48). In early times this honour passed rapidly from one kingdom to another.

It is uncertain how extensively the Meroitic kingdom was overrun by barbarian invaders as its power declined into oblivion (W. Adams 1968). Nevertheless the Meroitic language vanished to be replaced by Nubian, and with it literacy, monumental architecture, and the Meroitic state religion disappeared. Various war-like political units emerged, which by the sixth century were consolidated into several kingdoms along the Nile south of Aswan. As in England, the administration of these states appears to have been of a rudimentary nature, with their stability depending largely upon the forcefulness of individual rulers.

Anglo-Saxon England

In the sixth century the traditional Germanic religion was deeply rooted throughout lowland England although Christianity survived among the Celtic peoples to the north and west. Yet the Germanic religion remained essentially a family and local one (Fisher 1973 : 63–64). Although kings may have exercised priestly functions and temples and priests were attached to royal courts, a state religion does not appear to have been present or developing. By an apparent contradiction, in spite of the devotion of the English to their gods, by the end of the sixth century Roman authorities regarded the English as ripe for conversion (Blair 1956 : 123; Whitelock 1974 : 23; Gwatkin and Whitney 1913 : 515).

Christianity was established institutionally in England

through the baptism of kings. This brought about the conversion of their courts and of dependent rulers and that in turn was followed by mass baptisms among their subjects. The first English king to be converted was Ethelbert of Kent in 597. He was the most powerful English ruler of his day and had married a Frankish princess for whom a Christian chapel had already been established at Canterbury. Ethelbert's example led to the baptism of the neighbouring and subordinate kings of Essex and East Anglia. Edwin of Northumbria, the most powerful ruler of his day, was baptised at York in 627, following his marriage to a Kentish princess. The king of Wessex became a Christian in 635, the future king of Mercia in 653, and the king of Sussex in 679. In none of these realms did kings force conversion on their subjects and some kings are reported to have sought the approval of their councils before personally agreeing to baptism. There were strong pagan reactions in the south of England following the death of Ethelbert and in the north after the death of Edwin, while the epidemic of 664 encouraged people to resume worshipping the old gods. Even in Kent it was nearly fifty years after the conversion of Ethelbert before, in accordance with Frankish practice, the destruction of idols was ordered throughout the kingdom along with the enforcement of the Lenten fast (Fisher 1974 : 66). Still another fifty years later penalties were being imposed for pagan worship (Whitelock 1974 : 156). Yet Christianity was soon reinstated in kingdoms whose rulers had rejected the church and within less than a century all of England was under Christian rule. In some cases, efforts were made to mollify local opinion by converting local temples into churches and by incorporating pagan observances into Christian festivals (Gwatkin and Whitney 1913 : 519).

Why did the English kings convert to Christianity at this time? The English clearly had close economic and political relations with the continent that would be improved by a common bond of religion. Yet the internal advantages to be derived from conversion were even greater. The *Cambridge Medieval History* informs us that missionaries from Italy and Gaul introduced to the English kings 'new ideals of what a state should be and of the part a king should play . . . encouraging [them to govern] their people after the fashion of the Caesars' (Gwatkin and Whitney 1913 : 549). The kings' chaplains acted as their secretaries, and priests were able to draw up wills and contracts and to record deeds of importance (Whitelock 1974 : 58). Hence their administrative value was very great. The clergy also used their literacy and administrative experience to draw up law codes and orderly systems for assessing and collecting tribute; activities which directly increased royal power (Gwatkin and Whitney 1913 : 550). At the same time, the bishops (most of whom were not English until after 693) viewed England as the single unit it had been in Roman times. They realized the advantages to be gained from larger polities and tacitly supported the political consolidation of the Anglo-Saxons. From the continent they brought with them the idea of a king who claimed autocratic powers (Gwatkin and Whitney 1913 : 528, 549). Rather than undermining the concept of the divine origin of kings, the church sought to enhance the dignity and sanctity of royal office. Christian kings ruled by the grace of God and towards the end of the eighth century began to be anointed in a coronation ritual. Contrary to Anglo-Saxon tradition, the church maintained that an anointed king could not be deposed (Whitelock 1974 : 52). Even a limited understanding of the advantages to be gained from the establishment of a church in England must have made ambitious rulers incline to conversion. Such knowledge could be derived from the close relations England had with Frankish Gaul.

The church was not acting disinterestedly in promoting secular power. In spite of being divided into two archbishoprics, the diocesan organization of the church was coextensive with England as a whole; hence the church had a strong interest in the emergence of larger states that could provide it with greater protection and endowments. The Christian clergy, unlike their pagan counterparts, were anxious to establish themselves as a separate class, superior to the laity and protected by special legal sanctions. At least part of their interest in codifying and altering laws was directed towards securing their own position (Gwatkin and Whitney 1913 : 548–549). Their success in doing so introduced into English society a lasting division between clergy and laity and created a dualism in government and society that was of far reaching importance. The king was relied on to punish the murder of priests, to protect church property, and to ensure the collection of tolls, fees, and rents owed to the church, the evasion of which was punished with increasing severity through time (Whitelock 1974 : 42, 167). The growing exactions of the church reflected the increasing strength of the state.

In the sphere of social behaviour the church had to strike a compromise between Christian ideals and Anglo-Saxon customs. An effort was made to enforce church laws concerning marriage and divorce, while the church's prohibition against trading on Sundays and other holy days was upheld by secular authorities. The traditional bond between a man and his lord was strengthened by an oath sworn over holy relics. Although the church strove to encourage the acceptance of compensation (*wergild*) in place of blood revenge for murdered kinsmen, it did not dare to try to eliminate such revenge entirely (Whitelock 1974 : 37, 42–44, 122, 150). The development of monasteries and the encouragement of pilgrimages to Rome and Jerusalem were new and influential aspects of Anglo-Saxon social life (Whitelock 1974 : 169–177).

The effects of Christianity are also apparent in material culture and hence in the archaeological record. Grave goods were common in pagan cemeteries but gradually disappear in Christian ones (David Wilson 1972 : 48). Stone masons were imported from France and Italy to build churches. Stone structures had not been erected in England since the Roman period and the reintroduction of this craft has been hailed as marking the start of a new period of civilization in Britain (Gwatkin and Whitney 1913 : 523). Only later was stone used to construct palaces and a few town houses. Glaziers also were introduced into England, while painting and stone carving were encouraged as arts of value to religion. The teaching of writing and book learning were also sponsored by the church, primarily for training its own personnel. English metal smiths, who already were renowned for their skills, were put to work manufacturing clerical paraphernalia, while scroll motifs and representational art were added to the traditional repertoire of Anglo-Saxon designs (David Wilson 1972).

The Anglo-Saxon states that had emerged in England by the sixth century had reached a point where their consolidation and further development required a more complex administrative structure. They had also reached a point where the development of a state religion would promote economic growth

222

and a further elaboration of society, which in turn would encourage the development of stronger secular authority. This did not, however, lead to the indigenous growth of a state religion in England. Instead it resulted in the adoption of a foreign religious institution and the integration of that institution into Anglo-Saxon society. The success of this project demonstrates that the Christian church filled an important structural need in society; yet there is no reason to believe that anything resembling the Christian church would have evolved spontaneously in England.

Christian Nubia

There is considerably less historical documentation for post-Meroitic Nubia than for Anglo-Saxon England. Yet striking parallels can be observed between the political development of Nubia in the Ballana period (which followed the decline of the Meroitic kingdom) and in early Anglo-Saxon England. A series of small, rudimentary states emerged in the Nile Valley south of Aswan which, by the middle of the sixth century, had been consolidated into three kingdoms: Nobatia, Makuria, and Alwa. Some of the smaller states probably survived, however, as vassal territories within the larger kingdoms. The power of at least the Nobatian king appears to have been based on military force and his ability to control lucrative Saharan trade routes (Trigger 1965 : 140–141). Nubia as a whole had been economically and culturally impoverished by the chaotic conditions following the collapse of the Meroitic kingdom. Nevertheless in the Ballana period excellent stone buildings were erected at fortified centres such as Qasr Ibrim, and the nascent royal courts were patronizing skilled craftsmen on an increasing scale. There is no evidence that the Ballana kings, anymore than the Anglo-Saxon ones, sought to establish or patronize a state religion (Adams 1965 : 164).

The Ballana period witnessed increasing familiarity with and employment of Christian iconography throughout northern Nubia, and there is fragmentary evidence of Christian worship, perhaps paralleling that found in Kent prior to its conversion (Adams 1965 : 172). Some Egyptian Copts, fleeing Orthodox persecution, also may have settled there. Unlike in England, popular support for paganism appears to have declined in northern Nubia during the Ballana period. This permitted the Byzantine government to close the temples at Philae without opposition c. 540, when a long-term treaty guaranteeing the right of Nubians to worship at this pagan centre finally expired. The greater popular appeal of Christianity may explain why there is no record of royal apostasies in Nubia as there was in England and why goods rapidly ceased to be placed in ordinary graves following conversion.

The conversion of Nubia, like that of England, is attributed to the baptism of kings (Kirwan 1937). The king of Nobatia was baptised in 543, the king of Makuria about 570, and the king of Alwa far to the south about 580. The intrigues between the Monophysite and Orthodox factions at the Byzantine court may have increased the political complexities of conversion but ultimately the Monophysite (Coptic) church prevailed throughout Nubia (Krause 1970). The Byzantines sought to convert neighbouring peoples as a means of promoting alliances that would secure their own frontiers. In the case of Nubia, this must have become increasingly desirable as political power became more consolidated there and as political and economic relations between the Nobatian court and Egypt grew in intensity. The Nubian kingdoms, like Anglo-Saxon England, reached the point where the introduction of Christianity would promote their consolidation and internal development.

The material effects of conversion soon became apparent. Beginning about 580, trained church architects arrived in Nubia. In the course of the next 200 years the largest and most ornate churches of Nubia were constructed including the cathedral at Qasr Ibrim with its dressed stone masonry. The earliest churches are indistinguishable from those in Egypt and probably were built by Egyptian architects despatched to Nubia by religious authorities or by the Byzantine government. Stone sculpture and eventually wall painting were also introduced into Nubia by the ecclesiastical authorities (Adams 1965 : 173–175). Soon after conversion a number of major towns in Lower Nubia were fortified with massive stone walls, seemingly built with the assistance of Byzantine architects. These towns no doubt enhanced the authority of the Nobatian kings and increased the security of the trade routes passing through their territory. The construction of these fortifications also may have been sponsored by the Byzantine government (Stenico 1960).

The Church re-introduced literacy into Nubia. Greek and Old Nubian both were written by native Nubians while Coptic seems to have been employed by Egyptian elements among the clergy. Greek survived as a language of the royal court until at least the twelfth century (Oates 1963). It is not known what effects the clergy had on laws, taxes, and property rights or from what sources their revenues were derived. Adams (1977 : ch. 15) has speculated that the pottery industry at Faras, which was established in a monastery, may have remained under ecclesiastical control and that vineyards also may have been owned by monasteries. Yet, if different in detail, the effects that the church had upon the economy and government of Nubia were probably as great as in England. Christianity also introduced into Nubia the division between church and state, clergy and laity. Kings do not seem to have had the right to appoint bishops, which generally was done by the Patriarch of Alexandria. Thus there was not a national church of Nubia. On the other hand, the king of northern Nubia at certain periods was regarded as a temporal protector of Christians in Islamic Egypt (Adams 1977 : ch. 15).

While guarding its own autonomy, the church strove to enhance the prestige of the Nubian kings who were its temporal protectors and benefactors. Kings were associated with saints in church paintings and Abu Salih reported that a king who had not shed blood could enter the sanctuary of a church and celebrate the liturgy. The church also may have encouraged patrilineal succession to the throne into the eleventh century. The union of Nobatia and Makuria not long after their conversion partly may reflect the activity of the clergy in promoting political unity on a larger scale. The archaeological record bears witness to the economic prosperity of Nubia in the centuries following the introduction of Christianity. The greater political stability and economic complexity that resulted from the development of the church as an institution within Nubia seem to have more than offset the not inconsiderable economic demands that it made upon the Nubian people. Among the many customs that Christianity introduced to Nubian society were monasticism and pilgrimages, especially to the Holy Land. The latter resulted in many architectural and artistic, as well as religious, innovations being introduced into Nubia.

The Kushite State

The borrowing of religious and cultural institutions is not simply a concomitant of missionary activity. This can be seen to best advantage by examining a situation in which the division between clergy and laity was of little importance.

About 250 years after the collapse of the Egyptian empire of the New Kingdom, a local family began to rise to power near the former Egyptian administrative centre of Gebel Barkal, in Upper Nubia. The earliest graves of this family, at El-Kurru, suggest that these rulers were little advanced beyond a tribal level, although they were already profiting greatly from trade with Egypt. Within a short period of time the successive heads of this family were recognized as high kings by the other rulers in Nubia and by the middle of the eighth century B.C. they were able to begin fishing in the troubled politics of a weak and divided Egypt. By posing as the champions of the god Amon, these Kushite kings were able to gain the support of the leading families of southern Egypt for campaigns against the Libyan dynasts to the north. In this way they managed to establish their suzerainty over the whole of Egypt for several reigns (Trigger 1976b : 138–148).

Control of Egypt provided these rulers with the resources to consolidate further their own position in Upper Nubia. Either voluntarily or by compulsion many Egyptian priests, administrators, artists, and craftsmen were resettled in Nubia. Egyptian was adopted as the written language of the hitherto illiterate state; Egyptian arts and crafts flourished; and large stone tombs and temples were erected to proclaim the glory of the new rulers. This period also saw the development of a state-controlled economy modelled along Egyptian lines and no doubt administered by Egyptian or Egyptian-trained bureaucrats. Similar craftsmen produced luxury goods for the enjoyment of the Kushite upper classes, while large amounts of standardized wheel-made pottery suggest that centralized control was exercised over the surpluses of many basic com-

226

modities. Temples honouring Egyptian gods were erected and endowed in all of the major towns of Upper Nubia; native deities being either ignored or silently syncretized with Egyptian ones. By creating an elite culture, patronized by and centering on the royal court, the Kushite kings ensured that their developing society was consolidated into sharply-differentiated upper and lower segments. This was done in imitation of the class-structured society of Egypt. Kushite civilization differed from that of Egypt primarily that in Egypt the life-style of the elite had arisen out of a way of life that in large measure survived among the peasantry, whereas in Nubia it was an importation from elsewhere.

The Kushite rulers succeeded in imposing significant elements of Egyptian-style political organization upon their homeland by implanting there the religious cults and other cultural values of Dynastic Egypt. This is so even if Kushitic monuments greatly overstate the Egyptianization of the Nubian upper classes. In so doing, the rulers of Kush, like those of Anglo-Saxon England and post-Meroitic Nubia were able to elaborate and consolidate the social and economic basis on which their power rested. In this manner they founded a kingdom that was able to survive expulsion from Egypt and to maintain itself for over 1000 years.

Conclusions

These three case studies make it clear that not only traits and innovations but also major institutions and whole cultural subsystems may be transferred from one culture to another. In each instance, political and economic development in the recipient culture had to reach a critical level before the integration of foreign institutions became possible or desirable. The adopted institutions in turn became important catalysts in promoting further development of the social system. They also introduced customs, practices, and a view of the world that were not of local origin or likely to have been paralleled at all closely by indigenous developments. Indeed, there is no formal evidence that further indigenous development would have occurred, rather than political and cultural stagnation or collapse.

Inter-Societal Transfer of Institutions

I am convinced that the study of societies and cultures as complex, evolving systems should be a major goal of archaeology. I am also convinced, as Childe was in 1929, that diffusion is an omnibus term that covers many different kinds of processes, each worthy of study in its own right. It is clear, however, that diffusion is not limited to isolated traits but, at least in complex societies, can embrace institutions and whole cultural subsystems. Nor does borrowing of this sort make the development of cultural systems any less orderly or systemic; one must firmly reject the argument that an interest in diffusion necessarily implies a view of culture as a thing of shreds and tatters. Assigning a major role to diffusion does, however, increase greatly the variety of socio-cultural elements that are recognized as capable of influencing the development of a cultural system. This inevitably makes the development of cultural sequences more variable and less predictable than do views which stress development mainly through internal factors. If diffusionary processes are to be integrated into the systemic investigation of socio-cultural development, archaeologists must cease minimizing the importance of diffusion and stop regarding it as the antithesis of social evolution. By incorporating diffusion into their investigations of societal development, archaeologists will be taking a major step towards abolishing the false dichotomy between what is called science and history.

Acknowledgements

THIS BOOK COMPRISES a selection of papers, four of which have not been printed before and eight of which are revised versions of ones that have appeared over the past ten years in journals or books. The new papers were written, the old ones revised, and the book edited while the author was recipient of a Canada Council Leave Fellowship in 1976–77.

'Current Trends in American Archaeology' is new. An earlier draft was presented to a seminar at the Institute of Archaeology in the University of London in March 1977 and at the University of Southampton in May 1977.

'Aims in Prehistoric Archaeology' appeared in *Antiquity* 44 (1970) 26–37. An earlier version of this paper was presented at the Research Seminar on Archaeology and Related Subjects held at the Institute of Archaeology in the University of London in May 1969.

'The Future of Archaeology is the Past' appeared in *Research and Theory in Current Archeology* (ed. C. L. Redman), pp. 95–111. New York: John Wiley Ltd., 1973. This paper was written while I was the recipient of a Killam Award and was first presented at the meeting of the American Anthropological Association held in New York in November 1971.

'Archaeology and the Idea of Progress' was written for this book.

'The Development of the Archaeological Culture in Europe and America' is new. It was first read at a seminar of the Institute of Archaeology in the University of London in May 1977. I wish to thank J. B. Griffin and I. Rouse for helping to clarify issues discussed in this paper.

'Major Concepts of Archaeology in Historical Perspective' appeared in *Man N.S.* 3 (1968) 527–541. It was read at the first annual meeting of the Canadian Archaeological Association held in Winnipeg in March 1968.

'The Concept of the Community' is extracted from chapter 3 of my book *Beyond History: The Methods of Prehistory*, pp. 18–23. New York: Holt, Rinehart and Winston, Inc., 1968.

'Race, Language, and Culture' is from my book *Beyond History: The Methods of Prehistory*, pp. 7–13. New York: Holt, Rinehart and Winston, Inc., 1968.

'Archaeology and Ecology' appeared in *World Archaeology* 2 (1971) 321–336. London: Routledge and Kegan Paul Ltd. It was written for the 1969–70 McGill University Faculty Seminar on Human Ecology.

'The Archaeology of Government' appeared in *World Archaeology* 6 (1974) 95–106. London: Routledge and Kegan Paul Ltd. It was written as a summary article for a number on Political Systems.

'The Determinants of Settlement Patterns' appeared in *Settlement Archaeology* (ed. K. C. Chang), pp. 53–78. Palo Alto: National Press (now Mayfield Publishing Company), 1968.

'Inequality and Communication in Early Civilizations' appeared in *Anthropologica* N.S. 18 (1976) 27–52. An earlier version was read to the Seminar on Social Inequality of the University of Western Ontario and to the Seminar on Stratification and State Formation of the Department of Anthropology, McGill University, both in February 1976.

'The Inter-Societal Transfer of Institutions' is new. It was read at the Symposium of the Faculty of Arts held to commemorate the 500th anniversary of the founding of Uppsala University in Uppsala, Sweden in June 1977.

The revised papers are reproduced by permission of the original editors and publishers, to whom grateful acknowledgement is made.

B.T.

References

ABERCROMBY, J. (1912) *A Study of the Bronze Age Pottery of Great Britain and Ireland and its Associated Grave Goods.* 2 vols. Oxford: Clarendon Press.

ABERLE, D. F. (1968) Comments. In S. R. and L. R. Binford, eds. *New Perspectives in Archeology*, pp. 353–359. Chicago: Aldine.

ADAMS, R. M.
(1965) *Land behind Baghdad.*
Chicago: University of Chicago Press.
(1966) *The Evolution of Urban Society: Early Mesopotamia and Prehispanic Mexico.* Chicago: Aldine.
(1972) Patterns of urbanization in early Southern Mesopotamia. In P. J. Ucko, R. Tringham and G. W. Dimbleby, eds. *Man, Settlement and Urbanism*, pp. 735–749. London: Duckworth.
(1974) 'Anthropological perspectives on ancient trade'. *Current Anthropology* 15: 239–258.
(1975) The emerging place of trade in civilizational studies. In J. A. Sabloff and C. C. Lamberg-Karlovsky, eds. *Ancient Civilization and Trade*, pp. 451–464. Albuquerque: University of New Mexico Press.

ADAMS, W. Y.
(1965) 'Post-Pharaonic Nubia in the light of archaeology', II. *Journal of Egyptian Archaeology* 51: 160–178.
(1968) 'Invasion, diffusion, evolution?' *Antiquity* 42: 194–215.
(1970) The evolution of Christian Nubian pottery. E. Dinkler, ed. *Kunst und Geschichte Nubiens in Christlicher Zeit*, pp. 111–123. Recklinghausen: Bongers.
(1977) *Nubia: Corridor to Africa.* London: Allen Lane.

AITKEN, M. J. (1961) *Physics and Archaeology.*
London: Interscience.

ALBRIGHT, W. F. (1960) *The Archaeology of Palestine.*
Harmondsworth: Penguin.

ASSMANN, J. (1972) 'Palast oder Tempel? Überlegungen zur Architektur und Topographie von Amarna'. *Journal of Near Eastern Studies* 31: 143–155.

BAER, K. (1960) *Rank and Title in the Old Kingdom.*
Chicago: University of Chicago Press.

BAILEY, A. G. (1969) *The Conflict of European and Eastern Algonkian Cultures, 1504–1700.*
Toronto: University of Toronto Press.

BAKER, P. T. and SANDERS, W. T. (1972) Demographic studies in anthropology. In B. J. Siegel, ed. *Annual Review of Anthropology* I: 151–178. Palo Alto: Annual Reviews.

BALANDIER, G. (1972) *Political Anthropology.*
Harmondsworth: Penguin.

BARTHOLOMEW, D. J. (1967) *Stochastic Models for Social Processes.* London: Wiley.

BASCOM, W. (1955) 'Urbanization among the Yoruba'.
American Journal of Sociology 60: 446–454.

BAYARD, D. T. (1969) 'Science, theory and reality in the "New Archaeology"'. *American Antiquity* 34: 376–384.

BEAUCHAMP, W. M. (1900) *Aboriginal Occupation of New York.*
Albany: Bulletin of the New York State Museum, 7, no. 32.

BENNETT, J. W. (1943) 'Recent developments in the functional interpretation of archaeological data'.
American Antiquity 9: 208–219.

BERKHOFER, R. F. (1969) *A Behavioral Approach to Historical Analysis.* New York: Free Press.

BERNAL, I. *et al.* (1973) *The Iconography of Middle American Sculpture.* New York: Metropolitan Museum of Art.

BERNIER, FRANÇOIS (1916) *Travels in the Moghul Empire, A.D. 1656–1668.* London: Humphrey Milford.

BIBBY, G. (1956) *The Testimony of the Spade.* New York: Knopf.

BIEK, L. (1963) *Archaeology and the Microscope.*
London: Lutterworth.

BINFORD, L. R.
   (1962) 'Archaeology as anthropology'. *American Antiquity* 28: 217–225.
   (1963) '"Red Ochre" caches from the Michigan area: A possible case of cultural drift'. *Southwestern Journal of Anthropology* 19: 89–108.
   (1965) 'Archaeological systematics and the study of cultural process'. *American Antiquity* 31: 203–210.
   (1967a) Comment. *Current Anthropology* 8: 234–235.
   (1967b) An Ethnohistory of the Nottoway, Meherrin and Weanock Indians of Southeastern Virginia. *Ethnohistory* 14: 104–218.
   (1967c) 'Smudge pits and hide smoking: the use of analogy in archaeological reasoning'. *American Antiquity* 32: 1–12.
   (1968a) 'Some comments on historical vs. processual archaeology'. *Southwestern Journal of Anthropology* 24: 267–275.

(1968b) Archeological perspectives. In S. R. and L. R. Binford, eds. *New Perspectives in Archeology*, pp. 5–32. Chicago: Aldine.

BINFORD, L. R. and S. R. (1966) A preliminary analysis of functional variability in the Mousterian of Levallois facies. In J. D. Clark and F. C. Howell, eds. *Recent Studies in Paleoanthropology, American Anthropologist*, 68, part 2, no. 2: 238–295.

BINFORD, S. R. (1968) 'A structural comparison of disposal of dead in the Mousterian and the Upper Palaeolithic'. *Southwestern Journal of Anthropology* 24: 139–154.

BINFORD, S. R. and BINFORD, L. R., eds. (1968) *New Perspectives in Archeology*. Chicago: Aldine.

BLAIR, P. H. (1956) *An Introduction to Anglo-Saxon England*. Cambridge: Cambridge University Press.

BLOCH, MARC (1961) *Feudal Society*. Chicago: University of Chicago Press.

BOAS, FRANZ
(1887) 'Museums of ethnology and their classification'. *Science* 9: 587–589.
(1940) *Race, Language and Culture*. New York: Macmillan.

BOWEN, R. L. (1958) Ancient trade routes in South Arabia. In R. L. Bowen and F. P. Albright, eds. *Archaeological Discoveries in South Arabia*, pp. 35–42. Baltimore: Johns Hopkins Press.

BRAIDWOOD, R. J. (1967) *Prehistoric Men*. 7th edition. Glenview: Scott, Foresman.

BRONSON, B. (1972) Farm labor and the evolution of food production. In B. Spooner, ed. *Population Growth*, pp. 190–218. Cambridge, Mass.: MIT Press.

BROTHWELL, D. R. and E. S. HIGGS, eds. (1963) *Science in Archaeology*. London: Thames and Hudson.

BROWN, J. A. (1887) *Palaeolithic Man in N. W. Middlesex*. London: Macmillan.

BROWN, J. A. and S. STRUEVER (1973) The organization of archeological research: an Illinois example. In C. L. Redman, ed. *Research and Theory in Current Archeology*, pp. 261–285. New York: Wiley.

BURKITT, M. C. (1923) *Our Forerunners*. London: Williams and Norgate.

CALDWELL, J. R. (1966) The New American archaeology. In J. Caldwell, ed. *New Roads to Yesterday*, pp. 333–347. New York: Basic Books.

CARR, E. H. (1962) *What is History ?*. London: Vintage.

CASSON, S. (1939) *The Discovery of Man.*
London: Hamish Hamilton.

CHAMBERLAIN, T. C. (1944) 'The method of multiple
working hypotheses'. *Scientific Monthly* 59: 357–362.

CHANG, K. C.

(1958) 'Study of the neolithic social grouping'. *American
Anthropologist* 60: 298–334.

(1962a) 'A typology of settlement and community patterns in
some circumpolar societies'. *Arctic Anthropology* 1: 28–41.

(1962b) China. In R. J. Braidwood and G. R. Willey, eds.
Courses Toward Urban Life, pp. 177–192. Chicago: Aldine.

(1963) *The Archaeology of Ancient China.*
New Haven: Yale University Press.

(1967a) 'Major aspects of the interrelationship of archaeology
and ethnology'. *Current Anthropology* 8: 227–43.

(1967b) *Rethinking Archaeology*. New York: Random House.

ed. (1968) *Settlement Archaeology*. Palo Alto: National Press.

CHANTRE, E. (1875–76) *L'Age du Bronze*. 3 vols. Paris: Baudry.

CHILDE, V. G.

(1925) *The Dawn of European Civilization.*
London: Kegan Paul.

(1926) *The Aryans*. London: Kegan Paul.

(1928) *The Most Ancient East*. London: Kegan Paul.

(1929) *The Danube in Prehistory*. Oxford: Clarendon Press.

(1930) *The Bronze Age.*
Cambridge: Cambridge University Press.

(1931) *Skara Brae*. London: Kegan Paul.

(1933) 'Is prehistory practical?' *Antiquity* 7: 410–418.

(1934) *New Light on the Most Ancient East.*
London: Kegan Paul.

(1935) 'Changing methods and aims in prehistory'.
Proceedings of the Prehistoric Society 1: 1–15.

(1936) *Man Makes Himself*. London: Watts.

(1942) *What Happened in History*. Harmondsworth: Penguin.
(pages cited from first U.S. edition, 1946).

(1944) *Progress and Archaeology*. London: Watts.

(1946a) *Scotland Before the Scots*. London: Methuen.

(1946b) 'Archaeology and anthropology'. *Southwestern
Journal of Anthropology* 2: 243–251.

(1947) *History*. London: Cobbett Press.

(1950a) *Prehistoric Migrations in Europe*. Oslo: Aschehaug.

(1950b) *Magic, Craftsmanship and Science*. Frazer Lecture.
Liverpool: Liverpool University Press.

(1951) *Social Evolution*. New York: Schuman.

(1953) The constitution of archaeology as a science. In
E. A. Underwood, ed. *Science, Medicine and History*, pp. 3–15.
Oxford: Oxford University Press.
(1956a) *Piecing Together the Past: the Interpretation of
Archaeological Data*. London: Routledge and Kegan Paul.
(1956b) *Society and Knowledge*. New York: Harper.
(1956c) *A Short Introduction to Archaeology*. London: Muller.
(1958a) *The Prehistory of European Society*.
Harmondsworth: Penguin.
(1958b) 'Retrospect'. *Antiquity* 32: 69–74.
(1958c) 'Valediction'. *Bulletin of the Institute of Archaeology*
1: 1–8.

CLARK, J. G. D.
(1939) *Archaeology and Society*. London: Methuen.
(1952) *Prehistoric Europe: the Economic Basis*.
London: Methuen.
(1953) 'The economic approach to prehistory'. *Proceedings of
the British Academy* 39: 215–238.
(1954) *Excavations at Star Carr*.
Cambridge: Cambridge University Press.
(1957) *Archaeology and Society*. 3rd edition. London: Methuen.
(1970) *Aspects of Prehistory*.
Berkeley: University of California Press.
(1974) Prehistoric Europe. In G. R. Willey, ed.
Archaeological Researches in Retrospect, pp. 31–58.
Cambridge, Mass: Winthrop.
(1975) *The Earlier Stone Age Settlement of Scandinavia*.
Cambridge: Cambridge University Press.
(1976) 'Prehistory since Childe'. *Bulletin of the Institute of
Archaeology* 13: 1–21.

CLARK, K. (1962) *The Gothic Revival*. 2nd edition.
London: John Murray.

CLARKE, D. L.
(1967) Review of K. C. Chang: *Rethinking Archaeology*.
Antiquity 41: 237–238.
(1968) *Analytical Archaeology*. London: Methuen.
(1972) A provisional model of an Iron Age society and its
settlement system. In D. L. Clarke, ed. *Models in
Archaeology*, pp. 801–869. London: Methuen.
ed. (1977) *Spatial Archaeology*. London: Academic Press.

CODRINGTON, R. H. (1957) *The Melanesians*.
New Haven: HRAF Press.

COE, M. D. (1961) 'Social typology and tropical forest civilisations'. *Comparative Studies in Society and History*. 4: 65–85.

(1969) Photogrammetry and the ecology of the Olmec civilization. Paper read at Working Conference on Aerial Photography and Anthropology, Cambridge, Mass., 10–12 May.

(1972) Olmec jaguars and Olmec kings. In E. P. Benson, ed. *The Cult of the Feline*, pp. 1–18. Washington: Dumbarton Oaks.

COE, M. D. and K. V. FLANNERY (1964) 'Microenvironments and Mesoamerican prehistory'. *Science* 143: 650–654.

COHEN, M. N. (1977) *The Food Crisis in Prehistory: Overpopulation and the Origins of Agriculture*. New Haven: Yale University Press.

COLE, S. M. (1954) *The Prehistory of East Africa*. Harmondsworth: Penguin.

COOK, S. F. and R. F. HEIZER (1968) Relationships among houses, settlement areas, and population in aboriginal California. In K. C. Chang, ed. *Settlement Archaeology*, pp. 79–116. Palo Alto: National Press.

CORNWALL, I. W.

(1956) *Bones for the Archaeologist*. London: Phoenix.

(1958) *Soils for the Archaeologist*. London: Phoenix.

(1964) *The World of Ancient Man*. London: Phoenix.

COWGILL, G. (1975) 'On causes and consequences of ancient and modern population changes'. *American Anthropologist* 77: 505–525.

CRAWFORD, O. G. S.

(1921) *Man and his Past*. Oxford: Oxford University Press.

(1926) Review of V. G. Childe: *The Dawn of European Civilization*. *The Antiquaries Journal* 6: 89–90.

(1932) 'The dialectical process in the history of science'. *Sociological Review* 24: 165–173.

(1953) *Archaeology in the Field*. London: Phoenix.

CROWFOOT, J. W. (1920) 'Old sites in the Butana'. *Sudan Notes and Records* 3: 85–93.

CUNLIFFE, B. (1974) *Iron Age Communities in Britain*. London: Routledge and Kegan Paul.

DALTON, G. (1975) Karl Polanyi's analysis of long-distance trade and his wider paradigm. In J. A. Sabloff and C. C. Lamberg-Karlovsky, eds. *Ancient Civilization and Trade*, pp. 63–132. Albuquerque: University of New Mexico Press.

DANIEL, G.

(1943) *The Three Ages*.
Cambridge: Cambridge University Press.
(1950) *A Hundred Years of Archaeology*. London: Duckworth.
(1963) *The Idea of Prehistory*. Cleveland: World Publishing.
(1966) *Man Discovers his Past*. London: Duckworth.
(1967) *The Origins and Growth of Archaeology*.
Harmondsworth: Penguin.
(1968a) *The First Civilizations*. London: Thames and Hudson.
(1968b) One hundred years of Old World prehistory.
In J. O. Brew, ed. *One Hundred Years of Anthropology*,
pp. 57–93. Cambridge, Mass.: Harvard University Press.

DARBY, H. C. (1956) The clearing of the woodland in Europe.
In W. L. Thomas, ed. *Man's Role in Changing the Face of
the Earth*, pp. 183–216. Chicago: University of Chicago Press.

DAWKINS, W. B. (1880) *Early Man in Britain and his Place
in the Tertiary Period*. London: Macmillan.

DEETZ, J.

(1965) *The Dynamics of Stylistic Change in Arikara
Ceramics*. Urbana: University of Illinois Press.
(1967) *Invitation to Archaeology*.
New York: Natural History Press.

DE LAET, S. (1957) *Archaeology and its Problems*.
London: Phoenix.

DETHLEFSEN, E. and J. DEETZ (1966) 'Death's heads,
cherubs and willow trees: experimental archaeology in
colonial cemeteries'. *American Antiquity* 31: 502–510.

DEUEL, L. (1973) *Flights into Yesterday*.
Harmondsworth: Penguin.

DIMBLEBY, G. W. (1967) *Plants and Archaeology*.
London: Baker.

DIXON, R. B. (1913) 'Some aspects of North American
archaeology'. *American Anthropologist* 15: 549–577.

DONNAN, C. B. (1976) *Moche Art and Iconography*.
Los Angeles: UCLA Latin American Studies Center.

DORAN, J. (1970) 'Systems theory, computer simulations and
archaeology'. *World Archaeology* 1: 289–298.

DOXIADIS, C. A. (1968) *Ekistics: an Introduction to the
Science of Human Settlements*. London: Hutchinson.

DRAY, W. (1957) *Laws and Explanation in History*.
London: Oxford University Press.

DRIVER, H. E. (1974) Diffusion and evolution. In
J. G. Jorgensen, ed. *Comparative Studies by
Harold E. Driver and Essays in his Honor*, pp. 60–63.
New Haven: HRAF Press.

DRIVER, H. E. and W. C. MASSEY (1957) 'Comparative studies
of North American Indians'. *Transactions of the American
Philosophical Society* 47: 165–456.

DUMOND, D. E. (1972) 'Demographic aspects of the Classic
period in Puebla-Tlaxcala'. *Southwestern Journal of
Anthropology* 28: 101–130.

DUNNING, R. W. (1960) 'Differentiation of status in
subsistence level societies'. *Transactions of the Royal Society of
Canada* 54, sec. ii: 25–32.

DURKHEIM, E. (1933) *Division of Labor in Society*.
G. Simpson, trans. New York: Macmillan (orig. 1893).

DURKHEIM, E., and M. MAUSS (1963) *Primitive
Classification*. Chicago: University of Chicago Press.

DYSON, R. H., Jr. (1957) Review of V. G. Childe: *Piecing
Together the Past*. *American Antiquity* 23: 189.

EARLE, T. K. (1972) 'Lurin Valley, Peru: early Intermediate
period settlement development'. *American Antiquity*
37: 467–477.

EISENSTADT, S. N. (1963) *The Political Systems of Empires*.
New York: Free Press.

ELIADE, MIRCEA (1960) Structures and changes in the
history of religion. In C. H. Kraeling and R. M. Adams, eds.
City Invincible, pp. 351–366.
Chicago: University of Chicago Press.

ELTON, G. R. (1969) *The Practice of History*. London: Collins.

ERASMUS, C. J.
(1965) 'Monument building: some field experiments'.
Southwestern Journal of Anthropology 21: 277–301.
(1968) 'Thoughts on upward collapse: an essay on explanation
in anthropology'. *Southwestern Journal of Anthropology*
24: 170–194.

ERIKSON, E. H. (1959) *Young Man Luther*. London: Faber.

EVANS, A. J. (1890) 'Late-Celtic Urn-field at Aylesford, Kent'.
Archaeologia 52: 317–388.

EVANS-PRITCHARD, E. E. (1940) *The Nuer*.
Oxford: Clarendon Press.

FEI, HSIAO-TUNG (1953) *China's Gentry*.
Chicago: University of Chicago Press.

FEWKES, J. W. (1896) 'The Prehistoric culture of Tusayan'.
American Anthropologist 9: 151–173.

238

FISCHER, J. L. (1961) 'Art styles as cultural cognitive maps'. *American Anthropologist* 63: 79–93.

FISHER, D. J. V. (1974) *The Anglo-Saxon Age, c. 400–1042*. London: Longman.

FITCH, J. M. and D. P. BRANCH (1960) 'Primitive architecture and climate'. *Scientific American* 203, no. 6: 134–144.

FLANNERY, K. V.
(1967) 'Culture history vs. cultural process: a debate in American archaeology'. *Scientific American* 217: 119–122.
(1968) Archaeological systems theory and early Mesoamerica. In B. Meggers, ed. *Anthropological Archaeology in the Americas*, pp. 67–88.
Washington: Anthropological Society of Washington.
(1972) The cultural evolution of civilizations. *Annual Review of Ecology and Systematics* 3: 399–426.
Palo Alto: Annual Reviews, Inc.
(1973) Archeology with a capital 'S'. In C. L. Redman, ed. *Research and Theory in Current Archeology*, pp. 47–53.
New York: Wiley.
(1976) *The Early Mesoamerican Village*.
New York: Academic Press.

FLANNERY, K. V. and J. MARCUS (1976) 'Formative Oaxaca and the Zapotec cosmos'. *American Scientist* 64: 374–383.

FLEURE, H. J. and W. E. WHITEHOUSE (1916) 'The early distribution and valley-ward movement of population in South Britain'. *Archaeologia Cambrensis* 16: 101–140.

FORDE, C. D. (1934) *Habitat, Economy and Society*. London: Methuen.

FORGE, ANTHONY (1972) Normative factors in the settlement size of neolithic cultivators. In P. J. Ucko, R. Tringham and G. W. Dimbleby, eds. *Man, Settlement and Urbanism*, pp. 363–376. London: Duckworth.

FOSTER, G. M. (1960) 'Interpersonal relations in peasant society'. *Human Organization* 19: 174–178.

FOX, C.
(1923) *The Archaeology of the Cambridge Region*.
Cambridge: Cambridge University Press.
(1932) *The Personality of Britain*. Cardiff: National Museum of Wales.
(1959) *Life and Death in the Bronze Age*. London: Routledge and Kegan Paul.

FRANKFORT, H. (1956) *The Birth of Civilization in the Near East*. New York: Doubleday.

GIMBUTAS, M. (1963) 'The Indo-Europeans: archaeological problems'. *American Anthropologist* 65: 815–836.

GLADWIN, W. and H. S. (1934) *A Method for the Designation of Cultures and their Variations*. Globe: Medallion Papers 15.

GOBINEAU, J. A. DE (1856) *The Moral and Intellectual Diversity of Races*. Philadelphia: Lippincott. (originally published 1853–55).

GOLDSCHMIDT, W. (1959) *Man's Way*.
New York: Holt, Rinehart and Winston.

GREENBERG, J. H. (1957) *Essays in Linguistics*.
Chicago: University of Chicago Press.

GRUBER, J. (1965) Brixham cave and the antiquity of man. In M. Spiro, ed. *Context and Meaning in Cultural Anthropology* pp. 373–402. Glencoe: Free Press.

GWATKIN, H. M. and J. P. WHITNEY, eds. (1913) *Cambridge Medieval History*, Vol. 2.
Cambridge: Cambridge University Press.

GUDSCHINSKY, S. C. (1956) 'The ABC's of lexicostatistics (glottochronology)'. *Word* 12: 175–210.

HÄGERSTRAND, T. (1967) *Innovation Diffusion as a Spatial Process*. Chicago: University of Chicago Press.

HARRIS, M.
(1966) 'The cultural ecology of India's sacred cattle'. *Current Anthropology* 7: 51–66.
(1968) *The Rise of Anthropological Theory*.
New York: Crowell.

HAWKES, C. F. C. (1954) 'Archaeological theory and method: some suggestions from the Old World'. *American Anthropologist* 56: 155–168.

HAWKES, J. (1968) 'The proper study of mankind'. *Antiquity* 42: 255–262.

HAWKES, J. and L. WOOLLEY (1963) *Prehistory and the Beginnings of Civilization*. New York: Harper and Row.

HEIDENREICH, C. E. (1971) *Huronia: A History and Geography of the Huron Indians, 1600–1650*.
Toronto: McClelland and Stewart.

HEIZER, R. F. (1969) *Man's Discovery of His Past*.
Palo Alto: Peek Publications.

HEMPEL, C. G. (1949) The function of general laws in history. In H. Feigl and W. Sellars, eds. *Readings in Philosophical Analysis*, pp. 459–471.
New York: Appleton-Century-Crofts.

HILL, J. N.
(1966) 'A prehistoric community in Eastern Arizona'. *Southwestern Journal of Anthropology* 22: 9–30.

(1968) Broken K Pueblo: patterns of form and function.
In S. and L. Binford, eds. *New Perspectives in Archeology*,
pp. 103–142. Chicago: Aldine.

HO, PING-TI (1959) *Studies on the Population of China,
1368–1953*. Cambridge, Mass.: Harvard University Press.

HODDER, I. (1977) Some new directions in the spatial analysis
of archaeological data at the regional scale (Macro).
In D. Clarke, ed. *Spatial Archaeology*, pp. 223–351.
London: Academic Press.

HODDER, I. and C. ORTON (1976) *Spatial Analysis in
Archaeology*. Cambridge: Cambridge University Press.

HODGEN, M. T. (1964) *Early Anthropology in the Sixteenth and
Seventeenth Centuries*.
Philadelphia: University of Pennsylvania Press.

HODGES, H. (1964) *Artifacts: an Introduction to Early
Materials and Technology*. London: Baker.

HOLMES, W. H.
(1903) *Aboriginal Pottery of the Eastern United States*.
Washington: Bureau of American Ethnology, 20th Annual
Report, pp. 1–201.
(1914) 'Areas of American culture characterization tentatively
outlined as an aid in the study of antiquities'.
American Anthropologist 16: 413–446.
(1919) *Handbook of Aboriginal American Antiquities, Part I:
Introductory: The Lithic Industries*. Bureau of American
Ethnology, Bulletin 60.

HOLLANDER, A. N. J. DEN (1960) The great Hungarian plain:
a frontier area. *Comparative Studies in Society and History*
3: 74–88; 155–169.

HOMANS, G. C. (1962) *Sentiments and Activities*.
Glencoe: The Free Press.

IBN KHALDUN, ABD-AR-RAHMAN (1967) *The Muqaddimah:
An Introduction to History*. Translated by F. Rosenthal,
abridged by N. J. Dawood.
Princeton: Princeton University Press.

INNIS, H. (1951) *The Bias of Communication*.
Toronto: University of Toronto Press.

JOHNSON, G. A. (1973) *Local Exchange and Early State
Development in Southwestern Iran*. Anthropological Papers
No. 51. Ann Arbor: Museum of Anthropology,
University of Michigan.

KAPLAN, D. (1963) 'Men, monuments, and political systems'.
Southwestern Journal of Anthropology 19: 397–410.

KEES, H. (1961) *Ancient Egypt: A Cultural Topography*.
Chicago: University of Chicago Press.

KEHOE, A. B. (1964) 'A worm's-eye view of marriage, authority,
and final causes'. *American Anthropologist* 66: 405–407.

KIDDER, A. V. (1924) *An Introduction to the Study of
Southwestern Archaeology*. New Haven: Papers of the
Southwestern Expedition, Phillips Academy, no. 1.

KING, T. F. (1971) 'A conflict of values in American
archaeology'. *American Antiquity* 36: 255–262.

KIRWAN, L. (1937) 'A contemporary account of the conversion
of the Sudan to Christianity'. *Sudan Notes and Records*
20: 289–295.

KLEINDIENST, M. (1976) Reflections of an alleged 'New
Archaeologist'. University of Toronto, mimeographed, 7 pages.

KLEJN, L. S.
(1973) Marxism, the systemic approach and archaeology.
C. Renfrew, ed. *The Explanation of Culture Change*,
pp. 691–710. London: Duckworth.
(1974) 'Kossinna im Abstand von vierzig Jahren'.
Jahresschrift für mitteldeutsche Vorgeschichte 58: 7–55.

KLEMM, G.
(1843–52) *Allgemeine Cultur-Geschichte der Menschheit*.
Leipzig: Teubner.
(1854–55) *Allgemeine Kulturwissenschaft*. Leipzig: Romberg.

KLINDT-JENSEN, O. (1975) *A History of Scandinavian
Archaeology*. London: Thames and Hudson.

KLUCKHOHN, C.
(1940) The conceptual structure in middle American studies.
In C. L. Hay *et al.*, eds. *The Maya and their Neighbors*,
pp. 41–51. New York: Appleton-Century.
(1962) *Culture and Behavior: Collected Essays of Clyde
Kluckhohn*. New York: Free Press.

KOHN, H. (1961) *The Mind of Germany*. London: Macmillan.

KOSSINNA, G.
(1911) *Die Herkunft der Germanen*. Leipzig: Kurt Kabitzsch.
(1926) *Ursprung und Verbreitung der Germanen in vor- und
frühgeschichtlicher Zeit*. Berlin: Germanen-Verlag.

KRAMER, S. N. (1963) *The Sumerians*.
Chicago: University of Chicago Press.

KRAUSE, M. (1970) Zur Kirchen- und Theologiegeschichte
Nubiens: Neue Quellen und Probleme. E. Dinkler, ed.
Kunst und Geschichte Nubiens in Christlicher Zeit, pp. 71–86.
Recklinghausen: Bongers.

KROEBER, A. L.
(1916) Zuni potsherds. New York: *Anthropological Papers of the American Museum of Natural History* 18, pt. 1: 7–37.
(1952) *The Nature of Culture.*
Chicago: University of Chicago Press.
(1953) *Cultural and Natural Areas of Native North America.*
Berkeley: University of California Press.
(1955) 'Nature of the land-holding Group'. *Ethnohistory* 2: 303–314.
KROEBER, A. L. and C. KLUCKHOHN (1952) *Culture – A Critical Review of Concepts and Definitions.*
Cambridge, Mass.: Harvard University, Papers of the Peabody Museum of American Archaeology and Ethnology, 47.
KUHN, T. S. (1970) *The Structure of Scientific Revolutions.*
Chicago: University of Chicago Press.
LAMBERT, W. G. (1964) The reign of Nebuchadnezzar I.
In W. S. McCullough, ed. *The Seed of Wisdom,* pp. 3–13.
Toronto: University of Toronto Press.
LANNING, E. (1967) *Peru Before the Incas.*
Englewood Cliffs: Prentice-Hall.
LAUFER, B. (1913) Remarks. *American Anthropologist* 15: 573–577.
LEACH, E. R.
(1954) *Political Systems of Highland Burma.*
Boston: Harvard University Press.
(1966) 'On the Founding Fathers'. *Current Anthropology* 7: 560–567.
LEE, R. B. and I. DEVORE, eds. (1968) *Man the Hunter.*
Chicago: Aldine.
LEONE, M. P. (1975) 'Views of traditional archaeology'.
Reviews in Anthropology 2: 191–199.
LÉVI-STRAUSS, CLAUDE (1953) Social Structure. In
A. L. Kroeber, ed. *Anthropology Today,* pp. 524–553.
Chicago: University of Chicago Press.
LEWIS, H. S. (1966) 'The origins of the Galla and Somali'.
Journal of African History 7: 27–46.
LLOYD, P. C. (1965) The political structure of African kingdoms: an exploratory model. *Political Systems and the Distribution of Power,* A.S.A. Monographs 2: 63–112.
London: Tavistock Publications.
LONGACRE, W. A.
(1966) 'Changing patterns of social integration: a prehistoric example from the American Southwest'. *American Anthropologist* 68: 94–102.

(1968) Some aspects of prehistoric society in East-Central Arizona. In S. and L. Binford, eds. *New Perspectives in Archeology*, pp. 89–102. Chicago: Aldine.

(1973) Comment. In C. L. Redman, ed. *Research and Theory in Current Archeology*, pp. 329–335. New York: Wiley.

LOUNSBURY, F. G. (1961) 'Iroquois-Cherokee linguistic relations'. *Bureau of American Ethnology, Bulletin* 180: 11–17.

LOWIE, R. H. (1937) *The History of Ethnological Theory*. New York: Farrar and Rinehart.

LUBBOCK, J.

(1882) *The Origin of Civilization*. 4th edition. London: Longmans, Green.

(1913) *Prehistoric Times as Illustrated by Ancient Remains and the Manners and Customs of Modern Savages*. 7th edition. New York: Holt.

LYNCH, B. D. and T. F. LYNCH (1968) 'The beginnings of a scientific approach to prehistoric archaeology in 17th and 18th century Britain'. *Southwestern Journal of Anthropology* 24: 33–65.

MCCALL, D. F. (1964) *Africa in Time-Perspective*. Boston: Boston University Press.

MACFARLANE, A. (1970) *Witchcraft in Tudor and Stuart England*. London: Routledge and Kegan Paul.

MACGAFFEY, W. (1966) 'Concepts of race in the historiography of Northeast Africa'. *Journal of African History* 7: 1–17.

MCKERN, W. C. (1939) 'The Midwestern taxonomic method as an aid to archaeological culture study'. *American Antiquity* 4: 301–313.

MACNEISH, R. S.

(1952) *Iroquois Pottery Types*. Ottawa: National Museum of Canada, Bulletin 124.

(1964) 'Ancient Mesoamerican civilization'. *Science* 143: 531–537.

(1974) Review of J. E. Fitting: *The Development of North American Archeology*. *American Anthropologist* 76: 462–463.

MCPHERRON, A. (1967) On the sociology of ceramics. In E. Tooker, ed. *Iroquois Culture, History and Prehistory*, pp. 101–107. Albany: University of the State of New York.

MACWHITE, E. (1956) 'On the interpretation of archaeological evidence in historical and sociological terms'. *American Anthropologist* 58: 3–25.

MARCUS, J.

(1973) 'Territorial organization of the Lowland Classic Maya'.
Science 180: 911–916.

(1974) 'The iconography of Power among the Classic Maya'.
World Archaeology 6: 83–94.

MARTIN, P. S.

(1971) 'The revolution in archaeology'. *American Antiquity*
36: 1–8.

(1974) Early development in Mogollon research.
In G. R. Willey, ed. *Archaeological Researches in
Retrospect*, pp. 3–29. Cambridge, Mass.: Winthrop.

MARTIN, P. S., G. I. QUIMBY and D. COLLIER (1947)
Indians Before Columbus. Chicago: University of Chicago Press.

MARTIN, P. S. and F. PLOG (1973) *The Archaeology of
Arizona*. New York: Natural History Press.

MASON, O. T. (1896) 'Influence of environment upon human
industries or arts'. Washington: *Annual Report of the
Smithsonian Institution for 1895:* 639–665.

MAYER-OAKES, W. J. (1959) A developmental concept of
Pre-Spanish urbanization in the valley of Mexico.
New Orleans: *Tulane University Middle American Research
Records* 18, p. 2.

MAYR, E. (1963) *Animal Species and Evolution*.
Cambridge, Mass.: Harvard University Press.

MEGGERS, B. J.

(1954) 'Environmental limitation on the development of
culture'. *American Anthropologist* 56: 801–824.

(1960) The law of cultural evolution as a practical research
tool. In G. E. Dole and R. L. Carneiro, eds. *Essays in the
Science of Culture*, pp. 302–16. New York: Crowell.

MILLS, W. C. (1903) 'Excavations of the Adena mound'.
Ohio Archaeological and Historical Quarterly 10: 452–479.

MONTELIUS, O.

(1899) *Der Orient und Europa*. Stockholm: Königl.
Akademie der schönen Wissenschaften, Geschichte und
Alterthumskunde.

(1903) *Die typologische Methode. Die älteren Kulturperioden
im Orient und in Europa*, I. Stockholm: Selbstverlag.

MOOREHEAD, W. K.

(1909) A study of primitive culture in Ohio. In F. Boas *et al*,
eds. *Putnam Anniversary Volume: Anthropological Essays*,
pp. 137–150. New York: Stechert.

(1910) *The Stone Age in North America.* 2 vols.
Boston: Houghton Mifflin.

MÜLLER, WERNER (1962) *Die Heilige Stadt.*
Stuttgart: Kohlhammer.

MURDOCK, G. P.

(1934) *Our Primitive Contemporaries.* New York: Macmillan.

(1949) *Social Structure.* New York: Macmillan.

(1957) 'World ethnographic sample'. *American Anthropologist* 59: 664–687.

(1959a) *Africa: Its Peoples and their Culture History.*
New York: McGraw-Hill.

(1959b) Evolution in social organization. In B. Meggers, ed.
Evolution and Anthropology: A Centennial Appraisal,
pp. 126–143.
Washington: The Anthropological Society of Washington.

(1971) 'Anthropology's mythology'. *Proceedings of the Royal Anthropological Institute* 1971: 17–24.

NADEL, S. (1951) *The Foundations of Social Anthropology.*
Glencoe: The Free Press.

NAGEL, E.

(1953) Teleological explanation and teleological system.
H. Feigl and M. Brodbeck, eds. *Readings in the Philosophy of Science,* pp. 537–558. New York: Appleton-Century.

(1961) *The Structure of Science.*
New York: Harcourt, Brace, and World.

NAROLL, R. (1956 'A preliminary index of social development'.
American Anthropologist 58: 687–715.

NARR, K. J. (1956) Early food-producing populations. In
W. L. Thomas, ed. *Man's Role in Changing the Face of the Earth,* pp. 134–151. Chicago: University of Chicago Press.

NILSSON, S. (1868) *The Primitive Inhabitants of Scandinavia.*
London: Longmans, Green.

OATES, J. F. (1963) 'A Christian inscription in Greek from Armenna in Nubia'. *Journal of Egyptian Archaeology* 49: 161–171.

OBERG, K. (1955) 'Types of social structure among the lowland tribes of South and Central America'. *American Anthropologist* 57: 472–487.

O'CONNOR, D. (1974) 'Political systems and archaeological data in Egypt, 2600–1780 B.C.'. *World Archaeology* 6: 15–38.

OLMSTEAD, A. T. (1948) *History of the Persian Empire.*
Chicago: University of Chicago Press.

OPPENHEIM, A. L. (1964) *Ancient Mesopotamia.*
Chicago: University of Chicago Press.

OZGUC, T. (1963) 'An Assyrian trading outpost'. *Scientific American* 208, no. 2: 96–106.

PALLOTTINO, M. (1956) *The Etruscans*.
Harmondsworth: Penguin.

PARKER, A. C. (1916) 'The origin of the Iroquois as suggested by their archaeology'. *American Anthropologist* 18: 479–507.

PARSONS, J. R. (1971) *Prehistoric Settlement Patterns in the Texcoco Region, Mexico*. Ann Arbor: Memoirs of the Museum of Anthropology, University of Michigan, no. 3.

PEAKE, H. (1922) *The Bronze Age and the Celtic World*.
London: Benn.

PERRY, W. J.
(1923) *The Children of the Sun*. London: Methuen.
(1924) *The Growth of Civilization*. London: Methuen.

PETRIE, W. M. F. (1939) *The Making of Egypt*.
London: Sheldon.

PIRENNE, H. (1925) *Medieval Cities*.
Princeton: Princeton University Press.

PIGGOTT, S.
(1950) *William Stukeley*. Oxford: Oxford University Press.
(1976) *Ruins in a Landscape: Essays in Antiquarianism*.
Edinburgh: Edinburgh University Press.

PITT-RIVERS, A. (1906) *The Evolution of Culture and Other Essays*. Oxford: Oxford University Press.

PLOG, F.
(1968) A study in experimental archaeology. *Bulletin of the American Anthropological Association* (Abstracts of the 67th A.G.M.) 1, no. 3: 110.
(1973) Diachronic anthropology. In C. L. Redman, ed.
Research and Theory in Current Archeology, pp. 181–198.
New York: Wiley.
(1974) *The Study of Prehistoric Change*.
New York: Academic Press.

POCOCK, J. G. A. (1962) 'The origin of the study of the past: a comparative approach'. *Comparative Studies in Society and History* 4: 208–246.

PRZEWORSKI, A. and H. TEUNE (1970) *The Logic of Comparative Social Inquiry*. New York: Wiley.

PUMPELLY, R., ed. (1908) *Explorations in Turkestan*. 2 vols.
Washington: Carnegie Institution.

PYDDOKE, E.
(1961) *Stratification for the Archaeologist*. London: Phoenix.
(1963) *The Scientist and Archaeology*. London: Phoenix.

QUIMBY, G. I. (1960) Habitat, culture, and archaeology.
In G. E. Dole and R. L. Carneiro, eds. *Essays in the Science of Culture*, pp. 380–389. New York: Crowell.

RADCLIFFE-BROWN, A. R.
(1952) *Structure and Function in Primitive Society*.
London: Oxford University Press.
(1958) *Method in Social Anthropology*.
Chicago: University of Chicago Press.

RAIKES, R. (1967) *Water, Weather and Prehistory*.
London: Baker.

RATHJE, W. L.
(1974) 'The garbage project: a new way of looking at the problems of archaeology'. *Archaeology* 27: 236–241.
(1975) The last tango in Mayapan: a tentative trajectory of production-distribution systems. In J. A. Sabloff and
C. C. Lamberg-Karlovsky, eds. *Ancient Civilization and Trade*, pp. 409–448.
Albuquerque: University of New Mexico Press.

RATZEL, F.
(1882–91) *Anthropogeographie*. Stuttgart: Engelhorn.
(1885–88) *The History of Mankind*. A. J. Butler trans.
London: Macmillan. (Eng. trans. 1896).

REDMAN, C. L., ed. (1973) *Research and Theory in Current Archeology*. New York: Wiley.

REID, J. J. *et al.* (1975) 'Behavioral archaeology: four strategies'.
American Anthropologist 77: 864–869.

RENFREW, A. C.
(1969) 'Trade and culture process in European prehistory'.
Current Anthropology 10: 151–169.
(1972) *The Emergence of Civilisation*. London: Methuen.
(1973a) *Before Civilization*. London: Cape.
(1973b) 'Wessex as a social question'. *Antiquity* 47: 221–225.
(1973c) *Social Archaeology*. Southampton: The University.
(1975) Trade as action at a distance: questions of integration and communication. In J. A. Sabloff and
C. C. Lamberg-Karlovsky, eds. *Ancient Civilization and Trade*, pp. 3–59.
Albuquerque: University of New Mexico Press.
(1977) Space, time and polity. In J. Friedman and
M. Rowlands, eds. *The Evolution of Social Systems*,
pp. 89–112. London: Duckworth.

REVERE, R. B. (1957) 'No Man's Coast': ports of trade in the Eastern Mediterranean. In K. Polanyi, *et al.*, eds. *Trade and Market in the Early Empires*, pp. 38–63.
Glencoe: The Free Press.

RITCHIE, W. A. (1932) 'The Algonkin sequence in New York'.
American Anthropologist 34: 406–414.

ROSENFELD, A. (1965) *The Inorganic Raw Materials of Antiquity*. London: Weidenfeld & Nicolson.

ROUSE, I.
(1958) The inference of migrations from anthropological evidence. In R. H. Thompson, ed. *Migrations in New World Culture History*, pp. 63–68.
Tucson: University of Arizona Press.
(1964) Archaeological approaches to cultural evolution.
In W. H. Goodenough, ed. *Explorations in Cultural Anthropology*, pp. 455–468. New York: McGraw-Hill.
(1965) 'The place of "peoples" in prehistoric research'.
Journal of the Royal Anthropological Institute 95: 1–15.
(1972) *Introduction to Prehistory*. New York: McGraw-Hill.

ROUSE, IRVING, and J. M. CRUXENT (1963) *Venezuelan Archaeology*. New Haven: Yale University Press.

ROWE, J. H.
(1944) An introduction to the archaeology of Cuzco.
Harvard University, *Papers of the Peabody Museum of American Archaeology and Ethnology*, 27, no. 2.
(1962) Alfred Louis Kroeber 1876–1960. *American Antiquity* 27: 395–415.

SABLOFF, J. A. and G. R. WILLEY (1967) The collapse of Maya civilization in the Southern Lowlands: a consideration of history and process. *Southwestern Journal of Anthropology* 23: 311–336.

SAHLINS, M. D. (1968) *Tribesmen*.
Englewood Cliffs: Prentice-Hall.

SAHLINS, M. D. and E. R. SERVICE, eds. (1960) *Evolution and Culture*. Ann Arbor: University of Michigan Press.

SALIM, S. M. (1962) *Marsh Dwellers of the Euphrates Delta*.
London School of Economics Monographs on Social Anthropology, 23.

SANDERS, W. T. (1968) Hydraulic agriculture, economic symbiosis and the evolution of states in Central Mexico.
In B. Meggers, ed. *Anthropological Archaeology in the Americas*, pp. 88–107.
Washington: Anthropological Society of Washington.

SANDERS, W. T. and B. J. PRICE (1968) *Mesoamerica: the Evolution of a Civilization*. New York: Random House.

SANSOM, G. (1958) *A History of Japan to 1334*.
Stanford: Stanford University Press.

SAPIR, E.

(1916) *Time Perspective in Aboriginal American Culture*.
Ottawa: Canada Department of Mines, Memoir 90.
(1921) *Language*. New York: Harcourt, Brace and World.

SARG, the Members of (1974) 'SARG: A co-operative approach
towards understanding the locations of human settlement'.
World Archaeology 6: 107–116.

SCHIFFER, M. B. (1975) 'Archaeology as behavioral science'.
American Anthropologist 77: 836–848.

SCHWARTZ, D. W. (1968) *Conceptions of Kentucky Prehistory:
A Case Study in the History of Archaeology*.
Lexington: University of Kentucky Press.

SEARS, W. H.

(1961) 'The study of social and religious systems in North
American archaeology'. *Current Anthropology* 2: 223–246.
(1968) The state and settlement patterns in the New World.
In K. C. Chang, ed. *Settlement Archaeology*, pp. 134–153.
Palo Alto: National Press.

SEGRAVES, B. A. (1974) 'Ecological generalization and
structural transformation of sociocultural systems'.
American Anthropologist 76: 530–552.

SEMENOV, S. A. (1964) *Prehistoric Technology*.
London: Cory, Adams and Mackay.

SERVICE, E. R.

(1966) *The Hunters*. Englewood Cliffs: Prentice-Hall.
(1971) *Primitive Social Organization: An Evolutionary
Perspective*. 2nd edition. New York: Random House.
(1975) *Origins of the State and Civilization*.
New York: Norton.

SHETRONE, H. C. (1920) 'The culture problem in Ohio
archaeology. *American Anthropologist* 22: 145–172.

SHIMKIN, D. B. (1973) Models for the Downfall: some
ecological and culture-historical considerations. In
T. P. Culbert, ed. *The Classic Maya Collapse*, pp. 269–299.
Albuquerque: University of New Mexico Press.

SILVERBERG, R. (1968) *Mound Builders of Ancient America:
The Archaeology of a Myth*.
Greenwich: New York Graphic Society.

SJOBERG, G. (1960) *The Preindustrial City*.
Glencoe: The Free Press.

SLOTKIN, J. S. (1965) *Readings in Early Anthropology*.
New York: Viking Fund Publications in Anthropology, 40.

SMITH, G. E.

(1923) *The Ancient Egyptians and the Origin of Civilization*.
London: Harper.

(1933) *The Diffusion of Culture*. London: Watts.

SMITH, H. I. (1910) *The Prehistoric Ethnology of a Kentucky Site*. New York: Anthropological Papers of the American Museum of Natural History 6, pt. 2.

SMITH, W. S. (1958) *The Art and Architecture of Ancient Egypt*. Baltimore: Penguin.

SOKAL, R. R. (1966) 'Numerical taxonomy'. *Scientific American* 215, no. 6: 106–117.

SOUSTELLE, JACQUES (1962) *The Daily Life of the Aztecs*. New York: Macmillan.

SPATH, C. D. (1973) 'The problem of the Calpulli in classic Nahuatlaca social structure'. *Journal of the Steward Anthropological Society* 5 (1): 25–44.

SPAULDING, A. C. (1968) Explanation in archeology. In S. and L. Binford, eds. *New Perspectives in Archeology*, pp. 33–39. Chicago: Aldine.

SPIER, L. (1917) An outline for a chronology of Zuñi ruins. *Anthropological Papers of the American Museum of Natural History*, 18, pt. 3.

SPOONER, B. (1972) *Population Growth: Anthropological Implications*. Cambridge, Mass.: MIT Press.

SPRIGGS, M. ed. (1977) *Archaeology and Anthropology*. Oxford: British Archaeological Reports, Supplementary Series, 19.

STEIGER, W. L. (1971) 'Analytical archaeology?' *Mankind* 8: 67–70.

STENICO, A. (1966) Ikhmindi. *Acme* 13.

STJERNQUIST, B. (1972) 'Archaeological analysis of prehistoric society'. *Norwegian Archaeological Review* 5: 2–26.

STERUD, E. L. (1976) 'Comments on relative chronology'. *Norwegian Archaeological Review* 9: 83–91.

STEWARD, J. H.
(1953) Evolution and process. In A. L. Kroeber, ed. *Anthropology Today*, pp. 313–326.
Chicago: University of Chicago Press.
(1955) *Theory of Culture Change*.
Urbana: University of Illinois Press.

STRUEVER, S.
(1968a) Problems, methods and organization: a disparity in the growth of archaeology. In B. Meggers, ed. *Anthropological Archaeology in the Americas*, pp. 131–151.
Washington: Anthropological Society of Washington.
(1968b) Woodland subsistence-settlement systems in the Lower Illinois valley. In S. and L. Binford, eds. *New Perspectives in Archeology*, pp. 285–312. Chicago: Aldine.

SUGGS, R. C. (1960) *The Island Civilizations of Polynesia*.
New York: Mentor.

TAYLOR, W. W.

(1948) *A Study of Archaeology*. Washington: American
Anthropological Association, Memoir 69.

(1967) The sharing criterion and the concept of culture.
In C. L. Riley and W. W. Taylor, eds. *American Historical
Anthropology* pp. 221–230.
Carbondale: Southern Illinois University Press.

(1969) Review of S. R. and L. R. Binford: *New Perspectives in
Archeology. Science* 165: 382–384.

THIEME, PAUL (1964) The comparative method for
reconstruction in linguistics. In D. Hymes, ed. *Language in
Culture and Society*, pp. 585–598. New York: Harper and Row.

THOMAS, C.

(1894) Report on the Mound explorations of the Bureau of
American ethnology. *Twelfth Annual Report, Bureau of
American Ethnology*, pp. 3–730.

(1898) *Introduction to the Study of North American
Archaeology*. Cincinnati: Clarke.

TOLSTOY, P. (1969) Review of W. T. Sanders and B. J. Price:
Mesoamerica. American Anthropologist 71: 554–558.

TOULMIN, S. E. (1967) 'The evolutionary development of
natural science'. *American Scientist* 55: 456–471.

TOULMIN, S. E. and J. GOODFIELD (1966) *The Discovery of
Time*. New York: Harper and Row.

TREVELYAN, G. M. (1949) *Illustrated English Social History*.
London: Longmans.

TRIGGER, B. G.

(1960) 'The destruction of Huronia'. *Transactions of the Royal
Canadian Institute* 33, pt. 1, no. 68: 14–45.

(1963a) 'Settlement as an aspect of Iroquoian adaptation at
the time of contact'. *American Anthropologist* 65: 86–101.

(1963b) 'Order and freedom in Huron society'. *Anthropologica*
N.S. 5: 151–169.

(1965) *History and Settlement in Lower Nubia*.
New Haven: Yale University Publications in Anthropology 69.

(1966) 'The languages of the Northern Sudan: an historical
perspective'. *Journal of African History* 7: 19–25.

(1967) 'Settlement archaeology – its goals and promise'.
American Antiquity 32: 149–160.

(1968a) *Beyond History: the Methods of Prehistory*.
New York: Holt, Rinehart and Winston.

(1968b) 'Major concepts of archaeology in historical
perspective'. *Man* 3: 527–541.

(1969a) *The Huron: Farmers of the North.*
New York: Holt, Rinehart, and Winston.
(1969b) 'The myth of Meroe and the African iron age'.
African Historical Studies 2: 23–50.
(1970a) 'Aims in prehistoric archaeology'. *Antiquity* 44: 26–37.
(1970b) The cultural ecology of Christian Nubia.
In E. Dinkler, ed. *Kunst und Geschichte Nubiens in
Christlicher Zeit*, pp. 347–379. Recklinghausen: Bongers.
(1970c) 'The strategy of Iroquoian prehistory'. *Ontario
Archaeology* 14: 3–48.
(1972) Determinants of urban growth in pre-industrial
societies. In P. J. Ucko, R. Tringham and G. W. Dimbleby,
eds. *Man, Settlement and Urbanism*, pp. 575–599.
London: Duckworth.
(1976a) *The Children of Aataentsic: A History of the Huron
People to 1660.* Montreal: McGill-Queen's University Press.
(1976b) *Nubia under the Pharaohs.*
London: Thames and Hudson.
(in press) Egypt and the comparative study of early
civilizations. In K. Weeks, ed. *Ancient Egypt: Problems of
History, Sources and Methods.*
Cairo: American University in Cairo Press.

TUGGLE, H. D. (1971) 'Trigger and Prehistoric Archaeology'.
Antiquity 45: 130–132.
TYLOR, E. B. (1871) *Primitive Culture.* London: J. Murray.
UCKO, P. J.
(1968) *Anthropomorphic Figurines of Predynastic Egypt and
Neolithic Crete.* London: Szmidla.
(1969) 'Ethnography and archaeological interpretation of
funerary remains'. *World Archaeology* 1: 262–280.
UCKO, P. J. and ROSENFELD, A. (1967) *Palaeolithic Cave Art.*
London: Weidenfeld and Nicholson.
UPHILL, E. P. (1970) 'The Per Aten at Amarna'. *Journal of
Near Eastern Studies* 29: 151–166.
VANSINA, J. (1965) *The Oral Tradition: A Study in Historical
Methodology.* Chicago: Aldine.
VOGT, E. Z. (1956) An appraisal of *Prehistoric Settlement
Patterns in the New World. Viking Fund Publications in
Anthropology* 23: 173–182.
WALLACE, A. F. C. (1961) *Culture and Personality.*
New York: Random House.
WATSON, P. J. *et al.* (1971) *Explanation in Archeology: An
Explicitly Scientific Approach.*
New York: Columbia University Press.

References

WEDEL, W. R. (1938) The direct-historical approach in Pawnee archaeology. Washington: *Smithsonian Miscellaneous Collections* 97, no. 7.

WEISS, A. H. (1961) 'The Roman walls of Barcelona'. *Archaeology* 14: 188–197.

WENDORF, F. (1969) Review of B. G. Trigger: *Beyond History*. *American Anthropologist* 71: 344–345.

WHEELER, MORTIMER (1960) *The Indus Civilization*. Cambridge: Cambridge University Press.

WHITE, L. A.
(1945a) 'Diffusion vs. evolution: an anti-evolutionist fallacy'. *American Anthropologist* 47: 339–356.
(1945b) 'History, evolutionism and functionalism'. *Southwestern Journal of Anthropology* 1: 221–248.
(1948) Review of V. G. Childe: *History. Antiquity* 22: 217–218.
(1949) *The Science of Culture*. New York: Farrar, Straus.
(1959) *The Evolution of Culture*. New York: McGraw-Hill.

WHITELOCK, D. (1974) *The Beginnings of English Society*. Harmondsworth: Penguin.

WILLETTS, WILLIAM (1958) *Chinese Art*. Harmondsworth: Penguin.

WILLEY, G. R.
(1953) *Prehistoric Settlement Patterns in the Virú Valley*. Washington: Bureau of American Ethnology, Bulletin 155.
ed. (1956a) *Prehistoric Settlement Patterns in the New World*. Viking Fund Publications in Anthropology 23.
(1956b) Problems concerning prehistoric settlement patterns in the Maya Lowlands. In Willey, 1956a, pp. 107–114.
(1968) One hundred years of American Archaeology. In J. O. Brew, ed. *One Hundred Years of Anthropology*, pp. 29–53. Cambridge, Mass.: Harvard University Press.

WILLEY, G. R. and P. PHILLIPS (1958) *Method and Theory in American Archaeology*. Chicago: University of Chicago Press.

WILLEY, G. R. and J. A. SABLOFF (1974) *A History of American Archaeology*. London: Thames and Hudson.

WILSON, DANIEL (1851) *The Archaeology and Prehistoric Annals of Scotland*. London: Macmillan.

WILSON, DAVID (1972) *The Anglo-Saxons*. Harmondsworth: Penguin.

WISSLER, C. (1914) 'Material cultures of the North American Indians'. *American Anthropologist* 16: 447–505.

WITTFOGEL, K. A. (1957) *Oriental Despotism*. New Haven: Yale University Press.

WRIGHT, G. A. (1971) The Origins of Food Production in Southwestern Asia. *Current Anthropology* 12: 447–477.

Index

N.B. In items with sub-entries, a final italic entry, *various*, gathers the remaining references.

264

migration
  American archaeologists' use
    of concept, 5
  as explanation of change, 29,
    63, 86
  -based view of culture, 113
  concept of, 98-9, 101
  cultural change and, 66, 78-9,
    94
  cultural development and,
    63, 94, 101
  settlement patterns and, 188
Millar, John, 59
models, archaeological, 11, 28,
  29
Mommsen, T., 25
morphological patterns, 141-2,
  146
Montelius, O., 80, 82, 135, 245
Moorehead, W. K., 88, 89, 245
Morgan, L. H., 64, 99
Moundbuilders, 64, 87, 89, 94
Müller, S., 81
Murdock, G. P., x, xi, 107,
  116, 118, 119, 127, 156, 173,
  176, 183, 246

Nagel, E., vii, 26, 27, 28, 246
Naroll, R., 156, 199, 246
natural event, 13
natural history, 97
natural sciences
  methods of, 23
  ties with archaeology, 97, 99,
    100, 112
Nelson, N. C., 90
New Archaeology
  ahistoricity of, x, 3-4, 23
  aims of, 20-2
  anthropology and, x, 3-4, 5, 21
  criticism of, vii, ix-xi, 2-3,
    13-17
  cultural ecology, 7-9, 140
  culture, view of, x, 5, 93

deductive reasoning, 6-7
effect on fieldwork, 14-15
ethnography and, x, 4, 5
evolutionism and, xi, 11-12
in America, 2-18
materialism of, 12-13, 70, 140
nomothetic goals of, 5, 6-7
practical problems of, 13-17
problem-orientated research,
  15-16
recent trends in, x, 1-18
social organization and
  ideology, 9-10
systems approach, 10-11
tenets of, 4-13
theoretical orientation of, x,
  5-6, 11, 20-1
Nilsson, S., 62, 63, 80, 246
nomothetic
  aims of archaeology, 5, 6-7,
    14, 20, 21, 22, 24, 30, 33-5,
    37, 51, 137, 138
  concept of evolution, 31-2
  explanation, 6-7, 42, 137
  history as, 27-8, 40, 44-5, 46
  idiographic and nomothetic
    aims, 31-3, 35, 38
  social sciences, xi, 5, 31, 37,
    40
Nubia, 218-19, 223-6

O'Connor, D., 158, 163, 246
Olmstead, A. T., 207, 211, 246
oral tradition, 44, 127-8
origins of archaeology
  antiquarianism, 55, 58, 59, 61
  change, influence of, 55-6
  Enlightenment and, 59-60,
    61, 62, 63, 64-5, 77
  evolutionary archaeology,
    61-4, 77
  human origins and, 56-7, 58,
    62-3

267   *Index*

273

Index